# Searches, Seizures, and Warrants

# Searches, Seizures, and Warrants

## A Reference Guide to the United States Constitution

Robert M. Bloom

Foreword by John Garvey

REFERENCE GUIDES TO THE
UNITED STATES CONSTITUTION, NUMBER 3
Jack Stark, *Series Editor*

**Westport, Connecticut**
**London**

**Library of Congress Cataloging-in-Publication Data**

Bloom, Robert M., 1946–
    Searches, seizures, and warrants : a reference guide to the United States Constitution /
Robert M. Bloom; foreword by John Garvey.
        p. cm.—(Reference guides to the United States Constitution, ISSN 1539-8986; no. 6)
    Includes bibliographical references and index.
    ISBN 0-313-31445-4 (alk. paper)
    1. Searches and seizures—United States. 2. Warrants (Law)—United States. 3. Privacy,
Right of—United States. I. Title. II. Series.
KF9630.B58 2003
345.73'0522—dc21          2003045534

British Library Cataloguing in Publication Data is available.

Library of Congress Catalog Card Number: 2003045534
ISBN: 0-313-31445-4
ISSN: 1539-8986

First published in 2003

Praeger Publishers, 88 Post Road West, Westport, CT  06881
An imprint of Greenwood Publishing Group, Inc.
www.praeger.com

Printed in the United States of America

The paper used in this book complies with the
Permanent Paper Standard issued by the National
Information Standards Organization (Z39.48-1984)

10  9  8  7  6  5  4  3  2  1

# Contents

# Series Foreword

JACK STARK

One can conceive of the United States Constitution in many ways. For example, noting the reverence in which it has been held one can think of it as equivalent to a sacred text. Unfortunately, most of its devotees have had less knowledge and even less understanding of the document than they have had reverence for it. Sometimes it is treated as primarily a political document and on that basis has been subjected to analysis, such as Charles Beard's *An Economic Interpretation of the Constitution of the United States*. One can plausibly argue that the Constitution seems most astounding when seen in light of the intellectual effort that has been associated with it. Three brief but highly intense bursts of intellectual energy produced, and established as organic law, most of the Constitution as it now exists. Two of those efforts, sustained over a long period of time, have enabled us to better understand the document.

The first burst of energy occurred at the Constitutional Convention. Although some of the delegates' business, such as the struggle between populous and nonpopulous states about their representation in Congress, was political, much of it was about fundamental issues of political theory. A few of the delegates had or later achieved international eminence for their intellects. Among them are Benjamin Franklin, Alexander Hamilton, and James Madison. Others, although less well known, had first-rate minds. That group includes George Mason and George Wythe. Many of the delegates contributed intelligently. Although the Convention's records are less than satisfactory, they indicate clearly enough that the delegates worked mightily to constitute not merely a polity—but a rational polity that would rise to the standards envisioned by the delegates' intellectual ancestors. Their product, though brief, is amazing. William Gladstone called it "the most wonderful work ever struck off."

Despite the delegates' eminence and the Constitution's excellence as seen from our place in history, its ratification was far from certain. That state of affairs necessitated the second burst of intellectual energy associated with that document: the debate over ratification. Soon after the convention adjourned, articles and speeches (some supporting the Constitution and some attacking it) began to proliferate. A national debate commenced—not only about the document itself but also about the nature of the polity that ought to exist in this country. Both sides included many writers and speakers who were verbally adroit and steeped in the relevant political and philosophical literature. The result was an accumulation of material that is remarkable for both its quantity and its quality. At its apex is the *Federalist Papers*, a production of Alexander Hamilton, James Madison, and John Jay that deserves a place among the great books of Western culture.

Another burst, although not as impressive as the first two but highly respectable, occurred when the Bill of Rights was proposed. Some delegates to the Constitutional Convention had vigorously asserted that such guarantees should be included in the original document. George Mason, the principal drafter of the Virginia Declaration of Rights, so held, and he walked out of the convention when he failed to achieve his purpose. Even those who had argued that the rights in question were implicit recognized the value of adding protection of them to the Constitution. The debate was thus focused on the rights that were to be explicitly granted, not on whether any rights ought to be explicitly granted. Again many writers and speakers entered the fray, and again the debate was solidly grounded in theory and was conducted on a high intellectual level.

Thus, within a few years a statement of organic law and a vital coda to it had been produced. However, the meaning and effect of many of that document's provisions were far from certain; the debates on ratification of the Constitution and the Bill of Rights had demonstrated that. In addition, the document existed in a vacuum, because statutes and actions had not been assessed by its standards. The attempt to resolve these problems began after Chief Justice John Marshall, in Marbury v. Madison, asserted the right of the U.S. Supreme Court to interpret and apply the Constitution. Judicial interpretation and application of the Constitution, beginning with the first constitutional case and persisting until the most recent, is one of the sustained exertions of intellectual energy associated with the Constitution. The framers would be surprised by some of the results of these activities. References in the document to "due process," which seems to refer only to procedures, have been held also to have a substantive dimension. A right to privacy has been found lurking among the penumbras of various parts of the text. A requirement that states grant the same "privileges and immunities" to citizens of other states that they granted to their own citizens, which seemed to guarantee important rights, was not held to be particularly important. The corpus of judicial interpretations of the Constitution is now as voluminous as that document is terse.

As judicial interpretations multiplied, another layer (interpretations of interpretations) appeared, and also multiplied. This layer, the other sustained intellectual effort associated with the Constitution, consists of articles, most of them published in law reviews, and books on the Constitution. This material varies in quality and significance. Some of these works of scholarship result from meticulous examination and incisive thought. Others repeat earlier work, or apply a fine-tooth comb to matters that are too minute even for such a comb. Somewhere in that welter of tertiary material is the answer to almost every question that one could ask about constitutional law. The problem is finding the answer that one wants. The difficulty of locating useful guidance is exacerbated by the bifurcation of most constitutional scholarship into two kinds. In "Two Styles of Social Science Research," C. Wright Mills delineates macroscopic and molecular research. The former deals with huge issues, the latter with tiny issues. Virtually all of the scholarship on the Constitution is of one of those two types. Little of it is macroscopic, but that category does include some first-rate syntheses such as Jack Rakove's *Original Meanings*. Most constitutional scholarship is molecular and, again, some fine work is included in that category.

In his essay, Mills bemoans the inability of social scientists to combine the two kinds of research that he describes to create a third category that will be more generally useful. This series of books is an attempt to do for constitutional law the intellectual work that Mills proposed for social science. The author of each book has dealt carefully and at reasonable length with a topic that lies in the middle range of generality. Upon completion, this series will consist of thirty-seven books, each on a constitutional law topic. Some of the books, such as the book on freedom of the press, explicate one portion of the Constitution's text. Others, such as the volume on federalism, treat a topic that has several anchors in the Constitution. The books on constitutional history and constitutional interpretation range over the entire document, but each does so from a single perspective. Except for a very few of the books the special circumstances of which dictate minor changes in format, each book includes the same components—a brief history of the topic, a lengthy and sophisticated analysis of the current state of the law on that topic, a bibliographical essay that organizes and evaluates scholarly material in order to facilitate further research, a table of cases and an index. The books are intellectually rigorous (in fact, authorities have written them) but, due to their clarity and to brief definitions of terms that are unfamiliar to laypersons, each is comprehensible and useful to a wide audience, one that ranges from other experts on the book's subject to intelligent non-lawyers.

In short, this series provides an extremely valuable service to the legal community and to others who are interested in constitutional law, as every citizen should be. Each book is a map of part of the U.S. Constitution. Together they map all of that document's territory that is worth mapping. When this series is complete, each book will be a third kind of scholarly work that combines the macroscopic and the molecular. Together they will explicate all of the important constitutional topics. Anyone who wants assistance in understanding either a topic in constitutional law or the Constitution as a whole can easily find it in these books.

# Foreword

JOHN GARVEY
Dean and Professor, Boston College Law School

The aspirations that fueled the American revolution were numerous, but Thomas Paine captured one of them in his memorable phrase, "That government is best which governs least." This is an ideal that we still hold fast. Our national anthem celebrates America as "the land of the free." Our pledge of allegiance speaks of a nation that offers "liberty and justice for all." Our constitution protects the people from government intrusion in a variety of ways, and one of the most important is the fourth amendment of the bill of rights. It promises that

The right of the people to be secure in their persons, houses, papers, and effects, against unreasonable searches and seizures, shall not be violated, and no Warrants shall issue, but upon probable cause, supported by Oath or affirmation, and particularly describing the place to be searched, and the persons or things to be seized.

In this wonderful little book Robert Bloom explains the origins and meaning of this guarantee. It could not come at a better time. For a variety of reasons, our culture has focused unprecedented attention on the constitutional guarantees about searches and seizures.

The most recent of these was the terrorist attacks on the World Trade Center and the Pentagon that took place on September 11, 2001. That tragedy reminded us that there is an inevitable tension between liberty and security. The fourth amendment strikes a balance between individual privacy in our "persons, houses, papers, and effects" and the effective operation of our domestic law enforcement and intelligence agencies. We cannot have the full measure of security in both directions—against depredations by the government and by criminal and terrorist actors. And we are currently engaged in a national debate about how best to achieve the fullest measure of freedom.

The second is that we are in the midst of an revolution in intellectual technology that is changing the way we think, communicate, do business, and live our private lives. In the span of three decades we have seen the invention of personal computers, the development of the internet, the routine use of e-mail, the proliferation of cell phones and personal data assistants, an explosion of audio and video technology, and a hundred other technologies undreamed of by our parents. These make the fourth amendment's reference to "papers, and effects" seem quaint by comparison. Our spheres of private activity have spread outward in all directions. At the same time, law enforcement agencies have begun to employ these new tools and media. They no longer need to rely on the unaided human faculties of the peeping Tom and the eavesdropper. They are capable of spectacularly intrusive invasions.

The third is the internationalization of public and private life that has come about in the same period of time and for some of the same reasons. To an unprecedented extent our ideas and culture, friends and business partners, cross borders and oceans. We travel abroad as easily as we fly from New York to Los Angeles. This exchange works in both directions. English has become the new lingua franca, and in other parts of the world there is a great deal of interest in the American legal system, especially the constitutional protections we have developed over the last two centuries. Our fourth amendment is one of these.

Professor Bloom's book is thus timely and important. And it provides a clear and elegant account of the rules governing our practice regarding searches, seizures, and warrants. The central feature of that practice is this: we have made the judicial branch of our government the principal check on the excesses of law enforcement. There are three features of this arrangement that deserve attention. The first is built into the fourth amendment itself. In many cases, though not all, the government may not invade our private lives without first securing a warrant from a judge or magistrate, and the warrant must meet constitutional requirements governing its foundation ("probable cause, supported by Oath or affirmation") and scope ("particularly describing the place to be searched, and the persons or things to be seized"). When a warrant is required, the judiciary decides how, when, where, and why the police can act.

The second feature of our practice is the institution of judicial review. In the latter half of the twentieth century the United States Supreme Court essentially undertook to create, case by case, a model code of pre-arraignment procedure that explained what the fourth amendment demanded of the police in a wide variety of situations. It was not inevitable that we should have done it this way. We could have put flesh on the constitutional bones through legislation or regulation. (The American Law Institute proposed a model for this in 1975.) But we leaned toward judicial governance because of the faith we put in the courts as a bulwark against executive overreaching.

The third feature that warrants mention is the exclusionary rule. In *Mapp v. Ohio*, 367 U.S. 643 (1961), the Supreme Court held that evidence seized by searches and seizures in violation of the fourth amendment is inadmissible in criminal trials in state courts. This was not the only tool available for enforcing the fourth amendment. We could have tried to deter violations by punishing the police. But that would have forced us to rely on the executive branch to police itself. And it would have made the judicial branch complicit in violations by entertaining improperly seized evidence at trial. So we turned once again to the courts for the most effective remedy.

In contemporary fourth amendment debates about the proper balance between liberty and security much of the tension concerns these features of the judicial role. It is a fairly precise rule of thumb that judicial intervention varies directly with our interest in liberty, and inversely with our interest in security. The more we worry about governmental threats to our liberty, the more we call on the courts to protect us. The more we worry about security against criminal behavior and terrorist threats, the more the judicial role diminishes. Consider first the warrant requirement. As Professor Bloom explains, the fourth amendment has a built-in ambiguity. It consists of two independent clauses separated by the word "and": the prohibition of unreasonable searches and seizures, and the warrant requirement. We might interpret it to mean that any search or seizure without a warrant is per se unreasonable. But the Court has concluded otherwise, and in recent years has enlarged the area within which the government may act without a warrant— and consequently without advance judicial consent.

The protection of post hoc judicial review is also subject to limitations. One of these is the requirement of standing—the notion that only certain people are entitled to complain about constitutional violations. The Burger and Rehnquist Courts have cut back on the size of this class, and established the rule that one cannot have standing without a legitimate expectation of privacy in the place searched.

The Court has also cut back on the exclusionary rule in a variety of direct and indirect ways. The most important has been the adoption of a balancing test that weighs the benefits of deterrence (of fourth amendment violations) against the costs of suppressing reliable probative evidence. We see this at work in proceedings other than criminal trials, and in the creation of good faith exceptions in cases like *United States v. Leon*, 468 U.S. 897 (1984). The Court has also cut back on the exclusion of derivative evidence—the "fruit of the poisonous tree." Derivative evidence may be admitted if it is sufficiently attenuated, it if has an independent source, if it would inevitably have been discovered, and so on.

Not all of these restrictions are unwise. But as Professor Bloom explains, taken together they show a trend in a certain direction. It is a trend that bears watching in the contemporary climate where the fear of international terrorism has been added to our commonplace concerns about domestic crime.

I need to add a word about the splendid bibliographic essay with which this volume concludes. This book is designed as an introduction to the fourth amendment field for those who do not have the advantage of Professor Bloom's wisdom and experience. One who ventures outside its covers for further enlightenment will find an almost overwhelming literature on searches, seizures, and warrants. This fairly extensive bibliographic chapter is a very useful road map to that literature. It is more than that. It is a thoughtful guide to the stops that are worth making and the things a traveller can find there—a kind of Baedeker's guide to the territory. Students of the fourth amendment owe Professor Bloom a double debt of gratitude for including this contribution at the end of a fine book.

# Introduction

The framers of the Constitution designed the Fourth Amendment to protect individual citizens from unfettered invasions by governmental actors into their homes or on their persons. In this way, it provides the individual with a general sense of security from arbitrary governmental incursions. The old maxim that "a man's house is his castle" and is thus free from governmental snooping captures the essence of the liberty interest that the Amendment was designed to protect.

In practice, the Fourth Amendment protects this liberty interest by controlling the activity of the police. However, controlling police activity raises issues related to crime management. Because our society is concerned about the ravages of crime and the ever present threat of terrorism, crime control is an important public policy objective. To the extent that constraints on the power and authority of the police seem to hamper their ability to make our streets safe and to protect the citizenry from danger, society currently tends to favor giving the police more latitude to do what is necessary for crime prevention.

Thus there is an inherent tension in the Fourth Amendment between individual liberty and crime management. On the one hand, we want to protect the privacy interest of the individual from governmental intrusions. On the other hand, we want the police to do whatever is required to solve crime. Greater controls on the power of the police provide more privacy protection to citizens. Reduced controls on police actions provide less privacy protection to citizens. This inverse relationship between two worthwhile society objectives is the tension inherent in the Fourth Amendment and one that is observable throughout this book.

Our founding ancestors, concerned about unfettered invasions of individual privacy by the government, enacted the Fourth Amendment to the U.S. Constitution, which states that, "The right of the people to be secure in their persons, houses, papers and effects, against unreasonable searches and seizures, shall not be violated, and no warrants shall issue, but upon probable cause supported by oath or affirmation, and particularly describing the place to be searched, and the persons or things to be seized." As one can see, it consists of two clauses joined by the conjunction *and*. The first clause prohibits unreasonable searches and seizures and the second clause describes the requirement for the issuance of a warrant. The term *unreasonable* is vague and does not lend itself to an easily definable meaning. The grammatical structure of the Fourth Amendment, two clauses joined by the conjunction *and* has provided at least a possible formula for defining "unreasonable searches and seizures." The interpretation of the relationship between the two clauses has occupied the Supreme Court's jurisprudence in this area for a number of years. There are two possible ways to read the Amendment, one way being that a search without a warrant is unreasonable per se (so that the definition of unreasonable is less flexible and is linked to whether the requirements for obtaining a warrant can be met) and the other being that a warrant is not necessary and does not determine whether a search is unreasonable, thus leaving the term *unreasonable* with a much vaguer and more flexible meaning. Though this question has occupied the Court's jurisprudence for much of the twentieth century, the present court has come down on the side of saying that the presence/absence of a warrant is of limited importance on determining whether a search is reasonable or not.

There is a basic formula to the analysis of most Fourth Amendment issues found in this book. The first question to address is the applicability of the Fourth Amendment. To answer this question, we must first determine whether there is governmental action. This means federal, state, and local government or private individuals acting at the request of the government. In addition, persons subject to, and acting pursuant to, the regulations of a heavily regulated industry like the railroad are regarded as government actors. Once we have found that there is governmental action, the second question to address is whether the victim has a legitimate expectation of privacy in the action taken by the government. A legitimate expectation of privacy is one that society would regard as reasonable.

When the answer to both of these questions is in the affirmative, the Fourth Amendment is applicable. If this is the case, we must then deal with the requirements of the Fourth Amendment. First, the government must have sufficient justification for its action. The justification found within the wording of the Fourth Amendment is probable cause. We will see that this justification is flexible, depending on the type and purpose of the government action. Second, we must determine whether there is a need for a warrant, which is also found within the wording of the Fourth Amendment. A warrant is a judicial authorization for the government action. Finally, we will look at the scope of the government action to determine if it is consistent with the justification and authorization provided by a warrant or if no warrant is required, then with the permissible scope of warrantless activity. These requirements found in the Fourth Amendment can be waived if there is a valid consent.

With regard to the justification requirement, we will see that this requirement is directly related to the type of intrusion (criminal versus noncriminal) and the scope of the intrusion. For a criminal full-scale search or arrest, probable cause is the standard to meet the justification requirement. For a criminal investigative stop, which is a lesser intrusion than an arrest, reasonable suspicion is the standard. For a search whose main objective is something other than solving crime (health inspections, sobriety checkpoints), a balancing approach is used in which the scope of the intrusion is weighed against the governmental interest. In this situation, individual suspicion is usually not necessary. Reasonable administrative regulations will provide sufficient justification. Analysis of the justification requirement is separate and distinct from the necessity for a warrant.

The warrant mentioned in the wording of the Fourth Amendment is usually not required, since a myriad of exceptions to a warrant have evolved over time. These exceptions usually have to do with practicality concerns. Depending on the justification and the necessity for a warrant, the scope of the search should then be considered. The scope is limited to the amount of the justification. It is also limited by the specifics described in the warrant or if no warrant is necessary, by the practicality concerns underlying the lack of necessity for a warrant.

Closely related to substantive Fourth Amendment concerns is the so-called exclusionary rule. The suppression of evidence is the major remedy for addressing a violation of the Fourth Amendment. If there is no violation of the Fourth Amendment, there is no exclusionary remedy. In our analysis of the Fourth Amendment, it is important that we explore the so-called exclusionary rule because it forms a basis for understanding the Court's attitude toward the Fourth Amendment. Without this remedy, as the Court observed in Mapp v. Ohio (1961), the Fourth Amendment is "a form of words valueless and undeserving of mention in a perpetual charter of inestimable human liberties." Early on, Justice Benjamin Cardozo posed the question that has preoccupied the Court. "Should the criminal go free because the constable has blundered?" The suppression of reliable evidence that affects the truth-finding objective of a criminal trial may at times have the effect of freeing the guilty. This has troubled the Court. The result has been both direct and indirect cutbacks on the applicability of the exclusionary rule. The direct cutbacks involve the general applicability of the exclusionary rule in certain situations. For example, the Court has held the exclusionary rule is not applicable to a civil trial. The indirect cutbacks have often involved substantive Fourth Amendment doctrine, for example, the standing doctrine. If one does not have the right (standing) to raise a Fourth Amendment issue, then the exclusionary rule will not be relevant. Thus the Court's jurisprudence with regard to the exclusionary rule presents a valuable barometer to its approach to the Fourth Amendment. For this reason, before we look at substantive Fourth Amendment issues, we will examine the amendment's history as well as the exclusionary rule.

# PART I

# Analysis — History

In analyzing the Court's Fourth Amendment jurisprudence, we will often return to the concept of reasonableness. What role does reasonableness play in the Court's analysis? How does the Court determine reasonableness? Is it determined in conjunction with warrants and probable cause, or is it separate and distinct? As we examine the history of the Fourth Amendment and its application by the Supreme Court, the question of what is reasonable will often arise.

## INTRODUCTION

The historical record of the Fourth Amendment is somewhat murky. This record, coupled with a puzzling text, has provided the Court opportunities to interpret the amendment in a results-oriented way. Consequently, the decisions using a historical base have often been inconsistent. Justice Felix Frankfurter observed that, "The course of true law pertaining to searches and seizures . . . has not—to put it mildly—run smooth" (Chapman v. United States, 1961). More recently Justice Antonin Scalia observed "inconsistent jurisprudence that has been with us for years" (California v. Acevedo, 1991).

Recent scholarship on the history has shed a new light on the motivation and intent of the Framers. It is unclear as the Court begins to digest the recent scholarship whether it will have an effect on future decisions. Much depends on how one approaches constitutional analysis. Most would agree that history is indeed important and that the Framers' original intent should be considered in contemporary constitutional decisions. However, how important a role the Framers' intent should play is a matter of considerable debate. In addition, recent scholarship has questioned some of the long-held historical theories. In fact, history has been an instrument to support a particular result and will likely continue to be used in this way.

In this chapter, we will discuss the reasons why the Court has not been consistent in its interpretation of the historical record. We will analyze the competing scholarly views and the effect these views have had on the Court's interpretation of history.

The peculiar wording of the Fourth Amendment accounts for much of the Court's difficulty in interpretation. "The right of the people to be secure in their persons, houses, papers and effects, against unreasonable searches and seizures, shall not be violated, and no warrants shall issue, but upon probable cause supported by oath or affirmation, and particularly describing the place to be searched, and the persons or things to be seized." It consists of two clauses joined by the conjunction *and*. The first clause prohibits unreasonable searches and seizures, and the second clause describes the requirement for the issuance of a warrant. Interpreting the relationship between the two clauses has occupied the Court's decision-making in this area for a number of years.

In addition to the Court's jurisprudence, constitutional scholars have also extensively debated the proper interpretation of the relationship between the reasonableness and the warrant clauses of the Fourth Amendment. Some scholars have argued that the Framers intended the reasonableness clause to be read in conjunction with the warrant clause so that warrantless searches are per se unreasonable and thus a warrant is necessary for a search to be reasonable. Thomas Davies[1] and Tracy Macklin[2] argue that the sentiment of the Framers against general warrants underlay the drafting of the Fourth Amendment, and that this sentiment indicated the desire of the Framers to limit the discretionary activity of the police. Because warrants are a mechanism to limit such activity, Davies and Macklin argue that the reasonableness clause and the warrant clause should be read together. Scholars on the other side of the debate argue that the two clauses should be read separately so that reasonableness is the only standard by which to determine the appropriateness of Fourth Amendment activity. Advocates of this approach view warrants only as one factor among many in determining reasonableness. Akhil Reed Amar[3] and Telford Taylor[4] in fact argue that the historical record indicates that the Framers were opposed to warrants, and therefore the reasonableness clause should not be read in conjunction with the warrant clause.

In order to gain insight into the scholarly debate over the historical roots of the Fourth Amendment, we will first explore its origins in the history of England and the colonies. Next, we will examine the statutes used as a basis for drafting the Fourth Amendment and the actual drafting process itself. Finally, we will analyze the Court's utilization of history in determining the current status of Fourth Amendment jurisprudence.

## ENGLISH HISTORY

From the English legal tradition, the colonists inherited a special appreciation for the sanctity of their homes. This is often expressed by the familiar phrase that "a man's house is his castle." William Pitt eloquently expressed this sentiment in a speech before the English Parliament in 1763. "The poorest man may in his cottage, bid defiance to all the forces of the Crown." William Blackstone expressed this view in his treatise. "For every man's house is looked upon by the law to be his castle of defense and asylum, wherein he should suffer no violence."[5] Despite this deeply rooted view, the Parliament made it possible through the authorization of general warrants and writs of assistance to search a home without much justification or specificity. General warrants required merely a report that a violation of the law or a suspicion of a violation had occurred. It was not necessary to designate the person or place in the warrant although it was generally done. Writs of assistance, however, were issued by the courts of the time without any justification or judicial supervision and were not limited in scope. The Navigation Act of 1662, for example, authorized a custom official armed with a writ of assistance to go anywhere, including a home, in search of uncustomed goods. In addition, these writs were effective during the life of the king and did not expire until six months after the king's death.

These writs of assistance were made applicable to the colonies in 1696 by an Act of William III. The Townsend Act of 1767, by giving authority to the highest court in each colony to issue writs of assistance to customs officers, expanded the procedural authority for issuing them. In 1760, when the Secretary of State ordered the strict enforcement of the Sugar Act of 1733, which put a high tariff on molasses, customs officials were issued writs of assistance that enabled them to search where they pleased. These types of actions caused widespread resentment among the colonists over the unlimited authority of tax collectors to search their homes. William Cuddihy,[6] commenting on the extensive search activity in his dissertation on the origins of the Fourth Amendment, reports that a "colonial epidemic of general searches existed indeed that until 1760s a man's house was even less of a castle in America than in England."

Thus, despite the widely held public feeling about the sanctity of one's home, the government had tremendous power to intrude on private homes. The Courts of England faced this issue in the case of John Wilkes. In 1763, Wilkes, a politician, and his supporters were accused of publishing insults against the King. As a result of this accusation, a general warrant was issued by the Secretary of State for the arrest and search of Wilkes and his supporters. Armed with these warrants that gave them considerable discretion, government officials arrested 49 people, including Wilkes, and searched numerous houses. Wilkes brought a successful civil trespass action against these officials who were ordered to pay damages to Wilkes and others. In a series of cases culminating with Money v. Leach (97 Eng. Rep. 1075, 1088) (K.B. 1765), Lord Mansfield said, "It is not fit, that the necessary or judging of the information should be left to the discretion of the officer. The magistrate ought to judge; and should give certain directions to the officer." Wilkes' success in challenging the government was widely reported in colonial newspapers that emphasized the sanctity of the home and strongly criticized general warrants. The newspaper reports were picked up in pamphlets and other journals that reached the colonies, and Wilkes emerged from that trial as a hero for liberty. Amar suggests that he was so popular that some colonists named their children after him. The Wilkes story was used to champion the cause of liberty against the oppression of government as manifested in the issuance of general warrants in the colonies.

## COLONIAL HISTORY

The colonists inherited their concern for the sanctity of the home from their English roots. They felt oppressed by the use of general warrants and writs of assistance, and they reveled at the actions of Wilkes who took on the British government to oppose the use of a general warrant. A case emanating from the Massachusetts Superior Court in 1761 also proved influential. As previously mentioned, writs of assistance would expire six months after the death of the King. In February, 1761, six months after the death of King George II, Charles Paxton, chief customs official in Boston, petitioned for new writs of assistance in the Massachusetts Court. This petition was opposed by a group of merchants represented by James Otis. James Otis attacked the "tyrannical nature of the writs, the absence of judicial supervision, and . . . their unlimited scope," and referring to the English tradition in his attack, he characterized the writ as encroaching on "one of the most essential branches of English liberty [which] is the freedom of one's house. A man's house is his castle . . . This writ, if it should be declared legal, would totally annihilate this privilege."

Although the Court was not persuaded by Otis's argument and issued the writ, Otis's argument became widely known throughout the colonies because many lawyers and merchants were present at the event and newspapers ran accounts of the argument. Present at the argument was John Adams who took notes and distributed them in 1773. Fifty-six years after the argument, Adams declared, "Otis was a flame of fire! . . . Then and there was the first scene of the first Act of Opposition to the arbitrary Claims of Great Britain. Then and there the child Independence was born." According to noted legal historian Leonard W. Levy, Adams found Otis's speech so inspiring that it led to his framing of Article XIV of the Massachusetts Declaration of Rights, which, in turn, led to the Fourth Amendment.

Not surprisingly, early legislation of colonial governments reflected strong opposition to these general warrants. The first of these can be found in the Virginia Declaration of Rights of May 6, 1776, which stated:

X. THAT general warrants, whereby an officer or messenger may be commanded to search suspected places without evidence of a fact committed, or to seize any person or persons not named, or whose offence is not particularly described and supported by evidence, are grievous and oppressive, and ought not to be granted.

Following the lead of Virginia, Pennsylvania adopted its own search and seizure legislation in 1776, which stated:

X. That the people have a right to hold themselves, their houses, papers, and possessions free from search or seizure; and therefore warrants without oaths or affirmations first made, affording a sufficient foundation for them, and whereby any officer or messenger may be commanded or required to search suspected places, or to seize any person or persons, his or their property, not particularly described, are contrary to that right, and ought not to be granted.

Although the term *general warrant* does not appear in the text as it does in the Virginia statute, it is clear that the language in the Declaration of Rights refers to the qualities inherent in general warrants. Also, one should take note of the first clause, which refers to "the people have a right." As we will see, this type of clause was incorporated into the Massachusetts legislation that became the model for the Fourth Amendment. This type of clause might indicate a general privacy right. However, Davies in his article argues that this statement of right was not intended to provide general protection for the individual against searches and seizures but merely protection against general warrants as indicated by the wording that emphasizes the nature of the protected right.

He disagrees with other commentators who argue that the statement was designed to regulate government action beyond the issuance of general warrants. He points out that these commentators have not demonstrated that the colonists had concerns other than for general warrants. He also explains that the reason for the right statement was to show that the warrant standard was more than just a legal formula but was a fundamental protection to the citizens worthy of inclusion in the Declaration of Rights. This factor becomes important when we look at the discussion as to the need for a bill of rights in the next section. Davies further points out the influence of the Wilkes cases, which were primarily concerned with searches occurring in the home. The language, "their house," and so on is indicative of this concern. This language suggests that searches of warehouses were appropriate. Philadelphia was the busiest port in the colony and general warrants were necessary for customs enforcement. This was demonstrated by a statute enacted in 1780 that required specific warrants to search houses but permitted warrantless searches or even writs of assistance for searches other than houses. This specification of the dwelling is also found in the Massachusetts Constitution, yet is not found in the constitutions of states like Virginia and Maryland that did not have significant ports.

The Massachusetts statute, relying mostly on the wording of the Pennsylvania statute and written by John Adams, was adopted in 1780. It became the foundation for the Fourth Amendment. Note the statement of rights along with the term *therefore* and the specification of house, papers, and so on:

XIV. Every subject has a right to be secure from all unreasonable searches and seizures, of his person, his houses, his papers, and all his possessions. All warrants, therefore, are contrary to this right, if the cause or foundation of them be not previously supported by oath or affirmation; and if the order in the warrant to a civil officer, to make search in suspected places, or to arrest one or more suspected persons, or to seize their property, be not accompanied with a special designation of the persons or objects of search, arrest, or seizure: And no warrant ought to be issued, but in cases, and with the formalities, prescribed by the laws.

In my analysis of the Massachusetts statute, I rely again on the superb work by Thomas Davies. Massachusetts added the last provision that no warrant ought to issue unless prescribed by law. This was probably as a result of Entick v. Carrington (1765), one of the Wilkes series of cases in which the English Court held that the power to issue warrants was limited by law. This is also the first time that the term *unreasonable* was used. Davies suggests that Adams was a careful draftsman who wanted to clarify the Pennsylvania language so as to specify the type of search from which a person was to be free. Otherwise the language, "hold themselves . . . free from searches or seizure" could be interpreted to mean any search or seizure. The term unreasonable was used to mean against reason or, in the historical context, violative of fundamental legal principles. It represented a synonym for that which was illegal. In this context it referred to general warrants. However, the current interpretation of the term *unreasonable* by the Court has a broader meaning than the original "violative of a fundamental legal principle." With this meaning in mind, the Court goes through a type of balancing, weighing a variety of factors including needs of law enforcement, as well as privacy concerns of the individual (Whren v. United States, 1996; New Jersey v. TLO, 1985).

## THE FOURTH AMENDMENT

Permeating the Constitutional Convention was a general concern for individual rights and the best mechanism for dealing with this concern. Thus, there was considerable discussion about the necessity for a bill of rights. On the one side, the Anti-Federalist proponents wanted to quell the concerns of people who feared that, without specifically elaborated protections, the central government might take away these rights. On the other side, the Federalists felt that a bill of rights was unnecessary because the federal government was only granted explicitly mentioned powers and everything else was reserved to the states. According to the Federalists, the purpose of the Constitution was to define the existence of the federal government rather than the rights of the people, which would in any case be impossible to detail in one bill of rights. Alexander Hamilton in *The Federalist Papers No. 84* argued that the Constitution did in fact contain a bill of rights by defining the elements of a bill of rights such as the political privileges of the citizens and certain immunities and modes of proceeding. Nevertheless, the Anti-Federalist proponents of a bill of rights won the day. With the strong support of most of the populace, adoption was politically necessary to ensure ratification of the Constitution. This debate is summed up admirably by Patrick Henry in the Virginia State Convention on June 24, 1788:

A bill of rights may be summed up in few words. What do they tell us?—That our rights are reserved. Why not say so? Is it because it will consume too much paper? Gentlemen's reasoning against a bill of rights does not satisfy me. Without saying which has the right side, it remains doubtful. A bill of rights is a favorite thing with the Virginians and the people of the other states likewise . . . A bill of rights, even if its necessity be doubtful, will exclude the possibility of dispute; and, with great submission, I think the best way is to have no dispute.[7]

Patrick Henry himself felt that a prohibition of general warrants "by which an officer may search suspected places, without evidence . . . of a fact, or seize any person without evidence of his crime" should be part of this bill of rights.

James Madison of Virginia, relying on the Massachusetts Constitution of 1780, brought the original draft of the Fourth Amendment to the First Congress on June 8, 1789:

The right of the people to be secure in their persons, their houses, their papers, and their other property from all unreasonable searches and seizures, shall not be violated by warrants issued without probable cause, supported by oath or affirmation, or not particularly describing the places to be searched, or the persons or things to be seized.

This draft suggests that the intent was to limit the use of general warrants. There is no indication that Madison wanted to encourage the use of warrants or, for that matter, wanted a global prohibition against unreasonable searches, but rather only those that involved general warrants. The term unreasonable seems to refer to general warrants. Further, Madison proposed that this draft be placed in Article I's limitation on Congressional power rather than in a stand-alone provision. It seems then that his intent was to limit the power of Congress to issue general warrants.

The term *probable cause* appears for the first time in the Madison draft. Davies theorizes that he may have found the term in a 1786 Pennsylvania customs statute that allowed a customs official to obtain a search warrant. He points out that this standard was less rigorous than the common-law standard, which required both the showing of a violation in fact as well as probable cause. Blackstone, in describing the issuance of an arrest warrant, mentioned the necessity of proving an actual crime committed, as well as the "probability suspecting the party."[8] Thus Madison's draft, without the requirement of an offense in fact, was geared to ensure custom searches that would be a major source of revenue for the colonies.

A House Committee of Eleven, made up of one representative from each state, reviewed the Madison draft and reported the following on July 28, 1789:

The right of the people to be secure in their persons, houses, papers, and effects, shall not be violated by warrants issuing, without probable cause supported by oath or affirmation, and not particularly describing the places to be searched, and the persons or things to be seized.

This draft eliminated the phrase "no unreasonable searches or seizures" and substituted effects for the term *property*. Davies points out that the purpose of changing the wording from "property" to "effects" was to narrow the applicability of the amendment to a dwelling. The term *property* could refer to any real property other than a dwelling while the term *effect* refers to movable goods and not real property. When the House considered the draft by the Committee of Eleven, the omission of the unreasonable phrase was characterized as a mistake, and it was reinstated.

Davies points out that the term *unreasonable* came from Sir Edward Coke and was a synonym for illegality. It was therefore not intended to be the flexible, more broadly applicable term envisioned by Nelson Lasson in his 1937 treatise.[9] Davies further points out that the construction afforded to reasonableness today affords more discretionary governmental power than the Framers had in mind. The Lasson interpretation has certainly enjoyed the support of members of the Court. For example, Justice John Paul Stevens quoted the Lasson treatise in Payton v. New York (1980). "The general right of security from unreasonable search and seizure was given a sanction of its own and the amendment thus intentionally gives broader scope."

There is considerable debate over the origin of the phrase "and no warrant shall issue," which appears in the Fourth Amendment. In his treatise, Nelson Lasson claims that Egbert Benson of New York wanted to give the amendment a broader scope so that it would function as more than just a prohibition of general warrants. The House rejected his proposal for the phrase "and no warrant shall issue," which created the two-clause amendment (one clause prohibiting "unreasonable searches and seizure" and the second clause specifying the requirement for a warrant), though this phrase was ultimately incorporated into the amendment. Lasson claims that Benson, who served as the chairman of the committee to present the amendment in its final form, surreptitiously changed the text and submitted the Fourth Amendment as we now know it. Davies takes issue with Lasson's account. He suggests that Lasson, relying on the Congressional record, might have been mistaken as the House reporter made numerous errors.[10] He cites the *Gazette of the United States*,[11] quoted in Cogan,[12] as well as newspaper accounts, to suggest that Elbridge Gerry of Massachusetts made the motion. Further, Davies points out that Gerry (who often offered motions to help clarify the proposed amendments) was a more active participant at the Constitutional Convention than Benson. He thus claims that there is a strong likelihood that Elbridge Gerry of Massachusetts proposed the amendment and that the House actually passed the amendment in this form.

The critical question that remains is what does "and no warrant shall issue" mean. Lasson argues that "although [the language] was good as far as it went, it was not sufficient."[13] Lasson went on to interpret the phrase as adding a reasonableness interpretation separate and distinct from the warrant standard. Davies takes issue with Lasson's interpretation that the phrase was designed to give broader meaning to the Madison draft. Davies argues that the phrase "and no warrant shall issue" was simply designed to make the prohibition against general warrants more explicit. To support this argument, Davies points out that Gerry wanted a provision that was a more imperative declaration against general warrants. Davies further suggests that Gerry, as an Anti-Federalist, held a "near-paranoid fear" of general warrants.[14]

## WARRANT REQUIREMENT

There is little dispute, as indicated both by Madison's initial wording of the Fourth Amendment and by state constitutional provisions, that the Framers were concerned with the abuses associated with warrants and not with warrantless searches. Further support for this proposition can be found in the newspapers and pamphlets of the time:

There are other essential rights, which we have justly understood to be the rights of free men, as freedom from hasty and unreasonable search warrants, warrants not founded on oath, and not issued with due caution for searching and seizing men's papers, property, and persons.[15]

That all warrants, without oath or affirmation, to search suspect places or seize any person, his papers or property, are grievous and oppressive.[16]

Thus the Framers were concerned about customs officials who were armed with writs of assistance and as a result had carte blanche to search anywhere, including a private home. The major dispute has to do with how one interprets the Framers' disdain for general warrants. Some historians would favor interpreting the reasonable clause on its own and without regard to the warrant clause. These historians would interpret this disdain as a sentiment against all warrants. Davies, who interprets it more literally, would see it as disapproval for general warrants with basically a neutral position on warrants in general and certainly without a preference for them. Macklin would look to the underlying intent of the Framers and see this position against general warrants as a sentiment against arbitrary police action. He would see a warrant preference approach as a way to limit this type of police action. A preference for a warrant would generally require the police to obtain a warrant from a neutral magistrate before they could act. This preference is not an absolute requirement and would consider practicality concerns in the obtaining of a warrant.

Amar provides a gloss against a warrant preference approach by arguing that the Framers disapproved not only of general warrants and writs of assistance, but also of any warrants because these would indemnify officials from a civil lawsuit for trespassing. These civil suits were the prime method for dealing with police misconduct. Other scholars, including Taylor, take a more generalized position and lump general warrants together with any form of warrant, arguing that the Framers never intended to require the use of warrants. Macklin takes a broader view of this disdain for general warrants and concludes that the Framers were most concerned with oppressive governmental action as manifested by the searches of customs officials. He suggests that the same concern for discretionary police authority applies to warrantless searches. He further suggests that the Framers were mainly concerned about the power of the police, not the power of judges. As a result, he concludes that warrants as specified by the second clause of the Fourth Amendment serve as the effective method to limit the discretionary power of the police official. Macklin's approach is to look at broad issues that motivated our founding ancestors. Macklin argues that Otis, who railed against writs of assistance, would oppose warrantless searches because both relate to discretionary police power.

Davies argues that the Framers approved of specific warrants because they favored the orderly process associated with specific warrants. They were not concerned with warrantless activity because at the time, police activity was usually associated with authorization in the form of a warrant. There simply was not much ex-officio police authority. The Court did not respond to warrantless activity until police power expanded in the nineteenth and twentieth centuries. Amar and Taylor accurately point out that the Framers were concerned about general warrants, but were not really worried about specific warrants. In his argument, Otis endorsed specific warrants, which Davies indicates did provide significant protection against arbitrary searches. Thus, because they valued specific warrants, one might conclude that the Framers took these warrants for granted because they were very important and only sought to regulate general warrants.

Historian Lawrence Friedman characterized law enforcement institutions that existed at the time the Fourth Amendment was drafted as "a business of amateurs."[17] During the nineteenth century, police institutions expanded greatly. The constables, sheriffs, and night watchmen, who were often unpaid volunteers, were replaced by the trained, salaried police forces that we know today. With uniforms, guns, and a military hierarchy, the police forces moved from a strictly peacekeeping function to investigating crimes and providing the necessary evidence to convict the perpetrators of these crimes.[18] Also, legislature and courts expanded opportunities for warrantless activity by police during the nineteenth century. Ironically, the warrantless officers posed a similar threat of unbridled discretionary police activity that the customs officials, holding a warrant, posed to our founding ancestors.

This concern can be found in the 1914 decision of Weeks v. United States. In this case, United States marshalls conducted a warrantless search of a home. Concerned about the discretionary power of law enforcement, the *Weeks* Court expressed a preference for the use of warrants, especially for searches of the home:

The United States Marshalls could only have invaded the house of the accused when armed with a warrant issued as required by the Constitution, upon sworn information and describing with reasonable particularity the thing for which the search was to be made. Instead, he acted without sanction of law . . . and under color of his office undertook to make a seizure of private paper in direct violation of the prohibition against such action.

Thus a warrant was seen as a protection against governmental invasion of privacy. In this way, *Weeks* moved from the ban against general warrants to interpret the Fourth Amendment warrant clause as a protection, especially in the home, against discretionary policy activity. Although eleven years later, in Carroll v. United States (1925), the Court recognized that it was impractical to secure a warrant for certain types of searches, such as a car search, so it indicated a preference for securing a warrant whenever it was reasonably practical. Johnson v. United States (1948) further demonstrates the importance of the warrant in Fourth Amendment jurisprudence:

The point of the Fourth Amendment which often is not grasped by zealous officers, is not that it denies law enforcement the support of the usual inferences which reasonable men draw from evidence. Its protection consists in requiring that those inferences be drawn by a neutral and detached magistrate instead of being judged by the officer engaged in the often competitive enterprise of ferreting out crime.

The Court has continued to articulate its preference for warrants through its words but not by its actual holdings. In Katz v. United States (1967), the Court said, "searches conducted outside the judicial process, without prior approval by judge or magistrate, are per se unreasonable under the Fourth Amendment—subject only to a few specifically established and well delineated exceptions." In Mincey v. Arizona (1978), the Court characterized this preference as a cardinal principle. Nevertheless, the Court has increased the opportunities for warrantless activity so that Justice John Paul Stevens, dissenting in California v. Acevedo (1991), characterized the preference for warrants as "lip service."

## THE REASONABLENESS APPROACH

The Court's warrant preference became enmeshed in the debate over how the Framers intended the two clauses to be read. In a series of cases commencing in 1946 and ending in 1950 with United States v. Rabinowitz, the Court debated the relationship between the two clauses of the Fourth Amendment. Justice Sherman Minton, for the majority, believed that the reasonableness clause should be read separately and distinctly from the warrant clause. This reading dictates that the reasonableness of a search should be determined without regard to the second clause that includes the requirements for a warrant. Justice Frankfurter argued that the two clauses should be read together so as to give meaning to the amorphous term *unreasonable*. According to this reading, searches without a warrant were *per se* unreasonable. Although the Warren Court adopted the Frankfurter approach, it provided the mechanism for the movement of the present Court to the reasonableness analysis that has become the touchstone of the Fourth Amendment. In Terry v. Ohio (1968), the Warren Court was faced with a situation that involved suspicious activity that did not amount to a crime. In this case, the suspect was acting suspiciously by continuously (24 times) walking past and peering into a jewelry store window. Although the police officer confronted and frisked the suspect, this activity lacked the probable cause justification normally required for police activity because no crime had yet been committed. Wanting this serious police intrusion to come under the Fourth Amendment umbrella, the Court used the reasonableness clause and weighed the government interest (preventing a crime before it happens) with the intrusion (a stop and frisk that was less intrusive then a formal arrest). In doing this weighing, the Court avoided the probable cause requirement in the second clause of the Fourth Amendment and came up with a new standard of justification. This weighing, or balancing, has become the foundation of the reasonableness approach. Focusing on the reasonableness of the activity has allowed the Court to move away from the warrant requirement found in the second clause of the Fourth Amendment and to consider the reasonableness clause on its own.

A majority of the Court has clearly indicated its preference for the reasonableness approach. For example, in the area of third-party consent (see Analysis—Consent), the Court said, "The touchstone of the Fourth Amendment is reasonableness. The Fourth Amendment does not proscribe all state-initiated searches and seizures; it merely proscribes those which are unreasonable."(Illinois v. Rodriguez, 1990). In discussing an automobile exception to the warrant requirement, the Court in California v. Acevedo (1991) (see Analysis—Warrant Exceptions) said, "the first principle that the reasonableness requirement of the Fourth Amendment affords the protection the common law afforded." Likewise, in determining the acceptability of drug testing at a high school in Vernonia School District 47J v. Acton (1995) (see Analysis—Administrative Searches—

Justification—Reasonable Suspicion), the Court said, "As the text of the Fourth Amendment indicates, the ultimate measure of constitutionality of a government search is reasonableness." Finally, in upholding a search that may have been based on a pretext, the Court in Whren v. United States (1996) (see Analysis—Arrest and Criminal Searches—Justification—Probably Cause) said, "It is of course true that in principle every Fourth Amendment case, since it turns upon a reasonableness determination, involves a balance of all relevant factors."

Davies has expressed considerable concern for the emergence of reasonableness in Fourth Amendment analysis because in his opinion it provides too much discretionary power to the police and allows greater governmental intrusions. He argues that this ignores the "right to be secure" language of the Fourth Amendment, that focuses on the protection to be afforded to the individual. "The trajectory of doctrinal evolution has been away from a sense of the individual's right to be secure from government intrusion and toward an ever-enlarging notion of government authority to intrude."

Amar, on the other hand, supports the approach of the Court and points out the historical basis of this approach. He argues that the Fourth Amendment does not express a preference for a warrant or even probable cause but does specifically mention the requirement of reasonableness.

In light of the tragic attack of September 11, 2001, and the resulting legislation in the Patriot Act or United and Strengthening America Act of 2001, the reasonableness approach to the Fourth Amendment provides the potential for pernicious results that undermine individual liberties. At this time of great national concern, the reasonableness approach that balances the government interest with the intrusion of the individual is highly likely to favor the government at the expense of individual liberties.

## UTILIZATION OF HISTORY IN RECENT CASES— ORIGINAL INTENT

The Court continues to use historical rationales for their decisions. In Wilson v. Arkansas (1995), Justice Clarence Thomas pointed out that to give meaning to the reasonableness term, it is useful to determine the intent of the Framers. In this case, as well as in Kyllo v. United States (2001), the Court continues to recognize the importance of the home. In the unanimous decision by Justice Thomas, the Court upheld the importance of knocking and announcing a home search in determining Fourth Amendment reasonableness. At common law, although there was a recognition that an officer could break into a home, he "ought to signify the cause of his coming." In *Kyllo*, a case involving thermal imaging information emanating from a home, Scalia, writing for the majority, held that the applicability of the Fourth Amendment turned on what he perceived to be the original meaning of the amendment, which drew a "firm line at the entrance of the home" (Payton v. New York, 1980).

In Atwater v. City of Lago Vista (2001), Justice David Souter, for a 5-4 majority, turned to the history of the Fourth Amendment to determine the power of an officer to make an arrest without a warrant for a misdemeanor that did not involve a breach of the peace. The petitioner argued that founding-era common law forbade a warrantless misdemeanor arrest unless it involved a breach of the peace. Souter found that common law rules were not so clear with regard to warrantless arrests. He reviewed the history thoroughly and concluded that the evidence suggested that the Framers did not view a warrantless arrest for misdemeanor unaccompanied by real or threatened violence as unreasonable.

## CONCLUSION

The history of the Fourth Amendment in contemporary times has focused mainly on the meaning of the reasonableness clause and the importance of a warrant. The history has provided considerable data to support whatever position a justice of the Court has chosen to take with regard to these issues. Whether one relies exclusively on the narrow view of original intent (condemnation of general warrants), a broader view of original intent (limiting discretionary power of the police), or the specific wording of the Fourth Amendment, most would agree that the text and history are important sources for judicial decision making. How text and history are used is the subject of much debate. Justice Frankfurter once said, "it is true of journeys in the law the place you reach depends on the direction you are taking. And so where one comes out on a case depends on where one goes in."[19]

The problem with the utilization of history and the original wording is that there has been considerable debate both as to historical events and to the meaning of the wording of the Fourth Amendment. Thus the works of Thomas Davies of the University of Tennessee College of Law and Akhil Amar of the Yale Law School have been deliberately highlighted because their historical analysis has generated a great deal of attention. They also present different views of the Fourth Amendment. Although some of Amar's positions with regard to warrants and probable cause have not gained many followers, his position with regard to his emphasis on the reasonableness clause is the prevailing view of the present Court. Davies, however, has effectively pointed out that the Court's position with regard to the reasonableness clause lacks a historical basis.

## ENDNOTES

1. Thomas Davies, *Recovery of the Original Fourth Amendment*, 98 Mich. L. Rev. 547 (1999).

2. Tracy Macklin, *Central Meaning of the Fourth Amendment*, 35 Wm. & Mary L. Rev. 197 (1993) and Tracy Macklin, *When the Cure for the Fourth Amendment is worse than the disease*, 68 USC 1 (1994).

3. Akhil Reed Amar, *Fourth Amendment First Principles*, 107 Harv. L. Rev. 757 (1994).

4. Telford Taylor, *Two Studies in Constitutional Interpretation* (1969).

5. Neil H. Cogan, *The Complete Bill of Rights.* Oxford Press (1997).

6. William John Cuddihy, *The Fourth Amendment: Origins and Original Meaning.* Unpublished dissertation from Claremont Graduate School.

7. Cogan at 238.

8. Cogan at 243.

9. Nelson B. Lasson, *The History and Development of the Fourth Amendment to the United States Constitution* (1937). Baltimore, The Johns Hopkins Press. New York: BasicBooks.

10. Davies at 717, FN 479 & 480.

11. Davies at 717, FN 479 & 480.

12. Cogan at 237.

13. Lasson at 103.

14. Davies at 721.

15. The *Federal Farmer* No. 4, Oct. 12, 1787, cited Cogan at 239.

16. *Centinel* No. 2, Oct. 24, 1787, cited Cogan at 239.

17. Lawrence M. Friedman, *Crime and Punishment in American History* at 27 (1993).

18. Carol S. Steiker, *Second Thoughts About First Principles*, 107 Harv. L. Rev. 820 (1994).

19. United States v. Rabinowitz, 339 U.S. 56 (1950) Frankfurter dissent at 69.

# Analysis—Exclusionary Rule

## INTRODUCTION

We look at the Fourth Amendment first in the context of the exclusionary rule, the remedy created to address Fourth Amendment violations. If the U.S. Supreme Court finds a violation of the Fourth Amendment, the evidence resulting from the violation will be excluded. Without this remedy the Fourth Amendment, as the Court observed, is "a form of words valueless and undeserving of mention in a perpetual charter of inestimable human liberties" (Mapp v. Ohio, 1961).

The Court's approach to the exclusionary rule provides valuable insight into their attitude with regard to substantive Fourth Amendment doctrine. Is it more important to protect individual privacy values, or should we defer to the needs of law enforcement? As the Court has cut back on the applicability of the exclusionary rule, it has also cut back on when there is a viable remedy for a violation of the Fourth Amendment. We will see that the present Court has directly cut back on the exclusionary rule through a so-called balancing approach, which, in essence, is a cost/benefit analysis. This approach has limited the remedy to certain contexts. It has also indirectly cut back on the exclusionary rule by limiting the scope of derivative exclusion. The so-called "fruits of the poisonous tree doctrine" allowed for exclusion of not only the direct result of an illegality but also that which flowed from the illegality. We will see that it has expanded the exception to the fruits of the poisonous tree doctrine, thus limiting its thrust. In addition it has indirectly cut back on the exclusionary rule by limiting the standing doctrine that deals with the individuals who can raise Fourth Amendment objections.

## SCOPE

The first ten amendments to the Constitution, often referred to as the Bill of Rights, were enacted to protect the individual from the central federal government. Gradually, through the interpretation of the Fourteenth Amendment, that had been ratified in 1868, these amendments were made applicable to the states. We will see that the Fourth Amendment was incorporated through the Fourteenth Amendment in 1949 (Wolfe v. People of the State of Colorado, 1949). Initially, however, the Fourth Amendment exclusionary rule applied only to federal prosecutions.

Weeks v. United States (1914) was a case that involved a prosecution for using the mail for purposes of conducting a lottery, a violation of federal law. The evidence for the trial was obtained by two sources: searches conducted by a U.S. marshall and state police officers. The Court determined that each of these searches was an illegal, warrantless search. Because the Fourth Amendment was only applicable to federal government officials at that time, the Court recognized that it only had power to deal with the federal official. The defendant in the case petitioned for the return of the property illegally taken by these searches. In deciding to give back the property taken by the U.S. marshall and therefore prevent its use at the criminal trial, the Court seemed to rely on a rationale later described as judicial integrity. The Court did not want the trial courts to be in complicity with the illegal activity of the U.S. marshalls. This approach is reminiscent of the old unclean hands doctrine in Courts of Equity. One involved with illegal (unclean) activity was not entitled to relief in equity:

The tendency of those who execute the criminal laws of the country to obtain convictions by means of unlawful seizures . . . should find no sanction in the judgment of the courts which are charged at all times with the support of the Constitution . . .

This remedy of exclusion was expanded in Silverthorne Lumber Co. v. U.S (1920). In this case, the defendants were lawfully arrested and detained. Although they were detained, U.S. marshalls and representatives of the Department of Justice searched their office for books, papers, and documents. This search was conducted in the words of the Court, "without a shadow of authority." These illegally obtained items were returned but the information garnered from copying these papers was used to obtain additional indictments against the defendants. The grand jury, aware of these papers, subpoenaed the defendants to get the original copies of the papers that they previously had taken and copied. When the defendants refused to produce the papers, they were held in contempt of court. The Court, in an eloquent decision by Justice Oliver Wendall Holmes, held that not only evidence that was a direct result of an illegal search but any evidence derived from such illegality should be suppressed. "The essence of a provision forbidding the acquisition of evidence in a certain way is that no mere evidence so acquired shall not be used before the Court but that it shall not be used at all."

In *Silverthorne* and *Weeks*, one can see that the remedy created in *Weeks* for a Fourth Amendment violation had considerable thrust but, as we will see, this remedy was limited for many years to the control of federal law enforcement officials.

Because most criminal investigations and prosecutions in this country are performed by the state, the effect of the exclusionary remedy was not significant.

In Wolfe v. People of the State of Colorado (1949), the Supreme Court incorporated the guarantees of the Fourth Amendment into the Fourteenth Amendment, thus making them applicable to the states. In finding that a particular amendment to the Bill of Rights was applicable to the states, they found the right, in this case, the Fourth Amendment, to be "implicit in the concept of ordered liberty." However, the Court at the same time recognized that the specific requirements and restrictions placed on the federal authorities were not automatically applicable to the states, because the Fourteenth Amendment did not subject the states to specific limitations. Nevertheless, if a right was found to be basic to a free society, it was made applicable to the states. The security of one's privacy against intrusion by the state, as embodied in the Fourth Amendment, was found in *Wolfe* to be basic to a free society and therefore implicit in the concept of ordered liberty. As a result, this right was enforceable against the states through the Due Process Clause.

Despite making the Fourth Amendment applicable to the states, the Court refused to impose the exclusionary rule that the Federal courts used to enforce Fourth Amendment rights. In refusing to impose the exclusionary rule on the states, *Wolfe* characterized this as a remedy that was not derived from the specific wording of the Fourth Amendment but was rather a "matter of judicial implication." The Court, indicating that it did not favor the rule, pointed out that most of the English-speaking world did not have such a remedy and that, in fact, only 16 of 47 states had adopted it. Further, it indicated that other viable remedies were available, including private rights of action. The Court also expressed concern that the exclusionary remedy only benefits those persons who are charged with a crime and against whom incriminating evidence is sought to be used. Thus its benefits are limited to alleged wrongdoers. Finally, the Court, for reasons of federalism, felt that it could not impose this remedy on the states. "We cannot brush aside the experience of states which deem the evidence of such conduct by the police too slight to call for a deterrent remedy not by way of disciplinary measures but overriding the relevant rules of evidence."

Justice Frank Murphy, dissenting in *Wolfe*, pointed out the futility of addressing Fourth Amendment violations through other remedies, concluding that only through exclusion "can we impress on the zealous prosecutor that violations of the Constitution will do him no good." Justice Murphy characterized the alternative remedies as "no sanction at all." In dismissing the possibility of criminal sanctions, he pondered the question of what district attorney would prosecute himself or his associates for a search and seizure that he ordered. He further pointed out that a civil action in trespass would have limited damages, and therefore bringing charges would be futile.

Some twelve years after the *Wolfe* decision, the Supreme Court revisited the applicability of the Fourth Amendment to the states. In Mapp v. Ohio (1961), a 5-4 majority of the Court determined that the exclusionary remedy was an essential part of both the Fourth and Fourteenth Amendments and was therefore applicable to the states. Because of the controversy associated with the exclusionary rule, it is useful to look at this controversial decision in depth.

In *Mapp*, police officers in Cleveland, Ohio, stormed the home of Dorlee Mapp in search of a person wanted for questioning in connection with a recent bombing. The extensive search failed to turn up the bombing suspect but instead uncovered obscene material. Mrs. Mapp was charged under an Ohio statute with possession of obscene material. There was no dispute over the fact that the search violated the Fourth Amendment. Nevertheless, the evidence (obscene material) was admitted because the exclusionary rule was not applicable in the state of Ohio pursuant to *Wolfe*. Mrs. Mapp appealed her conviction for possession of obscene material, with the case ultimately reaching the Court. Mapp's primary argument to the Court had to do with the constitutionality of the Ohio obscenity statute. As a matter of fact, Justice Potter Stewart, who concurred in the majority decision in favor of Mrs. Mapp, did so because of the illegality of the statute and refused to join the five Justices who decided on the applicability of the exclusionary rule. Justice Stewart, subsequent to his retirement from the bench, described his shock when he received the opinion he thought would invalidate the Ohio statute:

I was shocked when Justice Clark's proposed Court opinion reached my desk. I immediately wrote him a note expressing my surprise and questioning the wisdom of overruling an important doctrine in a case in which the issue was not briefed, argued, or discussed by the state courts, by the parties counsel or at our conference following the oral argument.[1]

Justice John Marshall Harlan II, in his dissenting opinion, pointed out that the exclusionary argument was a subordinate point and that the pivotal issue that was decided by the Ohio Supreme Court was the constitutionality of the Ohio statute. As a matter of fact, the *Wolfe* decision was not even raised by Mrs. Mapp and was only raised by *amici* in a concluding paragraph of a brief without argumentation.[2] Justice Harlan characterized the five members of the Court who voted to extend the exclusionary rule as having "reached out" to overrule *Wolfe*.

The majority decision by Justice Tom Clark began by pointing out that there were some factors which had changed since the time of *Wolfe*. First, at the time of the decision, nearly two-thirds of the states were opposed to the use of the exclusionary rule. Now, more than half the states had adopted it. The majority then favorably cited the California Supreme Court decision in People v. Cahan (1955) for the proposition that other remedies had failed to secure compliance with constitutional provisions. Another factor that had changed since *Wolfe* was the confusion and inconsistency about the federal exclusionary rule that existed at the time of *Wolfe*. In *Mapp,* the Court concluded that later decisions of the Court had clarified the issue of standing in addition to discarding the so-called "silver platter" doctrine that had allowed the introduction of illegally seized evidence in federal trials if the seizure was by state officers. State officials not subject to the exclusionary remedy for violating the Fourth Amendment would give the illegally seized evidence ("on a silver platter") to federal officials. Thus the confusion existing at the time of *Wolfe* had largely been corrected. Though the majority pointed out these factual differences, the Court went on to conclude that they were not relevant or controlling for constitutional consideration. The Court determined that the exclusionary remedy is implicit in the concept of ordered liberty and a part of the Fourth Amendment. Otherwise the Fourth Amendment would be valueless and undeserving of mention, a "mere form of words."

Justice Hugo Black believed that he was bound by the specific wording of the Constitution. The Court, needing to gain the vote of Justice Black, tied the remedy of exclusion for Fourth Amendment violations with the Fifth Amendment prohibition of compelling testimony:

We find that, as to the Federal Government, the Fourth and Fifth Amendments and, as to the states the freedom from unconscionable invasions of privacy and the freedom from convictions based upon coerced confessions enjoy an intimate relation in their perpetuation of principles of humanity and civil liberty.

Justice Black, in his concurrence, indicated that, "when the Fourth Amendment's ban against unreasonable searches and seizures is considered together with the Fifth Amendment's ban against compelled self-incrimination, a constitutional basis emerges which not only justifies but actually requires the exclusionary rule."

*Mapp*, discussing the purpose of the exclusionary rule, relied on the rationale of judicial integrity introduced in the *Weeks* decision. The majority quoted Justice Louis Brandeis's dissent in Olmstead v. United States (1928):

Our government is the potent, the omnipresent teacher. For good or for all, it teaches the whole people by its example . . . If the government becomes a lawbreaker, it breeds contempt for law; it invites every man to become a law unto himself; it invites anarchy.

In addition to judicial integrity, the Court described the exclusionary remedy as a deterrent that would remove the "incentive to disregard" the Fourth Amendment. The deterrence rationale has been adopted by subsequent Court decisions.

Since *Mapp* there has been much debate over the efficacy of the exclusionary rule. The Fourth Amendment makes no mention of how the prohibitions stated within it should be enforced. Further, if the exclusionary remedy is regarded simply as a judicially created method to enforce the Fourth Amendment, what authority does the Court have to impose this remedy on the states? This question was answered in Ker v. California (1963), in which the Court stated the obvious proposition that it had no supervisory power over the state courts. Because our founding ancestors created two separate and distinct systems (federal and state), the power that the federal courts have over the states only involves interpreting the Constitution or federal laws that are the supreme law of the land. Thus, the implication in *Ker* was that the exclusionary rule had to be part of the Constitution for it to be applicable to the states.

Since the Warren Court's decision in *Mapp*, later Courts have not been particularly enamored with the exclusionary the rule. As we will see, they have sought to cut back on its applicability. Because the remedy is so important in preserving the guarantees of the Fourth Amendment, these cutbacks have had the effect of limiting the Fourth Amendment.

The first indication of the contempt in which the exclusionary rule is held can be found in the dissenting opinion of Chief Justice Warren Burger in Bivens v. Six Unknown Named Agents (1971). In the majority opinion, the Court created a civil damage remedy for a violation of the Fourth Amendment. Burger refused to join in the opinion, arguing that such a remedy was legislative and should be done by Congress. Then he took the opportunity, in a largely *ad hominem* way, to express his disdain for the exclusionary rule. He first points out that the only viable justification for the rule is deterrence. Given this limited justification for the exclusionary rule, he expresses concern that the amount of deterrence achieved does not justify the high societal price that he characterizes as "the release of countless guilty criminals." To support this argument, he points out that there are no direct sanctions on the wrongdoing of individual officers. In addition, it is the prosecutor who suffers the consequences of the exclusionary remedy by losing the case, and since law enforcement is not monolithic, the prosecutor has no power over police actions. Further, the educational effect of suppression is highly questionable given the fact that court decisions often come down years after the original police actions and police do not have the training, time, or inclination to read appellate decisions. Burger's final criticism of the rule has to do with proportionality. There is no consideration given to the wrongfulness of the police conduct or the offense with which the suspect is charged. Burger stated, "Freeing either a tiger or a mouse in a schoolroom is an illegal act, but no rational person would suggest that these two acts should be punished in the same way."

## DIRECT CUTBACKS TO THRUST OF EXCLUSIONARY RULE

### Balancing—Cost Benefit

For the last 30 years, the Court has focused exclusively on the deterrent rationale as the justification for the exclusionary rule. With this justification in hand, the Court has adopted a so-called balancing test, weighing the benefits of exclusion in deterring Fourth Amendment violations against the costs of suppressing reliable probative evidence. As we will see, if the benefits are limited, and are thus outweighed by the costs, the exclusionary remedy is not used. However, deterrence is difficult to measure because it applies to future acts and the Court has engaged in much speculation in analyzing the amount of deterrence gained by the exclusion of evidence. To the extent that the Court has actually measured the costs, it did not find Burger's comments in *Bivens* convincing, namely that the suppression of reliable evidence frees "countless guilty criminals." In *Leon*, the Court in a footnote reviewed various studies done to measure the costs of the exclusionary rule. The majority concluded that although a small percentage of cases actually result in the criminal going free, there are still a number of felons released because of the exclusionary rule (United States v. Leon, 1984).

The balancing test, because of its imprecision, often leads to a manipulation of results. This manipulation often benefits law enforcement at the expense of individual rights. In Massachusetts v. Sheppard (1984), Justice Brennan characterizes the balancing as follows:

. . . [T]he Court's decisions over the past decade have made plain that the entire enterprise of attempting to assess the benefits and costs of the exclusionary rule in various contexts is a virtually impossible task for the judiciary to perform honestly or accurately. Although the Court's language in those cases suggest that some specific empirical basis may support its analysis, the reality is that the Court's opinions represent inherently unstable compounds of intuition, hunches, and occasional pieces of partial and often inconclusive data.

Justice Brennan sees the balancing approach and the resulting limitation of the exclusionary rule as a way of placating the public's desire to combat crime. Although it may appear to be cost free, it results in a great loss of vital individual rights:

In the long run, however, we as a society pay a heavy price for each expediency, because [o]nce lost, such rights are difficult to recover. There is hope, however, that in time this or some later Court will restore these precious freedoms to their rightful place as a primary protection for our citizens against overreaching officialdom . . . (Justice William Brennan dissenting in *Leon*).

## Proceedings Other than Criminal Trial

United States v. Calandra (1974) introduced the use of the so-called balancing test in determining the applicability of the exclusionary rule. In this case, a witness summoned to a grand jury refused to answer questions based on evidence obtained in violation of the Fourth Amendment. This was a derivative use of the evidence that *Silverthorne* addressed. Not only was the direct evidence subject to suppression but anything derived from it could also be suppressed. Justice Powell, writing for the majority, indicated that the only purpose of the exclusionary rule was deterrence of Fourth Amendment violations. He seemed to discount the other rationale expressed in Mapp. Thus, though deterrence was mentioned but not highlighted in *Mapp*, it had become the major rationale for the exclusionary rule. Once this was established, he then balanced the benefits of exclusion in achieving deterrence against the cost of suppressing reliable evidence. He went through this balancing and concluded that the "extension of the exclusionary rule would seriously impede the grand jury" and that "(a)ny eventual deterrent effect which might be achieved by extending the rule to grand jury proceedings is uncertain at best." This balance has become the rationale for restricting the scope of the exclusionary remedy in a variety of settings.

In Stone v. Powell (1976), the Court, relying on the balancing analysis, restricted the possibility of raising the Fourth Amendment violation in a federal *habeas* proceeding, provided that there was a full, fair opportunity for a hearing during the state proceedings. *Habeas corpus* proceedings occur after the trial and direct appeal. It is brought by a prisoner who is claiming that he is being incarcerated in violation of his constitutional rights. The Court quoted *Calandra* to explain the justification for the exclusionary rule. "The rule is a judicially created remedy designed to safeguard Fourth Amendment rights generally through its deterrent effect . . ." (United States v. Calandra, 1974). The Court, although emphasizing the importance of excluding evidence at a criminal trial and its enforcement on direct appeal, prohibited the exclusionary remedy in *habeas*. The Court concluded that the additional benefits of exclusion for deterrence in collateral review would be outweighed by the costs. The costs, as articulated by the Court in *Stone*, include the diversion of the trial attention from guilt or innocence as the evidence to be excluded is reliable and probative of guilt or innocence. In this way, the Court concluded that "the rule thus deflects the truth-finding process and often frees the guilty." Given this test, the deterrence which might exist for the initial criminal trial, as evidence of guilt would be suppressed, would hardly seem to exist for proceedings substantially removed from the initial trial. There would hardly be much deterrence or discouragement of law enforcement officials from violating the Fourth Amendment when the proceedings are so remote from the trial determining guilt or innocence.

The same balancing analysis has resulted in the Court holding the exclusionary rule inapplicable in Internal Revenue Service (IRS)–initiated civil actions to collect taxes (United States v. Jarvis, 1976), in deportation administrative proceedings (I.N.S. v. Lopez-Mendoza, 1984), and finally and more recently, in parole revocation hearings (Pennsylvania v. Board of Probation and Parole v. Scott, 1998).

A closer look at *Scott* shows the subjective nature of this balancing approach. In the 5-4 decision authored by Justice Clarence Thomas, the Court concluded that the costs of disrupting the functioning of otherwise flexible administrative parole revocation proceedings would outweigh the minimal deterrence benefit. In analyzing the deterrence benefit, the Court indicated that a police officer would be sufficiently deterred by the use of exclusion at a criminal trial. The dissenters, in a decision written by Justice David Souter, disagreed with the majority's assessment of the deterrence benefit. The dissent pointed out the reality of the parole system. A police officer with knowledge of a parolee status is more likely to go through the administrative parole revocation process rather than a new prosecution with the resulting trial. Parole revocation "is often preferred to a new prosecution because of the procedural ease of recommitting the individual on the basis of a lesser showing by the state."

## Good Faith Exception: Exclusion at a Criminal Trial

The previous section dealt with the utilization of the balancing approach to limit the exclusionary remedy in proceedings other than a criminal trial. Given the Court's adherence to the deterrence rationale as the singular benefit of the exclusionary rule, it is not surprising that it would use the balancing approach to determine the applicability of the rule in a criminal trial when the police officers acted reasonably or in good faith. How, after all, do you deter an officer acting in good faith?

In *Leon,* the Court, in a 6-3 decision authored by Justice White, considered the issue of whether the Fourth Amendment exclusionary rule should be cut back so as not to preclude the prosecution from presenting evidence as part of its proof at trial when an officer was reasonably relying on a search warrant issued by a neutral magistrate, even though this search warrant was later determined to lack probable cause. The Court in *Leon* carefully chronicled the extensive police investigatory work done by the Burbank Police Department. As a result of an informant tip indicating a drug operation, the police undertook extensive surveillance of two locations. They observed several people, one of whom was known for his prior drug involvement, leaving the locations in question with small packages. Officer Romback, described as an experienced and well-trained narcotics investigator, prepared an application for a search warrant. A warrant was issued and executed, and drugs were found in the resulting search. The District Court, after an evidentiary hearing, found that there was insufficient probable cause for the warrant and suppressed the evidence. In response to a request by the government, the District Court found that Officer Romback acted in good faith. The Ninth Circuit affirmed. The government's petition for certiorari to the Court did not seek review of the probable cause issue but instead sought to challenge the exclusionary remedy when an officer acted in good faith reliance on a search warrant that was subsequently held to be defective.

To determine this issue, the Court went through the balancing test initiated in *Calandra*. In looking at the possible deterrent benefit, White raised the issue of whether the exclusionary rule had any deterrent value in a situation where the officer acted in an objectively reasonable manner and concluded that the possibility of deterrence was minimal. He further pointed out that the deterrent rationale was limited to police misconduct and was not applicable to the conduct of judges or magistrates.

In determining the cost of the exclusionary rule, the Court used some empirical data and found that the rule results in nonprosecution (some sort of plea bargaining or dropping of charges) or nonconviction of between 0.6 percent to 2.35 percent of arrested felons. Another study indicated that these figures were 2.8 percent to 7.1 percent for drug charges. Thus, while the cost does not result in the "freeing of countless criminals," there are costs nevertheless. Justice White concluded, based on the balancing test, that "the marginal or non-existent benefits produced by suppressing evidence obtained in objectively reasonable reliance on a subsequently invalidated search warrant cannot justify the substantial cost of exclusion."

In creating the good faith exception, the Court thought it could be easily applied by lower courts since obtaining a search warrant is an objective test. In creating this good-faith exception, JusticeWhite imposed some limitations on its applicability. The limitations arise when the magistrate "wholly abandons his judicial role" and thus could not be regarded as neutral and detached, when the magistrate was misled by an affiant who lied or recklessly disregarded the truth, or when "an affidavit was so lacking in indicia of probable cause as to render official belief in its existence entirely unreasonable."

The *Leon* decision presents some rather obvious concerns. Without the remedy of exclusion, what incentive would there be to request a review of a judge's decision to issue a warrant? Not only would the petitioner have to demonstrate a violation of the Fourth Amendment, but he would also have to fall within one of the limited restrictions on the good faith exception in order to have evidence suppressed. Another possible problem with this exception is that it might promote magistrate shopping by the police. Before *Leon*, an officer such as Romback, who did an extensive investigation, would have an incentive to find a demanding magistrate in order to ensure Fourth Amendment compliance and avoid later suppression. After *Leon*, this incentive is reduced considerably because now Romback will be insulated from later review by going to any magistrate with a request that might not comply with the Fourth Amendment. In addition, magistrates who feel that they will rarely be reviewed will have less incentive to devote as much care or attention to the issuance of warrants. Justice Brennan captures this concern in his dissent.

[C]reation of this new exception for good faith reliance upon a warrant implicitly tells magistrates that they need not take much care in reviewing warrant applications, since their mistakes will from now on have virtually no consequence: If their decision to issue a warrant is correct, the evidence will be admitted; if their decision was incorrect but [not "entirely unreasonable" and] the police rely in good faith on the warrant, the evidence will also be admitted. Inevitably, the care and attention devoted to such an inconsequential chore will dwindle.

One final point about *Leon* has to do with the dilution of the probable cause standard. In Illinois v. Gates (1983), the Court loosened the standard for probable cause. This lesser standard would only result in exclusion under *Leon* if the affidavit supporting the warrant was so lacking in indicia of probable cause (already a lesser standard) as to render official belief in its existence entirely unreasonable. This more flexible standard, coupled with the good faith exception, represents a double dilution of the justification (probable cause) for a Fourth Amendment search.

*Leon's* companion case, Massachusetts v. Sheppard (1984), involved a facially invalid warrant as opposed to lack of probable cause. In *Sheppard*, homicide detectives prepared a search warrant for a murder investigation, but because it was Sunday, they could only find a form warrant for drugs. The form and the affidavit were presented to a judge who assured the police that he would make the necessary changes to the search warrant so as to conform to the affidavit. Although some changes were made, the warrant still had language about controlled substances and therefore did not meet the particularity requirements of the Fourth Amendment. As a result, the state court suppressed the evidence. The Supreme Court reversed, holding that the officer acted in good faith reliance on the assurance of the judge.

Whatever an officer may be required to do when he executes a warrant without knowing beforehand what items are to be seized, we refuse to rule then an officer is required to disbelieve a judge who just advised him, by word and by action, that the warrant he possesses authorized him to conduct the search he has requested.

*Leon* created a good faith exception only in the context of a search warrant, however, as Justice Brennan observed, "I am not at all confident that the exception unleashed today will remain so confined." This comment by Justice Brennan proved prophetic. Illinois v. Krull (1987) involved an Illinois statute that required motor vehicle parts sellers to permit a search of certain records without a warrant or probable cause. The search was later found to be illegal when the statute was declared invalid. The Court, in refusing to apply the exclusionary rule, expanded the good faith exception to officers acting pursuant to a statute that was later held to be invalid. The majority stated:

The approach used in Leon is equally applicable in the present case. The application of the exclusionary rule to suppress evidence obtained by an officer acting in objectively reasonable reliance on a statute would have little deterrent effect on the officer's action, as would the exclusion of evidence when an officer acts in objectively reasonable reliance on a warrant.

A further extension of *Leon* can be found in Arizona v. Evan (1995). In this case, police, relying on a computer report that there was an outstanding warrant for the driver, arrested the driver and pursuant to a search incident to the arrest, found marijuana. It turned out that the computer was in error and the arrest warrant had been revoked. The error was the result of a clerical mistake by a court employee. The Court indicated that according to *Leon*, the exclusionary rule was designed to deter police misconduct. Because they were dealing with court employees, it would not have a deterrent effect on law enforcement personnel and therefore exclusion was not called for. The Court stated:

If it were indeed a court clerk who was responsible for the erroneous entry on the police computer, application of the exclusionary rule also could not be expected to alter the behavior of the arresting officer. . . . There is no indication that the arresting officer was not acting objectively reasonably when he relied upon the police computer record. Application of the *Leon* framework supports a categorical exception to the exclusionary rule for clerical error of court employees.

## INDIRECT CUTBACKS

### Standing

In civil cases, generally speaking, a person with an interest in the lawsuit has standing to be part of the case. In the criminal realm, in order for a person to complain about a constitutional violation, the individual must be a victim of the violation. This concept is reflected in the Federal Rules of Criminal Procedure (41 § e), which states "(only) a person aggrieved by an unlawful search and seizure" may seek to suppress the evidence illegally seized.

There is an important relationship between standing and the exclusionary rule. The greater the number of individuals who can litigate a Fourth Amendment violation, the more opportunity there is to exclude evidence. It is interesting to note that the most expansive standing case was decided by the Warren Court (Jones v. United States, 1960). As we will see, there have been substantial cutbacks to the decision as the Burger and Rehnquist Courts have expressed their concerns about the exclusionary rule.

Initially, standing concepts were closely related to the law of property. In order to complain about Fourth Amendment activity, an individual needed to have an ownership relationship with the item seized or the place searched. This approach to standing greatly limited the number of individuals who could raise Fourth Amendment violations. In *Jones*, the Court moved from arcane property law concepts to a broader approach to standing. The majority stated:

It is unnecessary and ill-advised to import into the law surrounding the constitutional right to be free from unreasonable searches and seizures subtle distinctions, developed and enforced by the common law in evolving the body of private property law.

In *Jones*, police found drugs in an awning just outside the window of an apartment. The defendant, Jones, was charged with possession of the narcotics and sought to suppress them. The government argued that Jones did not have standing to suppress the items found in the apartment because the apartment belonged to Jones' friend, who had given him a key and the use of the premises. He did not pay rent and had slept there for maybe a night. The district court held that Jones lacked standing because he did not have a substantial possessory interest in the locations searched.

The Court, in a decision by Justice Felix Frankfurter, gave Jones standing, finding that he was indeed a victim of the search and seizure. The first reason for conferring standing was based on logic. How could the government on the one hand claim that Jones possessed narcotics and on the other hand argue that he did not have standing? The Court reasoned here that:

To hold that petitioner's failure to acknowledge interest in the narcotics or the premises prevented his attack upon the search, would be to permit the Government to have the advantage of contradictory positions as a basis for conviction.

In addition, the Court did not think that it was fair for a defendant to take the stand and admit possession for purposes of standing only to have that testimony used against him to prove the substantive offense. Thus, the Court allowed for automatic standing to contest a Fourth Amendment violation when one was charged with possession of an illegal item.

The second ground for allowing standing was a shift from property law concepts of standing, such as an invitee as opposed to a trespasser, to conferring standing on anyone who was "legitimately on the premises" at the time of the search. However, this expansive approach to standing has been substantially reined in by the Burger and Rehnquist Courts, as we will see in Rakas v. Illinois (1978).

### Automatic Standing

In United States v. Salvucci (1980), the Court based its elimination of the automatic standing rule primarily on two of its prior decisions. In Simmons v. United

States (1968), the Court held that the defendant's pretrial testimony on a motion to suppress could not be used against him at trial. In light of *Simmons*, a defendant was no longer faced with the dilemma of incriminating himself (admitting that he possessed the drugs, the crime for which he was charged) in order to establish standing. In the second decision, Rakas v. Illinois (1978), the Court established legitimate expectation of privacy as the basis for determining standing. Thus, the government no longer held contradictory positions with regard to possession and standing because the Court held that it is possible for an individual to have an interest in seized property without necessarily being in possession of it. On the other hand, in the case of Rawlings v. Kentucky (1980), to be discussed later in this text, the Court specifically held that mere possessory interest in a seized item does not necessarily give one standing (no expectation of privacy) to challenge the search.

### Standing Merges With Fourth Amendment

In Rakas v. Illinois, the Court, feeling that the "legitimately on premises" standard was "too broad a gauge for the measurement of Fourth Amendment rights," decided to merge the standing analysis with the determination of Fourth Amendment applicability—that is, expectation of privacy, which is discussed in a later section of the analysis. It is interesting to note in *Rakas* that the Court recognized the close relationship between the exclusionary rule and the standing doctrine:

Each time the exclusionary rule is applied it exacts a substantial social cost for the vindication of Fourth Amendment rights. Relevant and reliable evidence is kept from the trier of fact and the search for truth at trial is defeated. Since our cases generally have held that one whose Fourth Amendment rights are violated may successfully suppress evidence obtained in the course of an illegal search and seizure, misgivings as to the benefit of enlarging the class of persons who may invoke the rule we properly considered when deciding whether to expand standing to assert Fourth Amendment violations.

In *Rakas*, the police, suspecting that a car was used for a robbery, stopped and searched the car. In searching the car, the police discovered a sawed-off rifle under the front passenger seat and a box of rifle shells in the glove compartment. Rakas, a passenger, sought to suppress the rifle and shells claiming that he was "legitimately on the premises." Rakas did not claim an ownership interest in either the vehicle, the rifle, or the shells. The Court, in denying standing, replaced the standing analysis with the Fourth Amendment analysis. "But we think the better analysis forthrightly focuses on the extent of particular defendant's rights under the Fourth Amendment, rather than on any theoretically separate, but invariably intertwined concept of standing."

Now, in order to have standing, the analysis is whether the person asserting it has a legitimate expectation of privacy in the place searched. In *Rakas*, the Court said that a passenger who asserted neither a property interest in the place searched (a car) nor the item seized had no expectation of privacy in the area searched. It is interesting to note that, although the Court in Jones abandoned the property concept for standing, *Rakas* seems to mark a return to that approach.

Although it is reasonably clear what *Rakas* did say, problems of interpretation arise when there are slight variations in the *Rakas* facts. In that case, the glove compartment and under the front passenger seat were the areas searched. It is not clear what the *Rakas* Court would rule with regard to the area on the seat next to the passenger, although in Wyoming v. Houghton (1999), the Court held that having probable cause to search a car allowed for the scope of that search to include a purse in the backseat owned by a passenger. The Court did not directly address whether the passenger could have contested that search, but it did indicate that the passenger had an expectation of privacy, albeit a reduced one, because of his relationship to the purse.

Despite the *Jones* Court's disillusionment with a property concept, ownership of the area searched was important to the *Rakas* Court. *Rakas* indicated that the owner of the vehicle, even if absent at the time of the search, would always have standing to contest the search. A person who borrowed the car from the owner and who had control (key) of the vehicle would also have standing to the extent of his access to the vehicle. Thus, if he did not have a trunk key, he would not have standing to contest a trunk search.

One final point about *Rakas* that should be made is that the Court was dealing with an automobile that, because it is heavily regulated (equipment and traffic laws), has enjoyed a lesser privacy expectation than a home. Justice Lewis Powell highlights this point in his concurrence:

Nothing is better established in Fourth Amendment jurisprudence than the distinction between one's expectation of privacy in an automobile and one's expectation when in other locations.

The distinction between an apartment and an automobile was one factor in upholding the *Jones* decision, as was the fact that Jones, because he possessed a key, had control of the apartment.

In Rawlings v. Kentucky (1980), the Court specifically held that a mere possessory interest in the item seized would not be sufficient to confer standing. Rawlings, the defendant, had placed assorted pills in the purse of a companion. At the time the purse was searched, Rawlings readily admitted an ownership interest in the pills. The Court, while indicating that this might be a factor in the standing equation, held that Rawlings had no expectation of privacy in the purse. His lack of control of the purse, including the ability to exclude others from searching it, appeared to be the most important factor for the Court. It is interesting to note Justice Marshall's dissent, in which he argues that the majority is ignoring the original intent of the Fourth Amendment:

The Fourth Amendment, it seems to me, provides in plain language that if one's security in one's 'effects' is disturbed by an unreasonable search and seizure, one has been the victim of a constitutional violation, and so it has always been understood. Therefore the Court's insistence that in order to challenge the legality of the search one must also assert a protected interest in the premises is misplaced. The interest in the item seized is quite enough to establish that the defendant's personal Fourth Amendment rights have been invaded by the government's conduct.

Two cases subsequent to *Jones* have elaborated on the Court's attitude with regard to standing as it related to a home. In Minnesota v. Olsen (1990), unlike Jones, the overnight guest was there with the owner. He never had a key or control over the home. Nevertheless, the Court allowed Olson to have standing. In a 7-2 decision by Justice Byron White, the Court said, "From the overnight guest's perspective he seeks shelter in another's home precisely because it provides him with privacy, a place where he and his possessions will not be disturbed by anyone but his host and those his host allows inside."

In Minnesota v. Carter (1998), the Court declared that a person visiting a home for business purposes, unlike a social guest, did not have an expectation of privacy. It is interesting to note that Justice Antonin Scalia, concurring with Justice Thomas, looked to the language of the Fourth Amendment and interpreted the term *home* to mean the place where one actually lives. Justice Scalia commented that the Court in Minnesota v. Olsen went to the absolute limits of that language in allowing standing to an overnight guest.

### Conclusion

The case of United States v. Payner (1980) graphically points out the dangers associated with the present standing limitations. In *Payner*, the IRS stole the briefcase of a Bahamian banker in order to convict *Payner* of tax fraud. Despite an outrageous violation of the banker's Fourth Amendment rights, *Payner* had no expectation of privacy in the banker's briefcase and had no standing to complain of the government's illegal activity. These types of standing limitations literally encourage deliberate Fourth Amendment violations.

How does one determine legitimate expectation of privacy and therefore standing? The focus should be on the place searched, not on the item seized. Thus, ownership of the place searched, as opposed to the item seized, is an important factor. Access and control of the place searched, through a key, also contributes to standing. The Court is less stringent about these factors when dealing with a home as opposed to an automobile, especially if the visitor to the home is a social guest.

## DERIVATIVE EVIDENCE

As mentioned earlier, in *Silverthorne,* the Court held that not only direct evidence, that which was found as an immediate result of the search, but also derivative evidence, that which flowed from the initial evidence, that resulted from a Fourth Amendment violation, would be excluded. This doctrine came to be known as the *fruit of the poisonous tree.* In Nardone v. United States (1939), the Court reasoned that once the accused has shown a violation of his Fourth Amendment rights, "the trial judge must give opportunity, however closely confined, to the accused to prove that a substantial portion of the case against him was a fruit of a poisonous tree." To give meaning to the exclusionary sanction, it was important to suppress not only the evidence found as a direct result of the violation but also the additional evidence obtained because of the knowledge gained from the initial violation.

Given the Court's disenchantment with the exclusionary rule, there have been exceptions created to restrict opportunities for excluding derivative evidence. One of these exceptions, "sufficient attenuation" to dissipate the taint, can be found in Wong Sun v. United States (1963). *Wong Sun* provides a good illustration of the fruits doctrine. In this case, Toy was illegally arrested, and during his arrest, he made a statement implicating Yee. The police immediately went to Yee's apartment and found narcotics. They wished to introduce the narcotics against Toy. The Court held that the illegal arrest represented the trunk of the tree, and the question that was asked was "whether, granting establishment of the primary illegality, the evidence to which instant objection is made has been come at by exploitation of that illegality or instead by means sufficiently distinguished to be purged of the primary taint." The Court held that the narcotics found at Yee's apartment were the result of the exploitation of the illegality, the illegal arrest.

Toy also implicated another individual named Wong Sun who was arrested without probable cause. Wong Sun was arraigned and later released on his own recognizance and returned voluntarily several days later to make a statement. With regard to the statement, the Court held that the connection between the Wong Sun's illegal arrest and his statement had become so attenuated as to dissipate the taint. The Court explained that, "We need not hold that all evidence is 'fruit of the poisonous tree' simply because it would not have come to light but for the illegal action of the police." Thus Wong Sun was unable to suppress the statement. With regard to the drugs found at Yee's apartment, Wong Sun was also unsuccessful in his effort to suppress them. Because the trunk of that tree came from Toy's illegal arrest, Wong Sun did not have standing to complain about the search for the drugs.

With regard to this particular exception, the Court has had opportunities to consider the issue of confessions resulting from an illegal arrest, a Fourth Amendment violation. When a suspect is arrested and interrogated, he is given certain warnings in order to neutralize the inherently coercive atmosphere of custodial police interrogation (Miranda v. Arizona, 1967). These warnings are: You have the right to remain silent. Anything you say can be used against you. You have the right to a lawyer during the interrogation. If you can't afford a lawyer, one will be appointed to represent you.

When an individual who has been arrested illegally and interrogated ultimately confesses, the fact that he has been given the *Miranda* warnings is not in itself sufficient to alleviate the taint of a Fourth Amendment violation. If this were not the case, the police could effectuate an illegal arrest and simply give a *Miranda* warning to dissipate the Fourth Amendment taint (Dunaway v. New York, 1979). "To admit petitioner's confession in such a case would allow law enforcement officers to violate the Fourth Amendment with impunity, safe in the knowledge that they could wash their hand with the procedural safeguards of the Fifth" (Dunaway v. New York, 1979 (quoting Comment, 25 Emory L.J. 227, 238 (1976))).

In Brown v. Illinois (1975) and Taylor v. Alabama (1982), the Court also addressed the insufficiency of *Miranda* warnings to act as a "cure-all" in the attenuation of the taint of Fourth Amendment violations. In *Brown,* officers investigating a murder broke into the defendant's apartment, searched it, and arrested the defendant all without probable cause or a warrant. The officers informed the defendant of his rights under *Miranda,* and within two hours, he made two inculpatory statements while in police custody. In confirming that *Miranda* warnings could not break the chain between the illegal arrest and the statements made, the Court explained that *Miranda* warnings were an important factor in the attenuation analysis. However, the majority also considered other factors in its attenuation analysis, including the temporal proximity of the arrest and confession (how long after the arrest was the confession made), the presence of intervening circumstances (did the suspect get to make a phone call or talk to anyone), and, perhaps most importantly, the flagrancy of the official misconduct.

*Taylor* also involved a confession obtained after an individual was illegally arrested. The Court observed that the fact that the defendant waited six hours after his arrest to confess, compared with the two hours in both Brown and Dunway, was insignificant because, during that entire period, the defendant was "in police custody, unrepresented by counsel . . . questioned on several occasions, fingerprinted, and subjected to a lineup." In each of these cases, the flagrancy of the police violation appears to have been an important factor in the Court's decision. The flagrancy consideration is not surprising, given that the purpose of the exclusionary rule is deterrence. This is highlighted by the case of Rawlings v. Kentucky (1980). In finding attenuation, even though the statement was made 45 minutes from the illegal arrest, the Court found the Fourth Amendment violation to be a good faith mistake as opposed to a flagrant violation.

In other derivative evidence cases, the Court has been reluctant to suppress the evidence. United States v. Ceccolini (1978) was a case involving the discovery of a live witness as a result of a Fourth Amendment violation. In *Ceccolini*, a police officer named Biro stopped by a florist shop to talk to an employee, opened an envelope with money lying on the cash register (an illegal search), and discovered not only money but also policy slips (betting slips). When the officer asked the employee to whom the envelope belonged, the employee responded that it belonged to Ceccolini, the owner of the shop. The employee was later asked to testify against Ceccolini, and Ceccolini moved to suppress her testimony as the fruit of an illegal search. Although Justice Burger indicated that he supported a per se exception to the fruits doctrine when the Fourth Amendment violation resulted in the finding of a live witness, the majority refused to adopt such an exception. Instead, in analyzing attenuation, the majority focused on the voluntary nature of the live witness' testimony and the flagrancy of the violation. In discussing the flagrancy of the violation, the Court harkened back to the deterrence rationale: "There is, in addition, not the slightest evidence to suggest that Biro entered the shop or picked up the envelope with the intent of finding tangible evidence bearing on an illicit gambling operation, much less any suggestion that he entered the shop and searched with the intent of finding a willing and knowledgeable witness to testify against the respondent. Application of the exclusionary rule in this situation could not have the slightest deterrent effect on the behavior of an officer such as Biro."

Another exception to the fruits doctrine, which was mentioned although not elaborated on in *Silverthorne*, is the independent source exception. Under this exception, the state can demonstrate that it found the secondary evidence through an independent source and did not rely on exploiting the initial illegality. The Court elaborated on this exception in Murray v. United States (1988), a case in which federal law enforcement agents forced entry into a warehouse, observed bales of marijuana in plain view, left to obtain a warrant, and then reentered and seized the marijuana. The majority determined that the fact the officers had illegally entered the warehouse was not important because the warrant that they ultimately obtained did not rely on their observations from the forced entry. In his dissent, Justice Marshall severely criticized the majority for "failing to provide sufficient guarantees that the subsequent search was, in fact, independent of the illegal search." Justice Marshall argued that, because obtaining a warrant is often inconvenient and time consuming, officers will now actually have an incentive to perform illegal searches simply to determine if obtaining a warrant is worth the effort. He stated: "the admission of the evidence reseized during the second search severely undermines the deterrence function of the exclusionary rule. Indeed, admission in these cases affirmatively encourages illegal searches."

One final exception involves evidence that would ultimately have been found by other means even though it was actually found by exploiting the initial illegality. This exception has been called the *inevitable discovery exception*. It stems from a case involving the Sixth Amendment, although the Court indicated that it was applicable to the Fourth. In Nix v. Williams (1984), a man who had abducted and murdered a young girl turned himself into police 160 miles from Des Moines, the town where the abduction had occurred. Police believed that the defendant had left the girl's body somewhere between the scene of the abduction and a rest stop where they discovered some of the girl's clothes, so they organized a large-scale search by 200 volunteers. Meanwhile, the officers who were transporting the defendant back to Des Moines interrogated the defendant in violation of his Sixth Amendment right to have counsel present. The defendant made several incriminating statements and eventually led the officers to the girl's body. Although the Court found that the statements made by the defendant could not be introduced at trial, they decided that evidence relating to the condition of the body as it was found, articles and photographs of her clothing, and results of a postmortem medical examination could be introduced. In so finding, the Court reasoned that the search parties would have discovered the body shortly anyway, and that the prosecution should not be put in a worse position simply because of earlier police error or misconduct. "If the prosecution can establish by a preponderance of the evidence that the information ultimately or inevitably would have been discovered by lawful means [in this case, the volunteers' search] then the deterrence rationale has so little basis that the evidence should be received. Anything less would reject logic, experience, and common sense." The fundamental problem with this doctrine is that it is speculative. The Court is basically guessing at a result that has not occurred.

In summary, seeking to limit the thrust of the exclusionary rule, the Court has liberally interpreted exceptions to the derivative evidence doctrine established in *Silverthorne*. They have readily found attenuation, especially when the police action is not particularly flagrant and thus not as subject to deterrence. It has established a new exception, inevitable discovery. Finally it has turned a blind eye even on flagrant police activity in finding the independent source exception.

## ENDNOTES

1. Potter Stewart, *The Road to Mapp v. Ohio and Beyond: The Origins, Development and Future of the Exclusionary Rule in Search and Seizure Cases*, 83 Colum. L. Rev. 1365 (1983) at 1368.

2. Mapp v. Ohio, 367 U.S. 643 FN5 at 674.

# Analysis—Government Action

## INTRODUCTION

The Bill of Rights, or the first 10 amendments to the U.S. Constitution, was designed as a method to protect citizens against the power of the central government. Thus, in order for the Fourth Amendment to apply, we must first have some sort of governmental conduct as opposed to private conduct. The second requirement is that the government conduct in question must be regarded as a search and seizure in order to implicate the Fourth Amendment. Conduct that is regarded as search and seizure is that conduct in which an individual has a reasonable expectation of privacy from intrusion. A reasonable expectation, discussed in the next section, is that which the majority of the Supreme Court says is reasonable.

## PRIVATE ACTION

As early as 1921, in Burdeau v. McDowell, the Court held that private procurement of evidence was not governed by the Fourth Amendment. In *Burdeau*, the petitioner had been discharged from the company he worked at for misconduct. When representatives of the company and their hired private detectives took possession of the petitioner's office, they removed papers from his desk and office safe. Shortly after discovering the papers, a representative from the company forwarded a letter found in the petitioner's desk to the U.S. Attorney General's office indicating that the company had papers in its possession that might prove useful to the Department of Justice's investigation of petitioner's alleged fraudulent use of the mails. In allowing the government to use the evidence, the Court said, "The Fourth Amendment gives protection against unlawful searches . . . its protection applies to governmental action. Its origin and history clearly show that it was intended as a restraint upon the activity of the sovereign authority." The Fourth Amendment, which was part of the so-called Bill of Rights, was designed to protect the individual from the power of the government. Although the property of the petitioner had been wrongly taken, no federal government official had participated in the wrongful seizure of the property or had any knowledge of the seizure until later. Therefore, "[t]here was no invasion of the security afforded by the Fourth Amendment against unreasonable search and seizure, as whatever wrong was done was the act of individuals in taking the property of another." Thus, the Court held that if a private individual unlawfully gathers evidence and turns it over to the government, the government is free to use it (Burdeau v. McDowell, 1921).

Coolidge v. New Hampshire (1971) demonstrates that this principle, sometimes referred to as the *silver platter doctrine,* is still applicable today. In this case, the wife of a murder suspect handed over her husband's guns and clothing to police officers for inspection, saying, "If you would like them, you may take them." The Court held that when a private party produces evidence for police inspection, it is "not incumbent on the police to stop her or avert their eyes." As long as the police did not coerce the wife into turning over the weapons, her voluntary act did not constitute an illegal search and seizure by the police.

The private action issue raises two primary issues. What entities constitute the government, and when does private action turn into government action because of the participation and encouragement of the government?

### What Constitutes Government?

It was initially thought that the Fourth Amendment was only applicable to police officers engaged in law enforcement activities like making arrests or searching as part of a criminal investigation. Warrantless safety inspections of a home not involving a search for evidence of a crime were found to be "touch[ing] at most upon the periphery" of constitutional safeguards (Frank v. Maryland, 1959). However, in Camara v. Municipal Court of the City and County of San Francisco (1967), the Court indicated that an individual's interest in protecting his or her private property extends beyond the criminal realm. Here, the Court held that the Fourth Amendment was applicable to other government officials, including building inspectors, saying that "even the most law abiding citizen has a very tangible interest in limiting the circumstances under which the sanctity of his home may be broken by official authority, for the possibility of criminal entry under the guise of official sanction is a serious threat to personal and family security." Accordingly, in order to inspect premises for violations of the housing code when a resident does not voluntarily authorize the inspection, the building inspector must conform to the requirements of the Fourth Amendment in obtaining a warrant for the inspection.

Similarly, although not involved in criminal activity, public school teachers and administrators are also subject to the Fourth Amendment:

Because the individual's interest in privacy and personal security suffers whether the government's motivation is to investigate violations of criminal laws or breaches of other statutory or regulatory standards, it would be anomalous to say that the individual and his private property are fully protected by the Fourth Amendment only when the individual is suspected of criminal behavior (New Jersey v. TLO, 1985).

The question becomes more problematic when dealing with the conduct of a private entity, which is part of an industry that is heavily regulated by the government (Skinner v. Railway Labor Executives Association, 1989). Although the Fourth Amendment does not protect against a private party acting on its own initiative, it does protect against searches and seizures by industrial entities when they are acting as instruments or agents of the government. In determining whether an entity is acting as an agent of the federal government (thus bound by the Fourth Amendment), the Court considers the circumstances particular to the situation such as the degree of the government's regulation in the industry's activities. When government participation in the private industry is high, the Court considers the private entity to be an instrument of the government, and thus subject to the requirements of the Fourth Amendment. Railroads, for example, appear to be instruments of the government because they are heavily regulated. In *Skinner*, the Court held that railroads were in fact instruments of the government. In this case, a federal regulation required railroads to administer breath and urine tests to employees who violated particular safety rules. The Court concluded that when a railroad administers the tests in accordance with the regulation, it does so "by compulsion of sovereign authority," namely as an agent of the government. Accordingly, the Court found that "the lawfulness of its [the railroad's] acts is controlled by the Fourth Amendment."

## When Does Private Action Turn into Government Action Because of the Participation and Encouragement of the Government?

The Court has had many opportunities to deal with the issue of when private individual action becomes government action because of the government's participation and encouragement. In Walter v. United States (1980), the issue concerned the scope of a governmental search conducted subsequent to a search by a private individual. In this case, several packages were mistakenly delivered to a company. Employees of the company opened the boxes, discovered individual boxes of film with suggestive drawings and explicit descriptions of the contents therein, and contacted the Federal Bureau of Investigation (FBI). However, the employees never viewed the films. FBI agents later viewed the films on a projector. In finding the FBI's viewing of the films to be an unconstitutional search and seizure, the

Court held that governmental searches conducted subsequent to private searches are limited to the scope of the initial private search saying the following:

Even though some circumstances—for example, if the results of the private search are in plain view when materials are turned over to the Government—may justify the Government's re-examination of the materials, surely the Government may not exceed the scope of the private search unless it has the right to make an independent search.

The Court explains this limitation in terms of the privacy that the owner of the films would expect. When the employee of the company that mistakenly received the packages opened the boxes and examined the contents, that initial search partially violated the box owner's expectation of privacy. However, the FBI's viewing of the tapes further violated the box owner's privacy. Although the FBI can benefit from the initial breach of privacy, that small breach does not remove all of the Fourth Amendment's protection of the contents of the box. "A partial invasion of privacy cannot automatically justify a total invasion." It should be pointed out that the Court's concern for the First Amendment might have played a role in this decision.

In contrast, if the governmental search was not "a significant expansion of the search which had been previously (privately) conducted" it would not violate the Fourth Amendment. In United States v. Jacobson (1984), the Court again tested the legality of the governmental search by measuring it against the scope of the prior private search. Federal Express employees opened a package that had been damaged by a forklift. When they discovered a white powdery substance inside the package, they notified Drug Enforcement Administration (DEA) agents. The federal agents examined the powder in the package and performed a field test that identified the powder as cocaine. The Court found that the field test performed by the FBI (but not by the Federal Express employees) was not a search and thus did not exceed the scope of the private search conducted by Federal Express. This holding was based on the fact that the chemical test only revealed whether the substance was cocaine but no other information about the substance. Secondly, the Court held that the defendant did not have a reasonable expectation of privacy in the chemical identity of the powder.

In his dissent, Justice William Brennan argued that this decision expanded the reach of the private-search doctrine beyond its logical bounds. However, he agreed that if the powder was in plain view of the officers, then the testing to determine whether the powder was cocaine would be acceptable under the Fourth Amendment. He would limit the holding to the fact that the DEA agents could identify the cocaine with "virtual certainty" just by looking at the substance. Thus the chemical test merely confirmed a fact that they already knew and did not provide the agents with any further information. Because the powder was plainly visible, Brennan asserted that the defendant could have no reasonable expectation of privacy in the identity of the powder. He distinguished this case, where the powder was wrapped in plastic bags in a Federal Express tube, a packaging technique unlikely to be used for a legal substance, from a hypothetical case where a defendant attempts to disguise the identity of the substance. Brennan gave the example of packaging the powder in a medicine vial (disguised as legitimate medication) as a situation where a chemical field test would be unreasonable.

The Court has not directly addressed the situation in which a private person acts at the behest of the government, as opposed to an industrial entity such as a railroad (Skinner v. Railway Labor Executives Association, 1989). When a private person acts at the behest of the government, this action creates an agency relationship resulting in Fourth Amendment involvement. In some cases, it is clear that a private party acted as a government agent. However, most situations fall into a "gray area between the extremes of overt governmental participation in a search and the complete absence of such participation."[1] In these circumstances, the Court must weigh the level of government participation in the search and determine whether the government was sufficiently involved in the search so as to create an agency relationship (United States v. Walther, 9th Cir., 1981). Circuit court case law sheds some light on the way the courts tend to define an agency relationship. In *Walther*, the Ninth Circuit explained their criteria for an agency relationship between the government and a private party:

De minimus or incidental contacts between the citizen and law enforcement agents prior to or during the course of a search or seizure will not subject the search to fourth amendment scrutiny. The government must be involved either directly as a participant or indirectly as an encourager of the private citizens' actions before we deem the citizen to be an instrument of the state.

The degree of governmental involvement in the private search is often difficult to gauge and varies from situation to situation. There is no bright-line test to determine whether a private individual acted as an agent of the government. Instead, the courts examine the totality of the circumstances surrounding the search. Several of the circuit courts consider two factors critical in determining whether the individual was acting as an instrument or agent of the government: "(1) the government's knowledge and acquiescence, and (2) the intent of the party performing the search" (United States v. Walther, 9th Cir., 1981). The courts seem to give greater weight to the intent of the party performing the search.

Although the government may know of a private search and may indeed quietly allow a private individual to conduct a search, the private individual's intent can be a critical factor. For example, in United States v. Feffer (1987), the Seventh Circuit found that an employee who turned over her employer's financial documents to the Internal Revenue Service (IRS) had not acted as an agent or instrument of the government. This employee met with IRS agents several times while furnishing the documents. IRS agents told the woman that they could not ask her for information but hinted as to what documents would be helpful. Although the facts suggested that the IRS clandestinely guided her search in the right direction, the Court did not find that she acted as an agent of the IRS. Instead, the Court found that she had turned over the documents to further her own ends (to protect herself from prosecution for tax fraud and to avenge the firing of a close friend). Thus, although the government knew that she was likely conducting questionable searches, her actions were voluntary, and therefore not at the request of the government.

Weighing the same two factors (government knowledge and acquiescence with intent of the private party), the Ninth Circuit came to the opposite conclusion in *Walther*. In this case, the Ninth Circuit found that an airline employee who opened a suitcase and turned over cocaine he discovered to the DEA had acted as an agent or instrument of the government. Like in *Feffer*, the intent of the private party proved critical to the Court's analysis. Because the airline employee who conducted the search had previously received rewards from the DEA for providing drug-related information, the Court found that he could have reasonably expected to receive a reward for this information. Additionally, he had no alternative personal or business-related motivation to search the bag. Thus, the Court found it likely that the employee searched the luggage in the hope of receiving another reward from the DEA. Since he acted like an "informant," he searched the bag as an agent or instrument of the government. As a result, the search implicated the Fourth Amendment.

## ENDNOTE

1. United States v. Walther, 652 F.2d 788 (9th Cir. 1981) at 792–793.

# Analysis—Applicability of the Fourth Amendment Expectation of Privacy

## INTRODUCTION

Initially, the applicability of the Fourth Amendment was governed by property concepts such as common law trespass. There needed to be an actual physical intrusion into a constitutionally protected area such as a home. The Supreme Court held that the tapping of a telephone wire (Olmstead v. United States, 1928) or a detechtaphone, a listening apparatus in the wall (Goldman v. United States, 1942), did not constitute a physical intrusion. On the other hand a spike mike inserted into the crevice of a heating duct constituted a physical penetration of the home and thus implicated the Fourth Amendment (Silverman v. United States, 1961).

As Fourth Amendment jurisprudence developed, however, the Court moved from an approach based on property law concepts to a more comprehensive theory of privacy. In Katz v. United States (1967), federal agents placed a listening device on the outside wall of a public telephone booth to listen to the defendant's conversation. Following common law trespass doctrine, the Ninth Circuit held that because there was no actual penetration of the booth, there was no trespass, and therefore no search. The Court reversed, ruling that because the Fourth Amendment "protects people, not places," it no longer made sense to rely on the antiquated property law concept of trespass.

Justice John Marshall Harlan's concurring opinion in *Katz*, relied on by later decisions of the Court, has become the basis for analyzing the rationale established by the decision. Harlon accepts the majority's ruling that the Fourth Amendment protects "people not places." He asks, however, "[w]hat protection [does] it afford to those people?" He then suggests a twofold analysis. First, did the individual exhibit an actual expectation of privacy? Second, was the expectation of privacy one that would be deemed reasonable by society? According to this analysis, it is not enough for the target of the intrusion to believe that he is acting in private; his belief must be recognized by society as reasonable.

For the most part, the courts have focused on the second prong of this analysis. How do we know what society is prepared to accept as reasonable? Because there is no straightforward answer to this question, "reasonable" has largely come to mean what a majority of the Supreme Court Justices says is reasonable, leading scholars to note that "when the court refers to society's judgment, it is looking in a mirror."[1] In this section, we will look at how the Court determines whether an expectation of privacy is reasonable. We will look at a variety of physical settings and observe the influence the home has on this analysis. We will also look at third-party disclosures and how the Court has expanded this concept.

## PHYSICAL CHARACTERISTICS

Each day, we present the same voice, face, handwriting, and fingerprints to the world. Because these physical attributes are constantly exposed to the public, the Court has held that there is no expectation of privacy in these characteristics. In United States v. Dionisio (1973), the Court held that "No person can have a reasonable expectation that others will not know the sound of his voice, any more than he can reasonably expect that his face will be a mystery to the world." In this case, a defendant objected to being asked to read in front of a grand jury so that the grand jury could compare his voice with recorded conversations (called a *voice exemplar*). The defendant argued that requiring him to make a voice recording for the grand jury violated his Fourth Amendment rights. The Court rejected his argument because by providing a voice exemplar, the defendant would not expose anything to the grand jury that had not already been exposed to the public:

Except for the rare recluse who chooses to live his life in complete solitude, in our daily lives we constantly speak and write, and while the content of a communication is entitled to Fourth Amendment protection . . . the underlying identifying characteristics—the constant factor throughout both public and private communications—are open for all to see or hear.

Following the reasoning in *Dionisio*, in United States v. Mara (1978) the Court placed handwriting in the category of physical characteristics not protected by the Fourth Amendment because one's handwriting, like one's voice, is constantly exposed to the public.

Fingerprints likewise are physical characteristics not protected by the Fourth Amendment. In Davis v. Mississippi (1969), the defendant, accused of rape, sought to have his fingerprints suppressed on the grounds that fingerprinting him constituted an unreasonable search under the Fourth Amendment. The Court found that individuals have no reasonable expectation of privacy in their fingerprints because fingerprinting does not involve probing into an individual's private life and thoughts as an interrogation or search does.

## THIRD-PARTY DISCLOSURE

In the *Katz* decision, the Court stated that the Fourth Amendment does not protect that which a person knowingly exposes to the public. Even before *Katz*, the Court applied this concept to information that defendants conveyed to a third party. In Hoffa v. United States (1966), the Court held that one has no expectation of privacy in a private conversation with a confidant. Misplaced confidence in a false friend is not subject to Fourth Amendment protection. Here, the defendant, Hoffa, faced trial for Taft-Hartley violations. Over the course of the investigation of these charges, a friend visited Hoffa in his hotel room. During their conversation in the hotel room Hoffa made many incriminating statements to this friend. However, this friend was in fact a government informant who helped secure Hoffa's conviction. Hoffa sought to suppress the informant's statements based on an expectation of privacy in his discussions with the informant. However, the Court declined to reward misplaced confidence in friends, explaining that the Fourth Amendment protects individuals only from unwanted governmental intrusion, not from voluntary statements made to friends. This was particularly true in this case, where the defendant had invited the informant voluntarily into his hotel suite and then discussed incriminating matters. The majority held that the informant was not eavesdropping or spying in any way.

The lack of Fourth Amendment protection from informants in *Hoffa* was extended to electronically wired informants in United States v. White (1971). This case involved misplaced confidence in a wired friend. In *White*, the informant consented to placing an agent with a radio receiver in the closet of his home. When the defendant visited the informant in his home, the two had incriminating conversations that were transmitted by the radio receiver to FBI agents waiting outside in a car. Extending the reasoning from *Hoffa*, the Court held that the Fourth Amendment does not protect a "wrongdoer's misplaced belief that a person to whom he voluntarily confides his wrongdoing will not reveal it." Logically, this lack of protection applies even when the informant "unbeknown to the defendant, carries electronic equipment to record the defendant's words and the evidence so gathered is later offered in evidence." The Court found that the use of electronic devices to record conversations merely bolstered the informant's credibility at trial without substantially changing the nature of the intrusion into the privacy of the defendant. The moral of the holdings in *Hoffa* and *White* is that wrongdoers should always contemplate the risk that their confidantes may divulge their crimes to the police.

It is interesting to note that Justice John Marshall Harlan's dissent in *White* is a good example of how the individual values of the Justices influence their views on what constitutes a reasonable expectation of privacy. "The impact of the practice of third-party bugging, must, I think, be considered such as to undermine that confidence and sense of security in dealing with one another that is characteristic of individual relationships between citizens in a free society." Justice William Douglas' dissent also paints an ominous future replete with privacy invasions and foreshadows the issues that the Court will face as technological innovations emerge:

Electronic surveillance is the greatest leveler of human privacy ever known. How most forms of it can be held "reasonable" within the meaning of the Fourth Amendment is a mystery. To be sure, the Constitution and Bill of Rights are not to be read as covering only the technology known in the 18th Century . . . At the same time the concepts of privacy which the Founders enshrined in the Fourth Amendment vanish completely when we slavishly allow an all-powerful government, proclaiming law and order, efficiency, and other benign purposes, to penetrate all the walls and doors which [citizens] need to shield them from the pressures of a turbulent life around them and give them the health and strength to carry on.

Furthermore, individuals concerned with divulging incriminating information must fear not only their friends, but other institutions as well. To the Court, it is the act of voluntary disclosure of information to a third party that is the important act. In United States v. Miller (1976), the Court held that there was no expectation of privacy with regard to bank records because the individual disclosed the information in these records to the bank:

The depositor takes the role, in revealing his affairs to another, that the information will be conveyed by that person to the Government . . . This court has held repeatedly that the Fourth Amendment does not prohibit the obtaining of information revealed to a third party and conveyed by him to government authorities, even if the information is revealed on the assumption that it will be used only for a limited purpose as the confidence placed in the third party will be betrayed.

The telephone company is sometimes a third party that is not subject to Fourth Amendment restrictions. Although an expectation of privacy with regard to telephone conversations is reasonable, no such expectation exists for the numbers dialed because those are automatically turned over to a third-party telephone company. In Smith v. Maryland (1979), the Court held that there was no expectation of privacy in the local numbers dialed as opposed to the actual conversation because the individual used the telephone company to dial the number. In this case, police used a pen register that was installed at the office of the telephone company to record the numbers that a particular customer dialed locally. Police used this information to secure a search warrant for the defendant's home.

In some cases, however, Congress has legislatively restored an expectation of privacy to information given to third parties. Although no Fourth Amendment violation was found in *Miller*, Congress subsequently passed legislation restricting government access to bank records without a search warrant or a subpoena (12 U.S.C. 3401-3422, 1996). Similarly, following *Smith*, Congress restricted the use of pen registers (18 U.S.C. 113, 1996).

Finally, an individual's garbage may subject him to a search that is not protected by the Fourth Amendment. Following the rationale that conveyance to a third party limits one's expectation of privacy, the Court in California v. Greenwood (1988) held that one did not have a reasonable expectation of privacy with respect to garbage conveyed to third-party garbage collectors. In this case, police suspected that the defendant was selling drugs. Hoping to find evidence, the police asked the local garbage collector to turn over the defendant's garbage bags. When the officers examined the contents of the garbage bags, they discovered drug paraphernalia that they used to secure a search warrant for the defendant's home. The defendant argued that he had a reasonable expectation of privacy in the garbage that he placed at the curb. The Court, however, rejected this argument for two reasons. First, the Court found that the defendant had "placed this refuse at the curb for the express purpose of conveying it to a third party, the trash collector," and therefore he "could have no reasonable expectation of privacy in the inculpatory items [he] discarded." Second, the Court found no reasonable expectation of privacy in garbage left curbside because bags that are left on the street are "readily accessible to animals, scavengers, snoops or other members of the public." Thus the Court found the defendant's expectation of privacy unreasonable because garbage left on the curb is both open to the public and conveyed to a third party.

## PHYSICAL SETTING

Whether an expectation of privacy is reasonable often depends on the physical setting involved. The Court has developed gradations of Fourth Amendment applicability. These gradations are called *zones of privacy expectation*. Certain locales have no expectation of privacy, whereas other locales enjoy a moderate expectation of privacy and thus some Fourth Amendment protection. The home enjoys the strongest expectation of privacy and maximum Fourth Amendment protection. This stems from the intent of the Framers to ensure the sanctity of the home from invasion by the government. Once we move from the immediate bounds of the home, we enter the court's designated zones of privacy expectations, which enjoy less protection than the home.

In the area just outside the home, called the *curtilage*, there is at least some expectation of privacy and therefore some Fourth Amendment protection. This is the area where the "intimate activity associated with the sanctity of a man's home and the privacies of his life" extend (Boyd v. United States, 1886). There is a heightened expectation of privacy because the curtilage is closely linked to the home both physically and psychologically. In United States v. Dunn (1987), the Court identified four considerations that are important in determining curtilage: (1) proximity to the home, (2) whether the area is enclosed, (3) nature of the area's use, and (4) the steps taken to protect the area. The fewer factors that are applicable to an area in question, the less Fourth Amendment protection is afforded to the area.

The Court has held that there is no expectation of privacy in an open field, and consequently such areas are not protected by the Fourth Amendment. A decision by Justice Oliver Wendall Holmes, indicated that the wording of the Fourth Amendment, "persons, houses, papers and effects," did not encompass open fields (Heake v. United States, 1924). In a more recent decision, police discovered marijuana growing in a field that was more than a mile away from the defendant's house. Affirming that the area was not protected by the Fourth Amendment, the Court held that "an individual may not legitimately demand privacy for activities conducted out of doors in fields, except in the area immediately surrounding the home." The Court reasoned that there is no societal interest in protecting activities that normally occur in fields outside the home, such as crop cultivation (Oliver v. United States, 1984).

Finally, there is no expectation of privacy in prison when a search is designed to maintain security. In Hudson v. Palmer (1984), the Court considered the important interest of society in the security of its penal institutions. Since the Fourth Amendment is "fundamentally incompatible with the close and continual surveillance of inmates and their cells required to ensure institutional security and internal order," the Court held that inmates surrender their Fourth Amendment rights when they enter the penal system. With regard to prisons, it is interesting to note that, in United States v. Cohen (2nd Cir., 1986), a prison search was conducted not for the security purposes mentioned in *Hudson* but rather to obtain information for a pending indictment. Given this purpose, the Second Circuit held that an incarcerated person did retain some protection of privacy, albeit diminished in scope.

## PHYSICAL SETTING AND ENHANCEMENT DEVICES

As technology rapidly advances, law enforcement has come to possess many sense-enhancing devices. In analyzing these enhancement devices, the Court has evaluated both their level of intrusiveness and the settings in which they are used. As we will see, the Court has largely accepted these devices when used in public settings, and often in the curtilage areas as well, but has been reluctant to accept these devices when they are used in the home. For example, in United States v.

Place (1983), the police used a trained dog to sniff luggage at an airport. In finding that there was no expectation of privacy, the Court emphasized the facts that the sniff was nonintrusive and the luggage was located in a public place.

When the setting is the curtilage, the Court has allowed the use of devices that enhance one's vantage point. In California v. Ciralo (1986), the Court found no expectation of privacy against an airplane flying over curtilage. In this case, police suspected that the defendant was growing marijuana but could not see it due to the ten-foot fence around the yard. They secured a private plane and flew over the defendant's house at 1,000 feet (within public navigable airspace). From the aircraft the officers observed marijuana plants growing in the defendant's yard. The defendant argued that because the marijuana grew in his curtilage, he had a reasonable expectation of privacy in his "illicit agricultural endeavor," especially given the fact that he had built a ten-foot fence. The Court disagreed, however, since the fence did not protect the plants from being seen by a police officer riding a double-decker bus or a neighbor peeking over from a second-story window. Although this justification seems to be a stretch, the Court held that the "test of legitimacy is not whether the individual chooses to conceal assertedly 'private activity,' but instead 'whether the government's intrusion infringes upon the personal and societal values protected by the Fourth Amendment.'" The Court further held that, because the observations were made with the naked eye in publicly navigable airspace, the expectation of privacy was unreasonable.

The Court upheld this principle with regard to helicopters in Florida v. Riley (1989). This was a 5-4 plurality decision. The plurality relied on the fact that the helicopter flying at 400 feet did not violate Federal Aviation Administration (FAA) regulations, that this type of helicopter flight was not rare, and that the flight did not interfere with normal use of the greenhouse and did not reveal intimate details connected with the use of the home. Justice Sandra Day O'Connor, who joined in the decision with the four-judge plurality, indicated that 400 feet was not rare but if it were less she would find an expectation of privacy even if it did not violate FAA regulations.

This case is particularly interesting because the owner of the curtilage took elaborate steps to protect his property from aerial view. The defendant grew marijuana in a partially enclosed greenhouse 10 to 20 feet behind his mobile home. Corrugated roofing panels (some clear, some opaque) covered the greenhouse roof. Finally, the greenhouse was surrounded by a wire fence with a "Do Not Enter" sign posted on it. A police officer who was circling the greenhouse in a helicopter observed marijuana plants growing inside through the openings in the roof. However, the Court again found that aerial observation of the curtilage did not implicate the Fourth Amendment.

Further, in Dow Chemical v. United States (1986), the government used an aerial magnifying camera to take pictures of a factory from the air. In allowing this device, the Court said it was not particularly sophisticated because it could be purchased by the public. Additionally, the area observed was "more comparable to an open field" than curtilage. The Court found that a large industrial complex was not like a home or an office where the common law curtilage law would apply because the traditional bases for curtilage protection (e.g., the "peculiarly strong concepts of intimacy, personal autonomy and privacy associated with the home") were not relevant to a large industrial complex.

The Court, however, distinguished visual inspection from tactile observation (touch) in Bond v. United States (2000). Although touch is not an enhancement device, the Court regarded it as an expansion or enhancement of a visual observation. In *Bond*, a customs agent boarded a bus for a standard immigration check and squeezed a canvas carry-on bag. On squeezing the bag, the agent noticed a brick-like object that turned out to be drugs. Finding the physical manipulation to be an unreasonable search, the Court indicated that physical inspection is more intrusive than visual inspection because it is not merely observation. The Court compared this search to a "frisk" (see the analysis of a *Terry* stop justification), that is a "serious intrusion upon the sanctity of the person." Thus, a frisk of luggage was an intrusion on the sanctity of an effect and thus subject to Fourth Amendment protection.

In United States v. Knotts (1983), police installed a beeper to monitor the location of an automobile. The Court held that since they were merely following a car over public roads, a device to enhance the senses was allowable, and thus this monitoring actually did not implicate the Fourth Amendment. However, in a similar case where the beeper ended up in the home, the Court did find a violation of a legitimate expectation of privacy (United States v. Karo, 1984). In this case, DEA agents used a beeper to verify the presence of illicit substances in a house. A government informant installed a beeper to monitor the movement of a canister containing ether, which was transferred to the defendant for use with cocaine. By tracking the movement of the ether canister, police were able to locate the suspects' residence and use the information to secure a search warrant. Although the initial placement of the beeper in the can was not a Fourth Amendment violation (as in *Knotts)*, the subsequent tracking of the canister to the suspects' home did violate the Fourth Amendment. In *Knotts*, the canister being tracked never entered a home, but instead remained in automobiles on public roads. In *Karo,* the Court found that the situation was substantially the same as if the agents had searched the houses themselves without a warrant. Thus, the Court again protected the sanctity of the home.

This brings us to the most recent case before the Court (Kyllo v. United States, 2001). In this case, police used a thermal imaging device to measure the amount of heat emanating from a home because the heat measurements would reveal whether the occupant was using high-intensity lamps to grow marijuana. In a 5-4 decision written by Justice Scalia, the Court determined that there was indeed an expectation of privacy in the heat emanating from a home and the Fourth Amendment was therefore applicable. He characterized the issue in terms of the limits that should be placed on emerging technology in order to preserve our privacy rights. In continuing to allow other types of enforcement devices, Scalia distinguished this case from *Dow Chemical*, which involved an industrial complex, not the area immediately adjacent to a home where there is a greater privacy expectation. "Enhanced aerial photography of an industrial complex . . . does not share the Fourth Amendment sanctity of the home." A prohibition on searching the interior of the home has its "roots deep in the common law," Scalia explained, and therefore "where as here, the Government uses a device that is not in general public use, to explore details of the home that would previously have been unknowable without physical intrusion, the surveillance is a 'search' and is presumptively unreasonable without a warrant." The dissent was concerned with the majority's comment about devices in general public use, arguing that once the same technology was in the general use by the public, the protection of the home might dissipate. It viewed this approach as somewhat perverse because "it seems likely that as intrusive equipment becomes readily available, the threat to privacy will grow, rather than recede."

What is clear from the *Kyllo* and *Karo* decisions is that the Court will be more vigilant when enhancement devices penetrate the sanctity of the home. What is unclear, however, is how enhancing the devices need to be in order to trigger Fourth Amendment concerns. What about binoculars used to look at a home? These are in general public use and would probably not implicate the Fourth Amendment. What about infra-red devices looking into a home? Are they in general public use? Do they otherwise enhance senses? The *Kyllo* decision left these questions open for further consideration.

## ENDNOTE

1. Johnson, P. Criminal Procedure, 3rd Ed. at 19 (2000).

# Analysis—Arrest and Criminal Searches—Justification— Probable Cause

## INTRODUCTION

The term *probable cause* is found within the second clause of the Fourth Amendment. In the wording of this clause *probable cause* refers to the amount of justification required for issuing a warrant: "No warrant shall issue but upon probable cause." Despite this specific wording indicating the applicability of probable cause only for warrants, probable cause also became the standard for justifying warrantless criminal searches and arrests. If a warrant is issued, a magistrate makes the determination of probable cause. If no warrant has been issued, an officer in the field generally makes the determination. The Court has held that the standard of justification for searches without a warrant cannot be less than if a warrant were required. In Henry v. United States (1959), the Court explained that "If the officer acts with probable cause, he is protected even though it turns out that the citizen is innocent . . . and while a search without a warrant is . . . permissible if incident to a lawful arrest, if an arrest without a warrant is to support an incidental search, it must be made with probable cause." In addition, a lesser standard would encourage warrantless activity.

The standard for probable cause is met when the facts and circumstances known to the police officer consist of sufficiently trustworthy information to warrant a reasonably prudent person in believing, in the case of a search, that an item related to criminal activity would be found in a certain place, or in the case of arrest, that the arrested person had committed, or was committing, a crime (Beck v. State of Ohio, 1964). This standard addresses both the amount of information the officer possesses, as well as the reliability of that information. In a search for items related to a crime that will be found at a particular place, the information required for a search is time sensitive because it is possible for an item to be moved from one location to another. In this situation probable cause to search, like bread, can go stale. On the other hand, for probable cause to arrest, the information to believe a particular person committed a crime does not deteriorate with time. Although the standard for probable cause seems clear, determining whether the standard has been met in a given case is often not so clear.

The information to establish probable cause can come from a variety of sources. Victims of crime or unnamed informants often provide police with information that is valuable in establishing probable cause. Other information comes from police officers' own observations.

In the next section, we will look at the probable cause standard to determine how much and what type of information is required to establish probable cause. We will then focus on informants, the subject of much of the Court's jurisprudence in this area.

## PROBABLE CAUSE—AN OVERVIEW ANALYSIS

Probable cause is the amount of justification necessary for law enforcement personnel to perform certain functions. To state it differently, how much information is needed before police officers can act in a certain way? The standard for probable cause must balance society's need to solve crimes against society's desire to protect individuals from government action. Requiring too much justification will adversely affect the ability of police to solve crimes. However, requiring too little justification for police action will adversely affect individual rights. In describing the difficulties inherent in accommodating both these interests, the Court in Brinegar v. United States (1949) remarked that "requiring more [than the accepted probable cause standard] would unduly hamper law enforcement. To allow less would be to leave law abiding citizens at the mercy of the officer's whim or caprice." The Court addressed this accommodation again in United States v. Ventresca (1965), this time remarking that:

This Court is alert to invalidate unconstitutional searches and seizures whether with or without a warrant. . . By doing so, it vindicates individual liberties and strengthens the administration of justice by promoting respect for law and order. This Court is equally concerned to uphold the actions of law enforcement officers consistently following the proper constitutional course. This is no less important to the administration of justice . . .

Thus, because probable cause represents a compromise between varying interests, there is a need for flexibility when the Court applies the probable cause standard.

The Court has been reluctant to define just how much information constitutes probable cause. It is clearly something less than that which is necessary to meet the beyond a reasonable doubt standard required for proof of guilt at a trial and something more than is necessary to establish reasonable suspicion (Texas v. Brown, 1983). In *Draper*, the Court explained that "a finding of 'probable cause' may rest upon evidence which is not legally competent in a criminal trial." In *Brinegar*, the Court elaborated on this difference in standards, explaining that if the standards used for judging guilt "were to be made applicable in determining probable cause for an arrest or for search and seizure . . . few indeed would be the situations in which an officer, charged with protecting the public interest by enforcing the law, could take effective action toward that end" (Brinegar v. United States, 1949).

The most recent statement by the Court respecting the quantity and type of information necessary to establish probable cause can be found in Illinois v. Gates (1983), in which the Court indicated that probable cause was a "fluid concept." "The central teaching of our decisions bearing on the probable cause standard is that it is a practical, nontechnical, conception." The standard has never been further explained. In *Gates*, the Court explained that a flexible, easily applied standard that takes into account the "totality of the circumstances" would best achieve the accommodation of the public and private interests embodied in the Fourth Amendment.

The type of information that goes into the probable cause equation should be factual as opposed to conclusive. This is particularly important when evaluating an affidavit. In *Spinelli*, a case involving a tip from an unnamed informant, the Court stressed that "though the affiant swore that his confidant was 'reliable,' he offered the magistrate no reason in support of this conclusion" (Spinelli v. United States, 1969). The conclusive nature of this information contributed to the Court's decision that the affidavit failed to meet the probable cause standard. Although hearsay information may be part of the probable cause equation, there must be some indicia that the information is reasonably trustworthy. Information that a victim tells police is likely to be trustworthy, especially since the victim is named in the affidavit and usually has no incentive to lie. Information from unnamed sources (confidential informants) does not automatically share this presumption of trustworthiness. Thus the conclusory language in *Spinelli* indicating that the confidant was reliable was not sufficient to establish reliability.

Among the factors that can be considered in the probable cause analysis are the suspect's prior criminal record and his reputation. However, information concerning the suspect's reputation must be factually detailed and trustworthy (United States v. Harris, 1971). A statement that the suspect had a relationship with the affiant going back four years could be used in the determination of probable cause, provided that there was a factual basis laid out in the affidavit for the reputation.

In addition, the suspect's flight alone cannot establish probable cause, especially where the police themselves bring on the suspect's conduct. In Wong Sun

v. United States (1963), a suspect fled down a hallway after a narcotics officer misrepresented his presence at the outset, claiming he wanted to pick up his laundry and dry cleaning and did not "adequately dispel the misrepresentation engendered by his own ruse" before the suspect fled down the hallway. The Court reasoned that the suspect's "refusal to admit officers and his flight down the hallway thus signified a guilty knowledge no more clearly than it did a natural desire to repel an apparently unauthorized intrusion." Illinois v. Wardlow (2000) involved the reasonable suspicion standard, but in this case, the Court did indicate a willingness to look at flight if there were sufficient other factors present: "Headlong flight . . . is the consummate act of evasion: it is not necessarily indicative of wrongdoing, but it is certainly suggestive of such." Among the factors mentioned in *Wardlow* were area of heavy narcotic trafficking, nervousness, and unprovoked flight.

Other factors that might be considered in establishing probable cause are presence in a high crime area and police officers' training and experience. In Brown v. Texas (1979), the Court decided that an individual's presence in an area of expected criminal activity, standing alone, is not enough to support a reasonable particularized suspicion that the person is committing a crime. In Illinois v. Wardlow, however, the Court held that "officers are not required to ignore the relevant characteristics of a location in determining whether the circumstances are sufficiently suspicious to warrant further investigation." In Texas v. Brown (1983), the Court also stressed the importance of the officer's prior experience in making determinations of probable cause. In *Brown*, a police officer conducting a stop at a routine driver's license checkpoint observed a party balloon tied at the end in the driver's hand. The balloon fell to the seat beside him. The Court explained that the officer had probable cause to believe the balloon contained an illicit substance because his participation in previous narcotics arrests and discussions with other officers had taught him that balloons tied in this manner were often used to carry narcotics.

The police may also rely on information from other police forces. For example, if the police receive a radio call or a flyer from another police department, the officers may, in reliance on the police department issuing the call or flyer, assume that probable cause exists for an arrest and search. However, the information from the source police department must itself meet the probable cause standard. In Whiteley v. Warden (1971), officers made an arrest and conducted a search of an automobile in reliance on a police bulletin issued by another department. Although the Court recognized that police officers called on to aid officers from another department are entitled to assume that the department requesting the aid had presented sufficient information to obtain a warrant supported by probable cause, "where, however, the contrary turns out to be true, an otherwise illegal arrest cannot be insulated from challenge by the decision of the instigating officer to rely on fellow officers to make the arrest." In United States v. Hensley (1985), the Court again stressed that "when evidence is uncovered during a search incident to an arrest in reliance merely on a flyer or bulletin, its admissibility turns on whether the officers who issued the flyer possessed probable cause to make the arrest." The officers who actually make the arrest do not themselves have to be aware of the specific facts on which the finding of probable cause was based.

## INFORMANTS

Much of the focus of the Court's probable cause jurisprudence has been on the role of informants. Informants are usually undercover individuals who provide information to law enforcement in return for money or concessions with regard to their own criminal activity. In Aguilar v. State of Texas (1964), the Court created a two-pronged test for the purpose of deciding whether information provided by informants should be used in probable cause determinations. The first prong focuses on the veracity of the informant (veracity prong), asking: Why should this unnamed individual be believed? The second prong analyzes the basis of the informant's knowledge (basis of knowledge prong), asking: How did the informant get the information? Specific factual detail as opposed to conclusion is necessary to satisfy the requirements of each of these prongs. So, for example, a statement that an informant was credible would be insufficient. The statement would instead need to say something as convincing as, "I have used the informant on the following occasions . . . and on each of these occasions this informant was credible."

For many years, the Court required substantiation of both prongs before the informant's information could be used in the probable cause equation. As a result, the Court has had occasion to address the methods by which the police could establish the sufficiency of either prong. For example, in Draper v. United States (1959), as interpreted in Spinelli v. United States (1969), the Court decided that an informant's very detailed account might well make up for a deficiency in the basis of knowledge prong. The Court reasoned that a magistrate presented with very detailed information "could reasonably infer that the informant had gained his information in a reliable way." In *Draper*, the informant described with great particularity the clothing the suspect would be wearing, his arrival in Chicago from a train originating in Denver, and the fact that he would be walking fast.

Independent police corroboration is another method to establish either prong, although the Court has indicated that merely corroborating innocent facts will not always amount to sufficient corroboration. In *Spinelli*, the police corroborated an informant's tip that the defendant had two phones in his apartment, but the Court explained that "there is surely nothing unusual about an apartment containing two separate telephones." The police also corroborated the informant's description of the defendant's travels to and from the apartment building and his entry into a particular apartment on one occasion. Again, the Court explained that "this could hardly be taken as bespeaking gambling activity." It should be pointed out that

*Spinelli* required a great deal of corroboration to satisfy the prong. In addition, *Spinelli's* analysis would indicate that the two prongs are separate and distinct so that the substantial satisfaction of one prong would not affect the second prong.

A plurality of the Court held that the veracity prong was satisfied when an informant made a statement against his own interests (United States v. Harris, 1971). In *Harris*, the informant admitted that over a long period, he had been buying illicit liquor on certain premises. The Court reasoned that "admissions of a crime, like admissions against proprietary interests, carry their own indicia of credibility—sufficient at least to support a finding of probable cause."

The Court's insistence that a deficiency in either of the two independent prongs would undermine the finding of probable cause eventually gave way to a more flexible approach. The Court adjusted the rigidity of this test, instead opting for a "totality of the circumstances" approach (Illinois v. Gates, 1983). The Court, in adopting this standard, recognized that the affidavits were often drafted by non-lawyers in the midst and resulting haste of a criminal investigation. In addition, the Court felt that a less flexible attitude toward probable cause would encourage police to resort to warrantless searches. The *Gates* approach allows for a deficiency in one prong to be compensated for by a strong showing in the other prong. Despite this more flexible approach, the *Gates* Court did indicated the continuing relevance of the two-pronged approach in evaluating informants. In fact, the Court engaged in a two-pronged analysis in its decision, and Justice Byron White's concurrence relied exclusively on the two-pronged test in finding probable cause. In addition, the two-pronged test retains considerable importance as many states have retained it in interpreting their own constitutional provisions (Commonwealth v. Upton, Mass., 1985).

Another related issue goes to the disclosure of informants. The Court in McCray v. State of Illinois (1967) refused to require the state to disclose the identity of an informant in a preliminary hearing held to determine whether probable cause existed for an arrest and search. The Court reasoned that when the issue is not guilt or innocence, but rather the question of probable cause for an arrest and search, officers need not disclose the informant's identity if the trial judge is convinced that officers relied in good faith on credible information supplied by a reliable informant. The rationale for this decision has to do with the Court's recognition of the importance of informants in solving crime. "The informer is a vital part of society's defensive arsenal. The basic rule protecting his identity rests upon that belief" (McCray v. State of Illinois, 1967 (quoting Chief Justice Weintraub in State v. Burnett, New Jersey, 1964)). However, the Court recognized in Roviaro v. United States (1957) that when the informant's identity is needed for the defense of the case in chief, as opposed to the issue of probable cause, the privilege of nondisclosure must give way. The Court explained that "we believe no fixed rule with respect to disclosure is justifiable. The problem is one that called for balancing the public interest in protecting the flow of information against the individual's right to prepare his defense. Whether a proper balance renders nondisclosure erroneous must depend on the particular circumstances of each case . . . ."

A related issue has to do with police lying about probable cause in order to procure a warrant. Often, this lying had to do with making up nonexistent informants or information claimed to be provided by informants. This issue was addressed in Franks v. Delaware (1978), in which the Court decided that the defendant bore the burden of showing both that the affidavit was knowingly and intentionally false or made with reckless disregard for the truth *and* that the false statement was necessary for the finding of probable cause. Thus in *Franks*, the defendant was first required to point out specifically, with supporting reasons and not simply conclusory statements, what portion of the warrant affidavit he claimed was false. The defendant then had to show that when the alleged falsity or reckless disregard was discounted, the remaining portion of the warrant affidavit was insufficient to support a finding of probable cause. If a defendant can show these two elements, he is entitled to a hearing at which he must establish both elements by a preponderance of the evidence in order to void the search warrant and exclude the fruits of the search from trial.

## MISCELLANEOUS ISSUES

The Court considers the probable cause standard to be based on articulated facts as opposed to the intent of the police. In Whren v. United States (1996), the Court refused to look into the subjective motivation of an individual police officer, indicating such motivation was irrelevant. This case raises an interesting issue involving racial profiling. Racial profiling occurs when an inordinate number of individuals are subject to police contact because of their race. This was graphically illustrated in a study done by the Orlando Sentinel. Studying 3,800 traffic stops between January 1996 and April 1997, the paper found that black drivers were 6.5 times more likely to be stopped than white drivers. In *Whren*, a plainclothes vice squad officer patrolling a high drug area in an unmarked car thought that a particular Nissan truck looked suspicious. When the truck took a turn without signaling and sped off at an unreasonable speed, the officer followed and stopped the truck at a red light. On approaching the truck, the officer observed two plastic bags of what appeared to be crack cocaine in the driver's hand. In seeking to suppress the drugs, Whren, the driver, argued that there was a lack of probable cause and the stop was pretextual. In other words, he argued that the police stopped him not for a traffic violation but because of drugs. Since many otherwise innocent individuals violate traffic and equipment laws, it presents a temptation to police officers to use seldom enforced traffic offenses to stop drivers. Whren, who was black, argued that police might decide to stop based on the race of the occupants. The Court, in a decision by Justice Scalia, refused to analyze the subjective intent of the police officer when probable cause exists.

The assessment of probable cause for arrest does not distinguish between minor or serious offenses. In Atwater v. City of Lago Vista (2001), the offender was arrested for not wearing a seatbelt, an offense that is punishable only by a fine. In a 5-4 opinion by Justice Souter, the Court ruled that, consistent with the Fourth Amendment, an officer armed with probable cause to believe that an individual committed even a nonjailable, minor offense may arrest the offender. Continuing the rationale of *Whren*, Justice Souter opted for a bright line or standardized rule with regard to probable cause. In dissent, Justice O'Connor distinguished *Whren* because it did not involve a fine-only offense and opted for a reasonableness analysis. She expressed concern that the approach by the majority would give the police "unfettered discretion" to decide whether to arrest and to do any number of things associated with arrest including a search incident to arrest that would include a search of the interior of the car (New York v. Belton, 1981).

In the section involving the exclusionary rule, we discussed the case of United States v. Leon (1984) in which the Court refused to apply the exclusionary remedy when a police officer acted in "good faith" in obtaining a search warrant. As a result of *Leon*, a warrant that later proves to be invalid because it lacked probable cause will not result in the exclusion of evidence unless there is no way for a reasonable officer to believe the warrant to be valid. A reasonable officer is only expected to question the validity of the warrant when the situation is "so lacking in indicia of probable cause as to render official belief in its existence entirely unreasonable." Because a magistrate's mistaken determination of probable cause will not result in the exclusion of evidence, this lack of enforcement represents a dilution in both the probable cause standard and the importance of probable cause. Further, faced with a standard "so lacking indicia of probable cause," it is unlikely that a defense attorney whose objective is exclusion would appeal the decision. Thus, there will not be much review of bad decisions by magistrates.

It should be pointed out that when we are dealing with major bodily intrusions that endanger life or health, the government is often required to show not only probable cause that evidence will be found from the intrusion, but also that the method of extraction was reasonable. In Winston v. Lee (1985), the government had probable cause that there was a bullet, that was valuable evidence to prove a robbery, lodged in defendant's chest. The Court weighed the intrusiveness (surgical procedure requiring anesthesia) with the government need for the bullet and concluded that the search would be unreasonable under the Fourth Amendment.

# Analysis—Stops—Justification— Reasonable Suspicion

## INTRODUCTION

Cleveland detective McFadden was an officer with 39 years of experience. One October afternoon, he observed two individuals walking back and forth 24 times, pausing briefly to look in a shop window. Based on his experience, McFadden became suspicious. He testified that after observing their elaborately casual and oft-repeated reconnaissance of the shop window, he suspected the two men of "casing a job—a stick-up." He approached the men and when they mumbled something in response to his inquiry, McFadden frisked Terry, one of the men, and found a .38-caliber revolver. Charged with possession of a concealed weapon, Terry sought to suppress the gun.

As we have seen thus far in the Fourth Amendment context, the justification for an arrest and most criminal searches is probable cause. With regard to an arrest, the police need probable cause that a particular individual has committed a crime. Thus McFadden, who had only observed suspicious activity, did not have probable cause to arrest Terry. The Supreme Court grappled with McFadden's activity in Terry v. Ohio (1968), considering whether actions by the police are appropriate even though no crime has yet occurred. The Court first determined that the Fourth Amendment should apply to such activity. In a decision by Justice Earl Warren, the Court recognized the conflicting tension between the importance of law enforcement intervention in preventing crimes and the protections afforded to an individual by the Fourth Amendment. The Court turned to the reasonableness clause of the Fourth Amendment to create a method to deal with "street encounters between citizens and police officers." Through the use of the reasonableness clause, the Court weighed the government interest in conducting investigations in the absence of specific crimes against the amount of intrusion such encounters would entail. The Court's solution reflects an attempt to balance the intrusion against an individual who is stopped and asked about his activities, a lesser intrusion than an arrest, with society's interest in public safety.

The Court characterized this activity as "an entire rubric of police conduct" not previously considered by the Court. The Court fashioned a lesser justification than probable cause to deal with activity that is less intrusive than a full scale search or arrest. The justification required "specific and articulable facts which taken together with rational inferences from those facts" result in reasonable suspicion that "criminal activity is afoot." Should the intrusion become greater, resulting in a pat down frisk similar to McFadden's frisk of Terry, then additional justification relating to safety concerns would be required. This justification would necessitate a reasonable suspicion based on facts, as opposed to a hunch that the suspect is armed and dangerous. It is a difficult standard to actually quantify. Keep in mind, however, that as the police activity becomes more intrusive, greater justification such as probable cause is required. Thus, the scope of the search is limited narrowly to the justification. It should be noted that a pat down frisk amounts to patting the outer clothing in search of a weapon, whereas a more intrusive search incident to an arrest allows for an extensive search of the arrestee that goes well beyond a pat down frisk for weapons:

[A protective search for weapons,] unlike a search without a warrant incident to a lawful arrest, is not justified by any need to prevent the disappearance or destruction of evidence of crime. The sole justification of the search in the present situation is the protection of the police officer and others nearby, and it must therefore be confined in scope to an intrusion reasonably designed to discover guns, knives, clubs or other hidden instruments for the assault of the police officer.

In this chapter, we will look at three issues. First, we will determine whether the stop implicates the Fourth Amendment, or stated differently, does the individual have a reasonable expectation of privacy with regard to the particular police activity? If the answer to this question is no, then no justification is required because the Fourth Amendment is not implicated. If there is indeed a stop implicating the Fourth Amendment, we will look then at the factors that determine whether the reasonable suspicion standard has been met. Finally, we will examine the scope of the activity that is supported by the reasonable suspicion standard.

## WHEN DOES A STOP IMPLICATE THE FOURTH AMENDMENT?

The initial encounter between the police and a citizen must first be evaluated. The question for the Court in evaluating this encounter is whether the police activity amounts to some kind of Fourth Amendment seizure. "It must be recognized that whenever a police officer accosts an individual and restrains his freedom to walk away, he has 'seized' that person." The *Terry* Court recognized that "not all personal intercourse between policemen and citizens involves seizure of persons." There is a wide variety of interactions between citizens and the police that do not amount to a seizure. A simple question or a direction by a police officer would not by itself amount to a seizure. If there is no seizure, the Fourth Amendment would not apply and no justification for the police activity would be required. Thus, it is important to determine when a citizen/police interchange becomes a seizure that implicates the Fourth Amendment.

*Terry* defined seizure as follows: "Only when the officer, by means of physical force or show of authority, has in some way restrained the liberty of a citizen." This standard was refined in United States v. Mendenhall (1980). In this case, two DEA agents approached a woman as she disembarked from a flight at the Detroit airport. On request, she provided them with her plane ticket and identification. They noticed a different name on the ticket. On inquiry, she appeared "quite shaken, extremely nervous . . . she had a hard time speaking." They returned her ticket and identification and asked her to accompany them. The issue was whether she was seized for Fourth Amendment purposes at the time of the request to accompany them. Justice Stewart formulated an objective standard that has come to be accepted by a majority of the Court. "A person has been 'seized' within the meaning of the Fourth Amendment only if, in view of all of the circumstances surrounding the incident, a reasonable person would have believed that he was not free to leave." The factors enumerated to evaluate the individual's belief included threatening presence of several officers, display of weapons, physical touching, and language or voice tone.

The *Mendenhall* Court concluded that no seizure had occurred as the confrontation took place in a public place with plainclothes agents (who had identified themselves) and with no display of weapons. In Florida v. Royer (1983), where the situation was similar to *Mendenhall*, except for the fact that the officers did not return the ticket or driver's license, the majority of the Court found a seizure:

Asking for and examining Royer's ticket and his driver's license were no doubt permissible in themselves, but when the officers identified themselves as narcotics agents, told Royer that he was suspected of transporting narcotics, and asked him to accompany them to the police room, while retaining his ticket and driver's license and without indicating in any way that he was free to depart, Roger was effectively seized for the purposes of the Fourth Amendment. These circumstances surely amount to a show of official authority such that "a reasonable person would have believed that he was not free to leave."

INS v. Delgado (1984) is a case that involved the questioning of factory workers by Immigration and Naturalization Services (INS) agents who were looking for illegal aliens. Some INS agents monitored the exits while others asked questions of the factory workers. The Court of Appeals weighted heavily the fact that agents were stationed at the door and therefore the workers were not free to leave. However, adopting the *Mendenhall* objective test, the Court rejected the Court of Appeals approach, indicating that mere questioning would not constitute a seizure. The Court pointed out that workers do not feel free to leave because of their work obligations and that the questioning was merely a brief encounter with no restriction of movement within the factory. "Ordinarily, when people are at work their freedom to move about has been meaningfully restricted, not by the actions of law enforcement officers, but by workers' voluntary obligations to their employers."

A bus confrontation presented an unusual seizure situation for the Court. In *Florida v. Bostick* (1991), as part of a drug interdiction effort, an armed uniformed officer approached Bostick, a bus passenger, during a stopover and requested consent to search his luggage. The Supreme Court of Florida, applying the *Mendenhall* standard, reasoned that a passenger would not feel free to leave in this situation. Thus a seizure had occurred and the police activity required justification. The Florida court created a categorical rule that "an impermissible seizure results when police conduct a drug search on buses during scheduled stops and question boarded passengers without articulable reasons for doing so." The Court refused to adopt this per se rule. The Court recognized that the standard created in *Mendenhall* would not work for a bus situation because a passenger in transit would never feel free to leave. Relying on the decision in INS v. Delgado, the Court found that the bus passenger's freedom of movement was not restricted by police action but by the circumstances of being a bus passenger in transit. The Court adopted the following approach for this situation:

We adhere to the rule that, in order to determine whether a particular encounter constitutes a seizure, a court must consider all the circumstances surrounding the encounter to determine whether the police conduct would have communicated to a reasonable person that the person was not free to decline the officer's requests or otherwise terminate the encounter.

Because of an insufficient record, the Court remanded the case to determine whether a seizure had occurred. It did note that the officer did not remove his gun and that the passenger was advised that he could refuse to consent. In United States v. Drayton (2002), also a bus search situation, the Court refused to find a seizure even though the suspect was not advised of his opportunity to refuse consent. In *Drayton*, three plainclothes police officers boarded a bus. With one officer at the back of the bus and the other at the front, a third officer moved through the bus indicating that they were conducting a "drug and weapons interdiction." He asked each passenger if he could search their bags. He further indicated that all the passengers consented to this request. Justice Anthony Kennedy, for 6-3 majority, in holding that there was no seizure in this situation even though there was no indication from the officer that passengers were not required to consent, noted that there were no threats, intimidation, or show of force and no blocked exits. He equated the confrontation with an officer approaching someone on the street. Justice Souter in dissent (joined by Justices John Paul Stevens and Ruth Bader Ginsburg) reasoned that, given the officer's position and the confined quarters of a bus, it was hard to imagine that the defendant felt free to decline the officer's request. This recent decision appears to be a relaxing of Fourth Amendment applicability to public transportation in light of the terrible events of September 11, 2001.

In California v. Hodari (1991), the Court further qualified the *Mendenhall* test of whether "a reasonable person would not feel free to leave." In this case, Hodari ran from an approaching police car. The police pursued him on foot and Hodari dropped some drugs during the pursuit. In his attempt to suppress the drugs, Hodari argued that he had been seized at the time of the drop and that there was insufficient justification for the seizure. The Court, in a 7-2 decision by Justice Scalia, held that the language of *Mendenhall* stated a "reasonable but not a sufficient, condition for seizure." There needed to be either physical restraint or a submission to the authority for a seizure to actually have taken place. Thus in order for there to be a seizure, a reasonable person, not on a bus or other location where he is not inclined to leave, must believe that he is not free to leave or he has submitted to police authority.

## REASONABLE SUSPICION

Assuming the Fourth Amendment applied to the activity, we must examine the justification for that activity to see if it meets the standard for reasonable suspicion. Reasonable suspicion, like probable cause, is difficult to quantify. We do know that it is a level of justification less than probable cause, but articulating a precise formula is not possible. Thus, it is useful to examine the characterization of reasonable suspicion in various Court decisions. Turning to Terry v. Ohio, Justice Harlan's concurrence seeks to fill in the gaps of the majority opinion. He would divide the justification into two discrete analyses. First he would determine whether there was justification for the stop. As he aptly points out, "if and when a policeman has a right instead to disarm such a person for his own protection, he must first have a right not to avoid him but to be in his presence." Then he would turn to the justification for a frisk. With regard to the stop, the *Terry* majority would require "specific and articulable facts" as opposed to a "inchoate and unparticularized suspicion or hunch." In addition, the officer may use his experience to draw inferences from the facts. The conclusion to be made is whether "criminal activity is afoot." For a pat down frisk, it is not necessary that the officer be absolutely certain that the individual is armed. The standard from *Terry* for a pat down weapon search is "whether a reasonably prudent man in the circumstances would be warranted in the belief that his safety or that of others was in danger."

Probably the best overview statement as to what justification is required can be found in United States v. Cortez (1981):

Courts have used a variety of terms to capture the elusive concept of what cause is sufficient to authorize police to stop a person. Terms like "articulable reasons" and "founded suspicion" are not self-defining; they fall short of providing clear guidance dispositive of the myriad factual situations that arise. But the essence of all that has been written is that the totality of circumstances—the whole picture—must be taken into account. Based upon that whole picture the detaining officers must have a particularized and objective basis for suspecting the particular person stopped of criminal activity.

The totality of circumstances was employed in the recent case of United States v. Arvizu (2002). In this case, a federal border patrol agent was patroling in Arizona 30 miles north of the United States–Mexico border. He received a report that sensors indicated that a vehicle was travelling a dirt road used by smugglers to avoid a checkpoint at a time when a shift change was occurring, thus leaving the road without patrols. The agent drove to the area and spotted a minivan occupied by a male driver, a female in the front passenger seat, and three children in the back. He noticed that two of the children's knees were elevated. When the driver of the van noticed that he had been spotted, the van slowed down, the driver's posture stiffened, and the children engaged in "odd" waving for 4 to 5 minutes. A check of the registration revealed that the van was registered to an address in an area notorious for alien and narcotic smuggling. The van was stopped and 100 pounds of marijuana was found. The Court of Appeals refused to weigh all the various factors in finding a lack of reasonable suspicion. Giving some of the factors no weight, the Court of Appeals felt that a multifactor test would result in "a troubling degree of uncertainty and unpredictability." The Court, in a unanimous decision by Chief Justice William Rehnquist, reversed the Court of Appeals, emphasizing that the Court should not eliminate any factor but look at all the factors under a "totality of the circumstances" test to see whether the officer has a "particularized and objective basis" for reasonable suspicion. The officer can rely on his experience and training in making this conclusion. Thus all the factors were weighed and found to be enough for the officer to conclude that reasonable suspicion existed.

As it has with the probable cause issue, much of the Court's attention has focused on whether information received from unnamed informants is sufficient to establish reasonable suspicion. Unlike with probable cause, however, the Court has shown a greater willingness to accept this information without various conditions (e.g. the two-pronged approach). The Court articulated this proposition in Alabama v. White (1990):

Reasonable suspicion is a less demanding standard than probable cause not only in the sense that reasonable suspicion can be established with information that is different in quantity or content than that required to establish probable cause, but also in the sense that reasonable suspicion can arise from information that is less reliable than that required to show probable cause.

The *White* Court allowed for an anonymous telephone call as the source of the information when the police were able to corroborate the information by observing the "innocent" activity specified in the telephone call. In this case, the phone call indicated that Vanessa White would be leaving a particular apartment at a particular time in a particular vehicle and that she would be going to a named motel with cocaine in her possession. In Florida v. J.L. (2000), however, an anonymous call stated that a young black male wearing a plain shirt at a particular bus stop was carrying a gun. Two officers observed a man fitting this description at the bus stop, approached J.L., frisked him, and found a gun. A unanimous Court held that the police lacked reasonable suspicion. The Court, in distinguishing Alabama v. White, characterized *White* as a close case for a finding of reasonable suspicion. The *J.L.* tip did not have the predictive information as to future acts as did the tip in *White*. This tip amounted only to an accurate description of the subject's readily observable location. The government in this case argued for a "firearm exception" to *Terry*, whereby a tip alleging the possession of a gun would automatically be considered reliable. The Court strongly rejected this argument. Such an exception would allow any person to harass another by simply placing an anonymous call.

In United States v. Hensley (1985), the Court addressed the issue of whether a wanted flyer could provide sufficient justification for a stop. The flyer was issued by a neighboring police department concerning the involvement of a particular person in an armed robbery. The Court allowed for the flyer to be the impetus for a stop when the information in the flyer was sufficient to establish reasonable suspicion. This case is similar to Whiteley v. Warden (1971), discussed in the section analyzing probable cause, in which the Court analyzed whether police acting pursuant to a police radio call had probable cause. As long as the genesis of the call provided a sufficient basis to establish probable cause, other police could act on it. Similarly, as long as the flyer was issued on the basis of articulable facts supporting reasonable suspicion that the person named committed the offense then other departments could act on it.

It should be pointed out that *Hensley* allowed for the *Terry* justification in the context of a completed crime. Terry involved the detention of an individual for an imminent or ongoing crime. The Court reasoned that given the strong government interest in solving crimes and bringing offenders to justice, law enforcement officers should not be prevented from stopping an individual because they lacked probable cause merely because the crime had been completed. Given the lack of probable cause, however, it is appropriate to focus on the scope of the intrusion.

The Court has spoken on a number of occasions with regard to the reasonable suspicion standard in the context of an airport search. In United States v. Sokolow (1989), the Court considered the applicability of the so-called drug courier profile. This is a group of factors put out by the DEA to assist law enforcement in detecting drug smuggling at airports. The factors include traveling from a narcotic source city, not checking luggage, using hard American Tourister luggage, and paying cash for tickets. The Court said that the law enforcement agent could certainly use these factors to establish reasonable suspicion. The dissent, however, felt that the profile would dull an officer's ability to make an otherwise fact-specific decision. Since none of the factors enunciated actually constitute criminal activity, the Court, as well as lower courts, have not been uniform in their determination of activity which constitutes reasonable suspicion. Paying cash for tickets and flying under an assumed name seem to be the most important factors considered by the Court in finding reasonable suspicion.

In Illinois v. Wardlow (2000), the Court dealt with the effect that unprovoked flight had on the determination of reasonable suspicion. In this case, uniformed officers were travelling in a four-car caravan in a heavy narcotics area. The defendant was spotted holding an opaque bag, and on seeing the caravan, he fled. The police chased him and found a gun when they stopped and frisked him. The defendant sought to suppress the gun, arguing that the police lacked reasonable suspicion to stop him. The Court, in a 5-4 decision by Chief Justice Rehnquist, first indicated that neither presence in a high crime area nor unprovoked flight alone were sufficient to establish reasonable suspicion. However, the Court reasoned that both of these factors were pertinent and could be considered along with other factors in determining whether there was sufficient justification for the stop. The Court deferred to the judgment of law enforcement officers in their "common sense judgment and inferences about human behavior," holding that the combination of these two factors was enough to establish reasonable suspicion. The dissent, although recognizing that flight could be a factor for a *Terry* stop, thought that the reasons for flight in this case could be innocent and therefore refused to find reasonable suspicion.

A number of cases have dealt with the *Terry* standard in the context of automobiles. In United States v. Brignoni-Ponce (1975), the Court refused to allow for a stop by a roving border patrol when the only justification for the stop was the ancestry of the occupants. In the analysis of administrative searches, we will see that these patrols do not fit the administrative search classification. Similarly, in Delaware v. Prouse (1979), a "discretionary spot check" was not characterized as administrative and thus the Court held that such discretionary stops of an automobile require "articulable and reasonable suspicion." In *Prouse*, the police were stopping vehicles for a routine license and registration check. The Court, in disallowing these random stops, was concerned with the intrusiveness of this police action and sought to limit this unconstrained discretion. Thus, for there to be a random stop of a vehicle, there must be observed violations amounting to articulable and reasonable suspicion.

## SCOPE OF A STOP UNDER *TERRY*

Earlier in the chapter, we discussed the circumstances under which an encounter implicates the Fourth Amendment. Assuming that the Fourth Amendment is implicated, when does an encounter become so intrusive (amounting to an arrest) as to require greater justification than the *Terry* standard? In Dunaway v. New York (1979), the police, acting with limited justification (less than probable cause), picked up a suspect who was not under arrest and brought him to the police station for an interrogation. They did not arrest him. The state sought to use the reasonable suspicion standard established by *Terry* to justify this activity. The Court first emphasized that the *Terry* standard represented an exception to the general rule of probable cause and was only applicable in limited situations that involved a lesser intrusion than an arrest. In this case, taking the suspect to the station house where he was interrogated, in essence, amounted to an intrusion with all the characteristics of an arrest. The Court refused to apply the *Terry* standard to this type of intrusion. "Indeed any 'exception' that could cover a seizure as intrusive as that in this case would threaten to swallow the general rule that Fourth Amendment seizures are 'reasonable' only if based on probable cause."

In Florida v. Royer (1983), the police removed a suspect by coercion (the police had his airline ticket and driver's license) to a separate interrogation room. The Court felt this removal from the scene was too great an intrusion to be justified by the *Terry* standard. This is similar to the *Dunaway* case. The *Dunaway* standard was upheld in the *per curium* decision of Kaupp v. Texas (2003) in which a 17 year old boy was awakened at 3 AM in his bedroom by three police officers. He was handcuffed and taken shoeless in his underwear to a patrol car and transported to the scene of the crime, then to the police station. The action, commented the court, "points to an arrest even more startling than the facts in *Dunaway* where the petitioner was taken from a neighbor's home to a police car, transported to a police station, and placed in an interrogation room."

The Court, in elaborating on the scope of a *Terry* stop, said, "This much, however, is clear; an investigative detention must be temporary and last no longer than is necessary to effectuate the purpose of the stop. Similarly, the investigative methods employed should be the least intrusive means reasonably available to verify or dispel the officer's suspicion in a short period of time." In looking at a *Terry* detention, keep in mind the principal that the scope should be limited to the justification. Courts weigh the duration and the alternatives available, as well as the force used in order to determine whether the intrusion was consistent with the *Terry* justification.

The Court, in United States v. Place (1983), held that a 90-minute detention of luggage, while awaiting the arrival of a narcotic detection dog, was too long absent of probable cause. In *Place*, the Court reasoned that the police knew of the arrival time of the luggage and should have been better organized in arranging for the dog. "[I]n assessing the effect of the length of the detention, we take into account whether the police diligently pursue their investigation." In United States v. Sharpe (1985), the Court considered whether the length of detention (20 minutes) transformed a roadside *Terry* stop into a de facto arrest. In assessing the length of the stop in *Sharpe*, the Court stated that "the question is not simply whether some other alternative was available, but whether the police acted unreasonably in failing to recognize or to pursue it." In Sharpe, the Court allowed for the 20-minute detention, concluding that the officer pursued the investigation in a diligent and reasonable manner.

With regard to a weapon search, the Court requires additional justification to meet the reasonable suspicion standard (officer has a fear for his safety) and in addition, the scope of the search is limited by the justification provided for conducting the search in the first place. In *Terry*, the Court described the scope of the search as a "limited search of the outer clothing . . . to discover weapons which might be used to assault him." In Adams v. Williams (1972), the Court allowed the police to expand the search beyond the outer clothing in order to immediately remove a gun from the waistband of the suspect. In *Adams*, the police receive a tip that the suspect in the parked car had a gun at his waistband. The Court found that dispensing with the pat down and allowing an officer to reach for the gun was reasonable, given that it was a limited intrusion and the gun posed a great threat to the safety of the officer.

In Minnesota v. Dickerson (1993), the Court indicated the limitations of the frisk, while at the same time suggesting a way to expand the frisk. In this case, the officer who was conducting a frisk felt a small lump in the suspect's front pocket. On further tactile examination, he concluded that the lump was crack cocaine. The Court, relying on the state court's finding of fact that the officer concluded it was cocaine only after "squeezing, sliding and otherwise manipulating the outside of defendant's pocket," held that this search surpassed the scope of a *Terry* weapon search. The Court did, however, in dicta, indicate that if the search was a lawful pat down search and the officer felt an object that he immediately recognized as contraband, he could seize that object. This plain feel approach is similar to the plain view doctrine.

The Court has been more lenient in applying the *Terry* standard to automobile stops in light of the greater dangers faced by police officers during these situations. If there is a lawful stop of an automobile, the police may automatically order the driver (Pennsylvania v. Mimms, 1977), and passenger (Maryland v. Wilson, 1997), out of the car. Even though this seems to be an extension of the *Terry* scope, the Court reasoned that this further intrusion was de minimus, given the great danger officers face during car stops. The Court indicated that the dangers involved the possibility of being shot or harmed by oncoming traffic. In Ohio v. Robinette (1996), the Court extended the scope of this car stop beyond its justification. In this case, the justification for the stop was speeding. However, after the police had issued an oral warning and returned the suspect's license, they continued to detain him as they sought consent to search his car. The Court refused to adopt the state court's per se rule that would require a statement that the suspect was free to go. Justice Stevens, in dissent, argued that without telling the suspect that he was free to leave, the suspect would still believe he was seized. As the seizure continued, it exceeded its lawful purpose and thus the consent was the fruit of an unlawful seizure. In addition, when the police have justification during an automobile stop to believe that the suspect is armed, they can do a frisk and search of the interior of the car (not the trunk) for weapons. In Michigan v. Long (1983), the Court, recognizing the unusual hazards associated with a roadside stop, allowed for this extension in the scope of a *Terry* search for weapons.

# Analysis—Administrative Searches— Justification—Reasonable Standards

## INTRODUCTION

These types of searches, sometimes called *administrative, regulatory,* or *special need searches,* all have one common element: they are not being done for the normal law enforcement needs of discovering crime, but for purposes that are not related to criminal investigation. These searches serve important societal needs other than crime control. The noncriminal purposes that we will discuss in this chapter include inspections of business establishments, drug testing programs, fire scene inspection, border searches, automobile checkpoint and inventory searches, probation supervision searches, and school disciplinary searches.

Initially such government activity was not governed by the Fourth Amendment. In Frank v. Maryland (1959), a case involving a Baltimore City Code provision allowing a health inspector to enter a home without a warrant if he had cause to suspect a nuisance, the Court upheld the validity of inspection without a warrant when it was part of a regulatory scheme designed to protect the general welfare of the community. In reaching this decision, the Court considered the long history of allowing this type of search, the magnitude of the problem the health inspection statute was designed to address, and the statutory safeguards that limited the demands actually imposed on the building owners. The Court decided that the Fourth Amendment did not apply because the search was not conducted to obtain evidence of criminal action. The Court reasoned that the primary purpose of the Fourth Amendment, like the Fifth Amendment, is to provide self-protection: "The right to resist unauthorized entry which has as its design the securing of information to fortify the coercive power of the state against the individual." Thus, unless the government wanted access for the purpose of securing evidence for criminal prosecution, the right to self-protection was not in jeopardy, and the Fourth Amendment did not apply.

This approach changed in Camara v. Municipal Court of San Francisco (1967), in which the Court considered the constitutionality of a statute similar to the statute in *Frank*. In finding the Fourth Amendment applicable, the Court reasoned that these regulatory searches can often result in criminal penalties and thus, requiring a warrant would give the occupant notice of its official authority. The Court held that a person has a constitutional right to insist, in a nonemergency situation, that an inspector obtain a warrant to conduct a search.

The traditional requirements for police activity implicating the Fourth Amendment are a warrant and probable cause. This justification does not work for administrative searches because individualized suspicion does not exist. For example, a health inspection is usually conducted in a large area of concern, not in an individual domicile. Realizing that the traditional justification for Fourth Amendment activity would not work for this type of search, the Court turned to the reasonableness clause of the Fourth Amendment and balanced the government purpose against the scope of the invasion to come up with a justification. In *Camara*, the Court observed that the intrusion to one's privacy is limited because the search is not directed at a particular individual and the purpose of the search is not to discover criminal evidence. On the other side of the equation, the government interest can be found in the long history of judicial and public acceptance, as well as the importance of addressing dangerous health conditions. The Court concluded that such searches could be conducted as long as "reasonable legislative or administrative standards for conducting an area inspection are satisfied with respect to a particular dwelling."

## ADMINISTRATIVE SEARCHES—YES OR NO?

Before examining the various categories of administrative searches, there are three broad issues on which to focus. When are searches appropriately regarded as administrative? What factors go into the balancing equation? And finally, when is a warrant required? Categorizing a search as administrative avoids the individualized suspicion requirement and the necessity for a warrant. In this way, an administrative search provides greater leeway to the government in conducting widespread search operations. A good example of this can be found every time we travel on an airplane. It is not possible to board a commercial plane without going through a metal detector or at times other, more intrusive search techniques.

Because the line between what is administrative and what is criminal has become blurry, the issue has generated considerable debate within the Court. For example, in New York v. Burger (1987), the Court held that a statute allowing police officers to conduct warrantless searches of automobile junkyards and seize stolen cars and property fell within the exception to the warrant requirement for administrative inspections. The Court reached this conclusion despite the fact that the purpose of the statute, the deterrence of car theft, was the same as the goal of the state's penal laws, and therefore the administrative inspection could disclose violations of the penal statutes. The Court of Appeals had held that the administrative goal of the statute, to ensure that vehicle dismantlers are legitimate business people and that vehicles and parts passing through junkyards can be identified, was pretextual, "designed simply to give the police an expedient means of enforcing penal sanctions for possession of stolen property." The Court found that a state could address a major social problem both through an administrative scheme and through penal sanctions. The fact that police officers, rather than administrative agents, conducted these searches and that those officers could discover evidence of crimes beyond violations of the scheme itself, was not problematic to the Court so long as the regulatory scheme was properly administrative. The Court found that the regulatory scheme contributed to a goal of ensuring that vehicle dismantlers were legitimate businesspersons.

More recently, the Court has been less willing to characterize something as administrative when the criminal purpose is apparent. For example, in Indianapolis v. Edmond (2001), the Court held that a traffic checkpoint program violated the Fourth Amendment when its primary purpose was indistinguishable from the general interest of crime control. The Court therefore distinguished the checkpoint in *Edmond*, both from the border checkpoints used to detect illegal aliens that reflected a "longstanding concern for the protection of the integrity of the border," and from sobriety checkpoints in which "there was an obvious connection between the imperative of highway safety and the law enforcement practice at issue." In the 6-3 decision in *Edmond*, Chief Justice Rehnquist's dissent stressed that it should not matter that the "primary purpose" of the roadblock was to interdict drugs because the roadblock was also used to check driver's licenses and registrations and to look for signs of a driver impairment. The stops therefore served an accepted and significant state interest in maintaining highway safety. Chief Justice Rehnquist explained the extrinsic limitation of the normal balancing test on roadblock seizures rendered the Court's "newfound non-law-enforcement primary purpose test" both "unnecessary to secure Fourth Amendment rights and bound to produce wide-ranging litigation over the purpose of any given seizure." The majority, however, was concerned that "without drawing the line at roadblocks designed to serve the general interest in crime control, the Fourth Amendment would do little to prevent such intrusions from becoming a routine part of American life."

Also, in Fergusen v. City of Charleston (2001), the participation of the police in drafting a policy for drug testing pregnant women, and in the day-to-day administration of that policy, appeared to be dispositive in the Court's refusal to regard the regulation as administrative. The Court found that the policy, although its ultimate objective was to use the threat of criminal prosecution to get women into substance abuse treatment, had an immediate objective of generating evidence for law enforcement purposes that was indistinguishable from the general interest in crime control. The majority viewed this distinction between ultimate and immediate objectives as critical. Justice Stevens explained that if only the ultimate purpose were considered, "Because law enforcement involvement always serves some broader social purpose or objective . . . virtually any nonconsensual suspicionless search could be immunized under the special needs doctrine by defining the search solely in terms of its ultimate, rather than immediate purpose." Although Justice Kennedy concurred in the Court's decision that the testing procedure could not be sustained under the Fourth Amendment, he felt the ultimate versus immediate objective distinction lacked foundation in the Court's previous special needs cases that all turned on the policy's ultimate goal. Justice Kennedy instead relied on the idea that "traditional warrant and probable cause requirements are waived in our previous case on the explicit assumption that the evidence obtained in the search is not intended to be used for law enforcement purposes." The fact that the positive drug tests were used to threaten women with criminal prosecution thus clearly distinguished *Ferguson* from prior cases (Skinner v. Railroad Labor Executives' Association, 1989 and Vernonia School District 47J v. Acton, 1995). The dissent, however, focused on the idea that the majority did not object to the search and seizure at issue—taking and testing the women's urine—but only to the hospital's reporting positive results to the police. After noting that the women provided the urine voluntarily and that urine cannot reasonably be considered an "effect" entitled to protection under the Fourth Amendment, Justice Scalia commented, "Until today, we have never held—or even suggested—that material which a person voluntarily entrusts to someone else cannot be given by that person to the police, and used for whatever evidence it may contain."

At times, to avoid the traditional requirement of probable cause, the Court seemed inclined to characterize a search as administrative even when a criminal purpose was at least part of the motivation. However, the two most recent decisions of the Court have taken a different approach in refusing to characterize a search as administrative when crime control was the primary motivation and when police are significantly involved in writing administrative regulations.

## BALANCING FOR THE REASONABLE STANDARD

As previously mentioned, the Court, realizing that probable cause would not work for administrative searches, turned to the reasonableness clause as it did in Terry v. Ohio (1968), and balanced the government purpose against the scope of the invasion to come up with a justification. In balancing the government's purpose against the scope of the intrusion, the Court has considered factors like the strength of the individuals' privacy expectations, the amount of discretion the government has, the search method used by the government, and the type of search. A good example of the elements of the balancing equation can be found in

*Vernonia.* In deciding that the school's drug testing policy did not violate student rights, the Court weighed the amount of intrusion, which included the nature of the students' privacy interests, against the important government interest in the prevention of drug use by our nation's school children. In weighing the students' privacy interests, the Court considered the students' decreased expectation of privacy, the relative unobtrusiveness of the search, the method of using a urine test to gather the information, as well as the amount of discretion that would be exercised by various school officials. In addition, the Court considered the lesser privacy expectations of student athletes. This particular concern was very important to Justice Ginsburg who indicated she would reserve the question of drug testing for all students attending schools. In a 5-4 decision in Board of Education of Independent School District No. 92 of Pottawatomie County v. Earls (2002), the Court accepted a drug testing policy that required drug testing for any middle or high school student participating in extracurricular activities. The Court discounted the lesser privacy expectation associated with athletes, focusing instead on lesser privacy expectation based on the school's custodial responsibility. This lesser expectation of privacy has been considered in weighing the intrusiveness of searches in the context of closely regulated businesses or occupations such as the railroad business (Skinner v. Railway Labor Executives' Association, 1989) or customs officers (National Treasury Employee Union v. Von Raab, 1989).

Therefore, in determining whether an administrative search is consistent with the Fourth Amendment, the Court engages in a process of balancing the government interest against the intrusiveness of the search. This is not, however, a precise formula. In his dissenting opinion in New Jersey v. TLO (1985), Justice Brennan characterized this balancing process as Rorschach-like. Brennan was concerned that the Court was casting aside the probable cause justification for a full-scale search. According to Brennan, given the scope of the intrusion, it was not appropriate to use an administrative search rationale and its lesser justification. In *TLO*, there was a very thorough search of the student's purse, and Justice Brennan pointed out that, in the other cases where a balancing test had been used, the intrusions were substantially less intrusive than a full-fledged search. Therefore, he was not prepared to treat the search in *TLO* as an administrative search because of its intrusive nature. In his dissent in *Skinner*, Justice Thurgood Marshall shared this sentiment. Justice Marshall felt that the collection of urine was the type of "full scale personal search[es]" that requires probable cause. He further argued that any type of personal search requires individualized suspicion.

## NECESSITY FOR A WARRANT

*Camara* indicated a strong desire for warrants. The companion case of See v. Seattle (1967), a case involving an attempt by a fire department representative to inspect a locked commercial warehouse without a warrant and without probable cause to believe a violation of any municipal ordinance existed inside, also indicates a strong preference for search warrants: "The businessman, like the occupant of a residence, has a constitutional right to go about his business free from unreasonable official entries upon his private commercial property. The businessman, too, has that right placed in jeopardy if the decision to enter and inspect for violation of regulatory laws can be made and enforced by the inspector in the field without official authority evidenced by a warrant."

Subsequent cases have created exceptions to the warrant requirement based on the nature of the business, practicality concerns in obtaining a warrant, and special needs situations. The nature of the business exception usually involves heavily regulated industries. In United States v. Biswell (1972), the Court held that a warrantless search of a pawn shop operator's locked storeroom, as authorized by the Gun Control Act of 1968, did not violate the Fourth Amendment. The Court reasoned that close scrutiny of interstate traffic in firearms was of central interest in the federal efforts to prevent violent crime, and warrantless inspections were a crucial part of the regulatory scheme. In Colonnade Catering Corp. v. United States (1970), which dealt with the statutory authorization for warrantless inspections of federally licensed dealers in alcoholic beverages, the Court emphasized the historically broad authority of the government to regulate the liquor industry. Although the Court found that Congress had ample power "to design such powers of inspection under the liquor laws as it deems necessary to meet the evils at hand," the Court concluded that, in this particular regulation, Congress had not expressly provided for forcible entry absent a warrant and had instead given Government agents a remedy by making it a criminal offense to refuse admission to the inspectors.

The nature of the business exception to the warrant requirement was also used in New York v. Burger (1987), in which the Court affirmed the validity of warrantless inspection of automobile junkyards for stolen cars and parts, and in Donovan v. Dewey (1981), in which the Court affirmed the validity of warrantless inspections of mining facilities for safety violations. In *Donovan*, Justice Marshall explained that "a warrant may not be constitutionally required when Congress has reasonably determined that warrantless searches are necessary to further a regulatory scheme and the federal regulatory presence is sufficiently comprehensive and defined that the owner of commercial property cannot help but be aware that his property will be subject to periodic inspections." The Court therefore found that the statute's inspection program provided a constitutionally adequate substitute for a warrant. However, in Marshall v. Barlow's Inc. (1978), the Court refused to dispense with the warrant requirement. The Court found that the Occupational Safety and Health Act (OSHA) (1970) failed to tailor the scope and frequency of administrative inspections to the particular health and safety concerns posed by the numerous and varied businesses regulated by the statute. The Court was concerned that a business owner not in an otherwise closely regulated industry had no real expectation that his business would be subject to inspection and that the provision of the Act authorizing administrative searches "devolves almost unbridled discretion upon executive and administrative officers, particularly those in the field, as to when to search and whom to search." The Court did, however, expressly limit their holding to OSHA, noting that, "The reasonableness of a warrantless search, however, will depend upon the specific enforcement needs and privacy guarantees of each statute."

In addition to the nature of the business exception, the Court has carved out an exception to the warrant requirement when it would not be practical to obtain a warrant because of the need for fast action (Skinner v. Railway Labor Executives' Association, 1989). In *Skinner*, the Court held that the Fourth Amendment did not require individualized suspicion or a warrant in order to perform drug and alcohol testing on railroad employees involved in certain train accidents. The Court reasoned that the burden of obtaining a warrant would likely frustrate the purpose behind the drug testing given the fact that alcohol and drugs gradually disseminate from the bloodstream and the delay necessary to procure a warrant could thus result in the destruction of valuable evidence.

The Court also recognizes an exception to the warrant requirement in situations where there is so-called "special need." For example, in New Jersey v. TLO (1985), the Court recognized that the special needs of a school environment make the warrant requirement unsuitable. Justice White explained that "Requiring a teacher to obtain a warrant before searching a child suspected of an infraction . . . would unduly interfere with the maintenance of the swift and informal disciplinary procedure needs in the schools." In Griffin v. Wisconsin (1987), the Court also recognized that a state's operation of a probation system presents special needs beyond normal law enforcement that may justify departures from the usual warrant and probable-cause requirements. The Court reasoned that the supervision necessary as part of probation is a "special need" of the State that justifies a degree of impingement on privacy that would not be constitutional if applied to the general public.

Thus, the Court has moved from a strong initial preference for administrative warrants and has created numerous exceptions to the need for warrants. These exceptions include the following areas: heavily regulated industries, practicality concerns, and special need situations.

## CATEGORIES OF ADMINISTRATIVE SEARCHES

This section is designed to show the application of the balancing test, as well as the need for warrants in a variety of categories of administrative searches. It is useful to divide it up by category, since the Court's approach to the importance of the governmental purpose varies with setting.

## Schools

In three cases involving public schools, *TLO*, *Vernonia*, and *Earls*, the Court has clearly recognized the need for administrative searches. *TLO* involved a vice principal's search of a student's purse for cigarettes after she was caught smoking in the lavatory in violation of school rules. As a result of this search, the vice principal found marijuana inside the purse along with note cards with names on them that indicated that the student had been selling marijuana. The Court decided that the special need to maintain school discipline required some easing of the restrictions to which searches by public authorities are ordinarily subjected. The Court thus found that school officials were not held to the standard of probable cause in conducting searches, but rather to a standard of reasonableness under all the circumstances. The Court required less than probable cause but still required some individualized suspicion. In developing this standard, the Court sought to allow teachers and administrators to conduct searches of students according to the dictates of reason and common sense while simultaneously ensuring that students' interests were invaded no more than necessary.

In *Vernonia,* no individualized suspicion was required for the mandatory drug testing of high school athletes. This lack of individualized suspicion was severely criticized by the dissent who did not approve of the idea of subjecting the nation's school children to mass suspicionless searches. Justice O'Connor felt that the personal intrusiveness of monitored urination and urine testing weighed heavily against the validity of evenhanded blanket searches. O'Connor stressed that if "an individualized suspicion requirement would not place the government's objectives in jeopardy, that requirement should not be forsaken." The dissent went on to explain that the effectiveness of an individualized suspicion requirement is particularly clear in the school context, where students are under constant supervision by teachers, administrators, and coaches. Although O'Connor explicitly acknowledged that a suspicion-based regimen would likely be less effective than a mass, suspicionless testing regimen, she stated, "There is nothing new in the realization that Fourth Amendment protections come with a price."

*Earls* went further than *Vernonia* by allowing the drug testing of any middle or high school student participating in extracurricular activities. In a 5-4 decision, Justice Ginsburg's dissent pointed out that the balancing equation was substantially different in *Earls* than in *Vernonia*. First, in terms of the government interest, there did not seem to be the substantial drug problem found in the Vernonia School District. Further, the intrusion was substantially greater because athletes who might be subject to injury are, according to *Vernonia*, similar to "adults who choose to participate in closely regulated industry." This particularized concern for physical safety among athletes using drugs did not exist for students participating in nonathletic extracurricular activities. Justice Thomas, however, for the majority, saw an important government interest because of a systemic drug problem in the schools and reasoned that the intrusion was minimal, given the custodial care-taking responsibilities inherent in attending a public school.

It is interesting to note that in Justice John Paul Stevens' dissent in *TLO*, he argued for greater Fourth Amendment protection so as to teach school children the value of the Constitution. "The school room is the first opportunity most citizens have to experience the power of government. Through it passes every citizen and public official, from schoolteachers to policemen and prison guards. One of our most cherished ideals is the one contained in the Fourth Amendment; that the government may not intrude on the personal privacy of its citizens without a warrant or compelling circumstances." Justice Ginsburg's dissent in *Earls* adds her voice to those advocating the importance of educating students. She cites the language of Justice Louis Brandeis in Olmstead v. United States (1928), stating "Our government is the potent, the omnipresent teacher. For good or for ill, it teaches the whole people by its example." She states, "that wisdom should guide decisionmakers in the instant case: The government is nowhere more a teacher than when it runs a public school."

## Borders

Borders have traditionally been recognized as a place at which administrative search standards are allowed. In United States v. Ramsey (1977), the Court explained that the executive has a longstanding right to conduct routine searches and seizures that are considered reasonable simply by virtue of the fact that they occur at the border. In *Ramsey*, a customs officer noticed eight envelopes in the same incoming bag of mail from Thailand, all of which appeared to have been addressed by the same typewriter and weighed more than normal international mail. He suspected that the envelopes might contain heroin. The Court held that the border search performed when the officer opened one of the letters did not violate the Fourth Amendment because it fit within the historically recognized "border search exception."

One issue that the Court has faced is the scope of these border searches. For example, in United States v. Montoya De Hernandez (1985), the Court held that when customs officials reasonably suspected a woman of being a "balloon swallower" and smuggling contraband in her alimentary canal, detaining the woman for 16 hours and then bringing her to a hospital for a rectal examination was not an unreasonable course of action. Although the Court recognized that the length of detention exceeded the detentions of others that the Court had approved, the majority emphasized that common sense, rather than hard-and-fast time limits, should govern the length of detention. The fact that alimentary canal smuggling presents few external signs as well as the woman's failure to comply with the official's request for an x-ray examination left officials with the option of a lengthy detention or releasing the woman into the interior carrying reasonably suspected contraband drugs. Under these circumstances, the Court concluded, the detention was reasonable in scope.

Another issue involving borders has to do with the stopping of vehicles not at the border, but at locations in the vicinity of the border. Some cases have involved roving patrols. In Almeida-Sanchez v. United States (1973), the Court held that a warrantless search of an automobile made without probable cause or consent at a point 20 miles north of the Mexican border was not a border search, or the functional equivalent, and violated the Fourth Amendment. The Court believed that the search was conducted at the "unfettered discretion" of the border patrol officers who had no reason to believe that the automobile had even crossed the border, much less that the driver possessed the marijuana the officers ultimately discovered in the truck. In United States v. Brignoni-Ponce (1975), the Court decided that a roving patrol could stop a vehicle and question its occupants concerning their citizenship and immigration status but only if the officers were aware of articulable facts, along with rational inferences therefrom, which would create reasonable suspicion that the vehicle contained illegal aliens. The Court further held that the fact that the occupants appeared to be of Mexican ancestry, although a relevant factor, was not itself sufficient to create a reasonable suspicion.

Other cases involve fixed checkpoints. In United States v. Ortiz (1975), a border patrol officer stopped the respondent's car at a fixed checkpoint, searched the car, and found three illegal aliens concealed in the trunk. The Court held that the Fourth Amendment prohibited border patrol officers from searching private vehicles at traffic checkpoints removed from the border in the absence of consent or probable cause. The Court concluded that the regularity of the stop, as compared with the random searches of roving patrols, did not mitigate the invasion of privacy that the search entailed, particularly because officers still exercised a substantial degree of discretion in deciding which cars to search. However, in United States v. Martinez-Fuerte (1976), the Court held that vehicle stops at a fixed checkpoint that only involved brief questioning of the vehicles' occupants were valid under the Fourth Amendment. In this case, the Court decided that the government interest in making the stops outweighed the constitutionally protected interests of the private citizens because these stops did not involve searches. The Court stressed that it would be impractical to require that these stops be based on reasonable suspicion because the amount of traffic did not allow for a particularized study of each vehicle.

## Automobiles

There are two types of administrative searches exclusively involving automobiles: the so-called checkpoint searches to discover drunk drivers and the inventory searches.

In Delaware v. Prouse (1979), the government sought to justify random stops of automobiles to check equipment and promote highway safety. The Court, in refusing to allow police officers to randomly stop cars to check licenses and registrations, balanced the intrusion on the individual's Fourth Amendment interests against its promotion of legitimate government interests. In this case, the Court determined that the marginal contribution to roadway safety that might possibly result from these spot checks could not justify subjecting drivers to the unbridled discretion of law enforcement officials. The randomness of the discretionary factors influenced the Court in finding the intrusion outweighed the government interest. The Court further stressed that no empirical evidence indicated that such stops would effectively promote roadway safety. The Court held that, except in those situations in which there is at least articulable and reasonable suspicion that a motorist is unlicensed or otherwise violating the law or that an automobile is unregistered, stopping and detaining the driver to check his license and registration is unreasonable under the Fourth Amendment. However, the Court explained that its decision did not preclude methods for spot checks that involved less intrusion or that did not involve the unconstrained exercise of discretion.

The Court later addressed the possibility of constitutional spot checks in Michigan v. Sitz (1990), when it upheld a drunk driving checkpoint search. The Court reasoned that, unlike Delaware v. Prouse, Michigan's sobriety checkpoints were created pursuant to guidelines and involved neither random stops (and thus no unbridled discretion) nor a complete absence of data indicating their effectiveness as a means of promoting roadway safety. The Court again performed a balancing test, resolving that the State's interest in preventing drunk driving and the extent to which the checkpoints were seen to advance this interest outweighed the degree of intrusion on the briefly detained motorists. It is interesting to note that Justice Rehnquist's dissent characterized the Court's conclusion that stopping motorists en masse was less intrusive than random individual stops as a new elevation of the "misery loves company" adage. In an attempt by the city of Indianapolis to extend *Sitz* to a drug detection checkpoint search, the Court held that since the primary purpose of the checkpoint was to detect evidence of ordinary criminal wrongdoing, there was not the same "obvious connection between the imperative of highway safety and the law enforcement practice at issue" as the Court found in *Sitz* (Indianapolis v. Edmond, 2000).

## Inventory Searches of Automobiles

With regard to inventory searches of automobiles that usually occur after an automobile has been impounded for traffic or parking violations, accident, or abandonment, the Court upheld such searches as administrative (South Dakota v. Opperman, 1976). In that case, while conducting a routine inventory search according to procedure to remove valuables from a locked automobile that had been impounded for parking violations, officers found a small amount of marijuana in the glove compartment. The Court found that the police inventory procedures were not unreasonable because they served three distinct needs: the protection of the owner's property while in police custody, the protection of the police against claims of lost or stolen property, and the protection of police from potential danger. The Court upheld the search because the strong government interest involved and the diminished expectation of privacy in an automobile reduced the nature of the intrusion. In addition, there was no indication that the procedure was a pretext for concealing an investigatory police motive.

This case was expanded somewhat in Colorado v. Bertine (1987) in which officers followed standardized inventory procedure when, after arresting a driver for drunk driving, they inventoried his van's contents. The officers opened a backpack found inside and then opened containers in the backpack that contained different drugs. In this case, the officers had discretion whether to impound the vehicle. The Court allowed for this discretion as long as it was exercised pursuant to standard criteria and not exercised based on suspicion of criminal action. The Court again emphasized that if a police inventory search is conducted according to standardized criteria and administered in good faith, the search will not violate the Fourth Amendment. In Florida v. Wells (1990), in which a large quantity of marijuana was discovered in a locked suitcase, the Court again stressed that an actual policy for opening closed containers during an inventory search was necessary to satisfy the Fourth Amendment. However, the Court did say that a police officer could have some discretion in deciding whether to open a specific container, if such discretion is provided for in the policy.

Both *Bertine* and *Opperman* seemed to limit inventory searches to areas where valuables were likely to be found. In Michigan v. Thomas (1982), however, the Court determined that once the standard inventory of a car revealed contraband in the glove compartment, probable cause existed to believe there was contraband elsewhere in the vehicle so that a warrantless search, which revealed a gun in the air vents under the dashboard, was justified. The Supreme Court held such a search was justified and overruled the Court of Appeals decision that the search was "unreasonable in scope" because it extended to the air vents, which, unlike the glove compartment or the trunk, were not a likely place for the storage of valuables or personal possessions. It should be pointed out that this *per curiam* opinion of the Court rested on the further justification of probable cause resulting from finding contraband in the glove compartment.

In addition, the Court allowed for these searches to be extended in terms of time in Florida v. Meyers (1984). In that case the Court held that a second search of the respondent's vehicle was constitutional even though it was conducted eight hours after his arrest and the impoundment of and first search of the vehicle. The Court relied on the rationale of Chambers v. Maroney (1970), that provided for an automobile exception to the warrant case. *Chambers* held that once there is probable cause to search a car, the search can occur later in time and at a different place (the station house). The existence of probable cause and not the time was the important factor for the automobile exception.

### Inventory Searches of Persons

In addition to inventory searches of cars, inventory searches have also been upheld to justify a search of an arrested individual. In Illinois v. Lafayette (1983), after a man was arrested for disturbing the peace and brought into the station, a police officer conducted an inventory search of his shoulder bag and discovered 10 amphetamine pills in a pack of cigarettes. The Court concluded that it is reasonable for the police to search the personal effects of a person under lawful arrest as part of their routine booking and jailing procedures. The procedures, designed to protect the suspect's property, to protect the police from false accusations of stolen or lost property, to protect the suspect and others, and to establish the identity of the suspect, were beneficial to both the police and the public. The Court indicated in a footnote that many of these interests would not be implicated if the suspect was not going to be incarcerated. The Court further explained that the possible existence of a less intrusive method for achieving these goals, namely sealing the entire shoulder bag as a unit, does not, by itself, render the search unreasonable.

### Public Employee Workplace Searches

Once again using the balancing approach previously discussed, the Court upheld workplace searches in O'Connor v. Ortega (1987). In that case, the Court decided that an employer's search of an employee's office, for both the noninvestigatory work-related purpose of inventorying state property and for the investigation of work-related misconduct, should be judged by a standard of reasonableness under all circumstances. Under the reasonableness standard, both the inception and the scope of the intrusion must be reasonable. The Court stressed that employee expectations of privacy may be reduced by the "operational realities of the workplace," and thus certain work-related intrusions by supervisors or co-workers would be entirely reasonable, though they might be viewed as unreasonable in other contexts. The Court then balanced the invasion of the employee's legitimate expectations of privacy against the government's need for supervision, control, and the efficient operation of the workplace. The Court emphasized the noncriminal value of the searches in order to justify such searches as administrative. "Even when employers conduct an investigation, they have an interest substantially different from 'the normal need of law enforcement.'" The Court reasoned that an employer's focus is on running his agency effectively and efficiently, and an employer must therefore be able to deal effectively with the incompetence, inefficiency, mismanagement, or other work-related misfeasance of his employees.

The Court has upheld such searches even when the searches became more intrusive and involved the testing of urine for drugs and alcohol. In *Skinner*, the Court upheld a regulation of the Federal Railroad Administration mandating and authorizing drug and alcohol testing of railroad employees. The Court reasoned that the compelling government interests in ensuring the safety of both the public and the employees themselves presented a "special need" beyond normal law enforcement that outweighed employees' privacy concerns. It should be pointed out that this happened in the wake of a railroad accident, after drug problems with railroad employees had been well documented. The Court again recognized that employees have diminished expectations of privacy, in this case by virtue of their participation in an industry that is pervasively regulated to ensure safety.

The Court applied the same reasoning in a close 5-4 decision in National Treasury Employee Union v. Von Raab (1989), when it decided that the Customs Service's policy of drug-testing employees applying for promotions or transfers to positions that involve the interdiction of illegal drugs or that require them to carry firearms, was reasonable under the Fourth Amendment. The Court noted that the testing program was not designed to serve the ordinary needs of law enforcement but was instead designed to ensure the effectiveness of the Customs Service and the safety of the public. The Court therefore performed a balancing test and concluded that the "extraordinary safety and national security hazards that would attend the promotion of drug users to positions that require the carrying of firearms or the interdiction of controlled substances" outweighed the employee's privacy interests. It is interesting to note that Justice Scalia's dissent in this case pointed out that, unlike the railroad situation, there was no documented drug problem among customs officials. Thus Justice Scalia was not convinced of the governmental interest: "I joined the Court's opinion [in Skinner] because the demonstrated frequency of drug and alcohol use by the targeted class of employees, and the demonstrated connection between such use and grave harm, rendered the search a reasonable means of protecting society. I decline to join the Court's opinion in the present case because neither frequency of use nor connection to harm is demonstrated or even likely. In my view, the Customs Service rules are a kind of immolation of privacy and human dignity in symbolic opposition to drug use."

The Court refused to extend the rationales of *Skinner* and *Von Raab* in Chandler v. Miller (1997). The Court held that requiring individuals to pass drug tests prior to qualifying for nomination or election did not qualify as a constitutionally permissible search. The Court felt that Georgia failed to show a "special need" sufficient to override the individual employee's privacy interests. Specifically, the Court emphasized that the case lacked the unique circumstances present in *Von*

*Raab*, in which employees worked directly with the interdiction of drugs, and employees could not be subjected to the day-to-day scrutiny of a traditional office environment. The Court concluded that the need addressed by the Georgia statute was not "special" but rather was symbolic of Georgia's commitment to the struggle against drug abuse, and the Fourth Amendment shields society from state action that diminishes personal privacy for the sake of symbolism.

## Miscellaneous Administrative Searches

### Fire

In Michigan v. Tyler (1978), the Court held that a fire presents an emergency of sufficient proportions to justify a warrantless entry, and that once inside officials may remain for a reasonable time to investigate the cause of the fire and seize evidence in plain view. Additional entries to investigate the cause of the fire, however, will require a warrant. The Court found that immediate investigation was justified because prompt discovery of a fire's source may be necessary to prevent its reoccurrence, evidence must be preserved from actual or intentional destruction, and the sooner officials complete their investigation, the less they will interfere with the privacy of the victim. The Court then reasoned that a warrant is required for subsequent entries because several factors may need to be weighed by a neutral magistrate to determine the reasonableness of these searches. These factors include the number of prior entries, the scope of the search, the time of day when it is proposed to be made, the lapse of time since the fire, the continued use of the building, and the owner's efforts to secure the building against intruders. Thus if after their initial immediate search investigators feel there is probable cause to believe arson has occurred and require additional entries to gather evidence, they must obtain a warrant. The administrative purposes of discovering and putting out the fire allow for these intrusions, but searches beyond the scope of this justification need Fourth Amendment protection, especially where the purpose of the search becomes criminal.

### Prison Searches

In Hudson v. Palmer (1984), the Court held that prison inmates have no reasonable expectation of privacy in their cells which would entitle them to the protections of the Fourth Amendment. Justice Warren Burger explained that, while prison inmates are afforded those rights not inconsistent with imprisonment or incompatible with the objectives of incarceration, the recognition of privacy rights is incompatible with the concept of incarceration and the needs and objectives of prison institutions. The Court reasoned that the Fourth Amendment protects those privacy expectations that society would view as reasonable, and "society would insist that the prisoner's expectation of privacy always yield to what must be considered the paramount interest in institutional security." Thus searches in prison for institutional safety purposes do not implicate the Fourth Amendment and do not have to satisfy administrative search requirements.

### Parole Violations

In Griffin v. Wisconsin (1987), the Court held that a regulation allowing a search of a probationer's home according to a "reasonable grounds" standard, instead of a probable cause standard, did not violate the Fourth Amendment. The Court reasoned that supervision of probationers created a "special need" for the state that would justify departures from the normal warrant and probable cause requirements. Just as they had done with prison inmates in Hudson v. Palmer, the Court, in this case, weighed the state interest in effectively running its system against probationers' individual privacy interests and struck the balance in favor of the state. The Court again reasoned that probationers, like prisoners, do not enjoy absolute liberty, but only conditional liberty.

In the case of United States v. Knight 534 US 112 (2001), the Court refused to be limited to the facts of *Griffin*, which involved a search conducted by a probation officer monitoring whether the probationer was following the conditions of probation. In Knight the search was conducted by a police officer investigating a crime.

### Public Benefit Cases

The most recent statement by the Court can be found in Ferguson v. City of Charleston (2001). In this case, a hospital, deeply concerned with what it saw as an increase in cocaine use by pregnant women, consulted with police and established a drug testing program for women who came to the hospital for prenatal care. Although the Court acknowledged that drug abuse during pregnancy was indeed a serious societal concern and both mothers and babies would benefit from drug abuse treatment, the Court held that testing the women's urine without their consent, and reporting positive results to the police, violated the Fourth Amendment. As Justice Stevens explained, "While respondents are correct that drug abuse both was and is a serious problem, 'the gravity of the threat alone cannot be dispositive of questions concerning what means law enforcement officers may employ to pursue a given purpose." Given the law enforcement involvement in designing the program, it was thought that the intrusion should not be subject to the lesser administrative search standard.

# Analysis—Warrants

## INTRODUCTION

The purpose of obtaining a warrant is to have a neutral person who is not involved in law enforcement evaluate the justification to determine whether there is probable cause for action that police wish to take. In Johnson v. United States (1948), the Supreme Court elaborated on this sentiment:

The point of the Fourth Amendment, which often is not grasped by zealous officers, is not that it denies law enforcement the support of the usual inferences which reasonable men draw from evidence. Its protection consists in requiring that those inferences be drawn by a neutral and detached magistrate instead of being judged by the officer engaged in the often competitive enterprise of ferreting out crime. The importance of such a neutral evaluation is understandable given the fact that, out of necessity, warrants are issued *ex parte* (the only party before the issuing person is the state). If this were not the case, the target of the search would receive advance warning and could take action to frustrate the search.

There are two types of warrants, arrest warrants and search warrants, although arrest warrants are rarely used or required. Although search warrants are often used, especially in cases where there is an extensive investigation, the Court has broadened the circumstances under which the police may conduct warrantless searches. This will be the topic of the analysis on exceptions to the warrant requirement. Unlike arrest warrants, however, search warrants can grow stale with the passage of time. This consideration is reflected in the Federal Rules of Criminal Procedure 41(c), which states, "It shall command the officer to search, within a specified period of time not to exceed 10 days . . . ."

It should be noted that it is possible to waive the warrant requirement for a search or arrest. In United States v. Knights (2001), a suspect had agreed, as a condition of his probation, that he would submit to a search at any time, with or without a search, arrest warrant, or reasonable cause. During his probation, officers searched his apartment based on the suspicion that he was involved in an act of arson. The Court held that the warrantless search was reasonable. The Court balanced the intrusion to the individual with the governmental interest in concluding it was reasonable. In evaluating the intrusion, the Court took account of the suspect's diminished expectation of privacy due to his having agreed to warrantless searches, as well as his probation status.

There are three basic requirements to a warrant that we will explore here. First, it must be issued by a *neutral and detached* magistrate. Second, there must be an adequate showing of *justification* to the magistrate, which is usually in the form of a sworn affidavit from a police officer. The Fourth Amendment specifically requires that "no warrants shall issue, but upon probable cause, supported by Oath and affirmation." Finally, as required by the Fourth Amendment, the warrant must describe in a *particular* way "the place to be searched and the persons or things to be seized." In addition to discussing the Court's decisions that establish the components of a lawful warrant, we will also discuss the decisions that relate to the police execution of these warrants.

## NEUTRAL AND DETACHED MAGISTRATE

In general, the Court considers whether the issuing party has a vested interest in the outcome of the decision to issue the warrant. As indicated by the *Johnson* decision, the Fourth Amendment requires the person issuing the warrant to be someone not involved in the "competitive enterprise of ferreting out crime." In Coolidge v. New Hampshire (1971), the state Attorney General had the power to issue search warrants. The Court held that such an individual was in charge of investigating and prosecuting a criminal act and thus could not be regarded as a "neutral and detached magistrate required by the Constitution." In Connally v. Georgia (1977), a Georgia statute provided that a magistrate would receive $5 for every warrant he issued. If no warrants were issued, there would be no compensation. The Court invalidated the statute, holding that a magistrate who had a pecuniary interest could not be neutral.

In Shadwick v. City of Tampa (1972), the Court addressed whether someone who was not a lawyer could issue a warrant. In this case, the clerk of the municipal court, a nonjudicial officer, issued an arrest warrant for a violation of a municipal ordinance. In holding that the clerk could issue a warrant, the Court stated, "The substance of the Constitution's warrant requirements does not turn on the labeling of the issuing party . . . [A]n issuing magistrate must meet two tests. He must be neutral and detached and he must be capable of determining whether probable cause exists." As a member of the judicial branch who was not associated with law enforcement, the clerk met the neutral and detached requirement. The ability to assess probable cause, even though one is not a lawyer, did not trouble the Court. The majority pointed out that the system has entrusted nonlawyers to evaluate complex issues. Although the Court has not dealt with the issue since *Shadwick*, it should be pointed out that the clerk in *Shadwick* was only dealing with an arrest warrant for a minor ordinance violation. The Court might require that more complicated probable cause determinations be made by a legally trained individual.

The final case involving the standard for neutral and detached relates to the actual execution of a search warrant. In Lo-Ji Sales v. New York (1979), a magistrate issued a warrant to search for obscene material at an adult bookstore. The warrant application specifically requested the Town Justice (Judge) to accompany investigators as they executed the warrant in order to assist them in determining what was obscene. The judge went to the bookstore along with law enforcement officers, where he viewed various obscene materials, including films and magazines. The Court held that the judge, "did not manifest that neutrality and detachment demanded of a judicial officer" as "[h]e allowed himself to become a member, if not the leader, of the search party." He had become an adjunct to the police rather than a neutral and detached judicial officer.

## JUSTIFICATION

The types and amount of information required to establish probable cause, the justification needed for most criminal searches and arrests, are discussed in the chapter on probable cause. However, as the administrative search chapter demonstrates, the level of justification necessary to obtain an administrative warrant differs from the probable cause justification needed for a criminal investigation. Justification for an administrative search is based on balancing the governmental interest in conducting the search against the amount of the intrusion imposed on the individual.

For the most part, judges or magistrates base their probable cause determination on sworn affidavits signed by police officers. This provides a written record if it is necessary to review the probable cause determination. A reviewing court will only review that information that was presented to the magistrate at the time the warrant was issued. Some jurisdictions, including the federal system, permit the issuance of a warrant on sworn oral communications, even if communicated by a telephone. In this situation, the judge will place the person applying for the warrant under oath and record the conversation when possible. If it is not possible to record the conversation, then the judge will create a longhand verbatim record. The recording and/or the longhand record must be filed with the court (Federal Rules of Criminal Procedure 41(c)).

Although traditional search warrants are supported by probable cause, lower courts have supported the issuance of anticipatory warrants. At the time of issuance, these warrants are not supported by traditional probable cause that a particular item is at a particular place. Instead, they are issued on a showing that a particular item *will* be at a particular place. This situation usually exists when contraband is in transit and is about to be delivered to a particular place United States v. Garcia, 2nd Cir., 1989). The Court, however, has not dealt specifically with anticipatory warrants.

As discussed in the analysis of the exclusionary rule, a warrant is rarely reviewed and invalidated for lack of probable cause. The Court has determined that it will not exclude evidence for lack of probable cause unless the affidavit is so lacking in indicia of probable cause so as to render belief in its existence entirely unreasonable (United States v. Leon, 1984). Thus incorrect probable cause determinations will not render a warrant invalid unless there is some evidence of a gross error. In addition, it is difficult to invalidate a warrant by challenging the truthfulness of a sworn affidavit (Franks v. Delaware, 1978). First, a defendant must make a substantial preliminary showing that the affiant made a false statement knowingly and intentionally or with reckless disregard for the truth. Second, a defendant must show that the false statement was necessary to the probable cause determination. Thus, even a knowingly false statement will not, by itself, invalidate the finding of probable cause. Once this preliminary showing is made, the defendant must prove by a preponderance of the evidence that a false statement was made that influenced the probable cause determination.

## PARTICULARITY

The history chapter indicated that our founding ancestors were concerned that custom officials holding writs of assistance or general warrants were allowed to search any location they chose. The Fourth Amendment reflects this concern for the unfettered discretion of government officials by requiring that warrants "shall issue . . . particularly describing the place to be searched and the person or things to be seized." As we will see in the chapter on administrative searches, however, administrative warrants need not be as specific and may authorize the search of an entire locale as long as the search is consistent with the administrative objectives.

The creation of a good faith exception to the exclusionary rule, an exception that the Court has interpreted quite broadly, has influenced the Court's findings with regard to particularity problems in warrants. The Court held that in order to avoid a good faith exception, the warrant must be "so facially deficient—i.e., in failing to particularize the place to be searched or things to be seized—that the executing officer cannot reasonably presume it to be valid." United States v. Leon (1984). Based on this standard, it is rare for the Court to invalidate a warrant on the basis of a particularity problem. *Leon*'s companion case, Massachusetts v. Sheppard (1984), highlights the good faith exception as it relates to particularity. In *Sheppard*, homicide detectives sought a search warrant for a murder investigation on a Sunday. Because the courts were closed, they could only find a form warrant for drugs. Although the judge assured the police that he would make the necessary changes, the actual warrant still contained language allowing for the seizure of drugs, thus violating the particularity requirement of the Fourth Amendment. The Court refused to apply the exclusionary rule to this situation because the officers acted in good faith, relying on the assurance of the judge. Thus the holdings in *Leon* and *Sheppard* provide a guideline for understanding the Court's current evaluation of particularity.

The impact of the *Leon* and *Sheppard* decisions on the particularity requirement can be seen in the Court's changing standard for this requirement. In Steele v. United States (1925), the Court held that the description of the place to be searched should be precise enough so that "the officer with a search warrant can with reasonable effort ascertain and identify the place intended." However, in Maryland v. Garrison (1987), a case decided after *Leon*, the police had a warrant that specifically described the third floor of a building as occupied exclusively by McWebb's apartment. After the police arrived and began to search, the officers realized that there were two apartments on the third floor, one occupied by McWebb and one by Garrison. In this case, Garrison sought to suppress contraband that an officer discovered in his apartment. The Court refused to suppress the evidence, finding that the officers basically made an honest mistake. The warrant was broader than appropriate because it was based on a mistaken belief that there was only one apartment on the third floor. Nevertheless, the Court held that the validity of the warrant was to be evaluated on the basis of the information provided to the magistrate at the time it was issued. The dissent indicated that this analysis was inconsistent with *Steele* because when dealing "with multiunit buildings courts have declared invalid those warrants that fail to describe the targeted unit with enough specificity to prevent a search of all the units."

The standard of particularity with regard to the items to be seized requires that nothing be left to discretion of the officer (Marron v. United States, 1927). The purpose of this was to prevent the evil of general warrants addressed by the Framers of the Constitution. The particularity clause of the Fourth Amendment places limitations and restraints on the power of the government officials. Therefore, items must be carefully described in the warrant. However, the courts have allowed for less specificity in the description of items to be seized when the items are readily identifiable as contraband (gun, drugs, and so on). On the other hand, when the items implicate First Amendment concerns, greater specificity is required. In Zucker v. Stanford Daily (1978), which involved a search of a newspaper, the Court indicated that "particular exactitude" is required "when First Amendment interests would be endangered by the search." Also, in Sanford v. Texas (1965), officers were enforcing a law making it an offense to be a member of the Communist Party. They obtained a warrant authorizing the search of "books, records, pamphlets, cards, receipts, lists, memoranda, pictures, recordings, and other written instruments concerning the Communist Party of Texas." Armed with this warrant, they seized books by "such diverse writers as Karl Marx

. . . Pope John XXIII and Mr. Justice Hugo Black." The Court, in invalidating this warrant, described it as a general warrant that the Fourth Amendment was designed to prevent. There was simply too much discretion given to the executing officer.

In Andreson v. Maryland (1976), the authorities obtained a warrant to investigate a fraudulent land transaction. The warrant provided an exhaustive list of particularly described documents. However, at the end of this list, the phrase "together with other fruits, instrumentality and evidence of crime at this (time) unknown." Rather than invalidating the warrant based on the inclusion of this phrase, the Court concluded that it referred to a specific lot of land and thus the warrant gave officers the authority to search only for items related to that land.

In sum, although the particularity requirement mandates the place searched and items seized be specifically and accurately described, the Court has been very strict in interpreting the standard when First Amendment issues are involved, lenient when obvious contraband is involved, and quite lenient in allowing the good faith exception to rescue a warrant that contained a reasonable mistake or which appeared facially valid and was executed in good faith.

## ARREST WARRANTS

As previously indicated with regard to the seizure of a person (arrests), arrest warrants are rarely used or required. In United States v. Watson (1976), the Court held that police may make an arrest in a public place as long as they have probable cause. The *Watson* Court, utilizing history, indicated that the cases construing the Fourth Amendment reflect a common-law rule allowing a peace officer to make a warrantless arrest for crimes committed in his presence or felonies not committed in his presence, provided there was sufficient justification. In addition, this common-law rule was reflected in 1792 by Congress, which invested United States marshals with this power to arrest. It was not important to the Court that the police had the time to seek a warrant. The Court indicated that it did not want "to encumber criminal prosecutions with endless litigation with respect to the existence of exigent circumstances, whether it was practicable to get a warrant, whether the suspect was about to flee, and the like." In interpreting public place, the Court, in United States v. Santana (1976), held that a front doorway was a public place for purposes of warrantless arrest. Even though it was private property, it could be viewed from a public vantage point, and thus there was no legitimate expectation of privacy in this area.

The only time that an arrest warrant is required is when the arrest occurs in the subject's home (Payton v. New York, 1980). In *Payton*, the police, having probable cause to arrest Payton, went to his apartment without a warrant. Some 30 minutes after receiving no response to their knock on the door, they broke open the door. No one was found, but a .30-caliber shell, which was later introduced into evidence against Payton, was in plain view. Payton sought to suppress the shell because of a lack of either an arrest or a search warrant. The Court, in recognition of the sanctity associated with a home, decided to impose an arrest warrant requirement. The arrest warrant provides the authorization to enter a dwelling and search for the suspect "when there is reason to believe the suspect is within." Thus it is not necessary to obtain both a search warrant and an arrest warrant. The arrest warrant is sufficient to protect the arrestee's Fourth Amendment rights. Thus, to use an arrest warrant to search in a home for a suspect, two requirements must be satisfied. First, there must be a reasonable belief that the location to be searched is the suspect's dwelling, and second, there must be a reasonable belief that the suspect will be found there.

Courts have indicated that the quantum of suspicion necessary for "reason to believe" that a suspect is within a dwelling in order to execute an arrest warrant may be something less than that of probable cause. Although not fully defined by the *Payton* court, reasonable belief exists when, given the totality of the circumstances known to the law enforcement officer, the common sense conclusion is that the suspect is inside the home.

Steagald v. United States (1981) dealt with the issue of an arrest of a suspect in the home of a third party. The Court held that a search warrant is required in this situation in order to protect the interests of the third party. This search warrant would be issued on a showing of probable cause that the suspect is on the premises. Keep in mind that the search warrant requirement is designed to protect the interest of a third party because the arrest warrant is all that is required to protect the arrestee. Justice Rehnquist, dissenting in *Steagald*, raises an interesting point as to what constitutes a suspect's home. He points out that, pursuant to *Payton*, only an arrest warrant is required to enter a suspect's home. If a suspect who is a fugitive lives in a place for a few days, even if a third party owns the premises, Chief Justice Rehnquist argues that this could be considered the suspect's house. He further argues that a suspect is inherently mobile and therefore the government has a compelling interest in being allowed to execute an arrest warrant without obtaining a search warrant. Therefore with regard to an arrest, the only time an arrest warrant is required to protect an individual's Fourth Amendment rights is for an arrest in his own house. A search warrant is required for the arrest of a suspect in the home of another (not his home) in order to protect the rights of a third-party homeowner. It should be pointed out that we will be exploring exceptions to this requirement based on practicality concerns in the analysis on exceptions to warrants section.

State courts and the United States Court of Appeals have grappled with the issues raised by *Payton* and *Steagald*. Often the issue will focus on whether a residence is a suspect's home.[1] If it is the home of the arrestee, a search warrant is not required. When "common authority" over the premises exists, courts have held that a third party has a diminished expectation of privacy, and thus a search warrant is not necessary to make an arrest or protect the third party.[2] Thus, when a third party is a co-habitant of the arrestee, evidence found during the arrest of a suspect can be used against that third party.

An arrest warrant with an erroneous address can still be valid, so long as there is probable cause to arrest the suspect in question regardless of the error. In United States v. Lauter (2nd Cir. 1995), police obtained an arrest warrant for a suspect that specified his residence with an apartment number. When police learned from the landlord that he had moved to a different apartment in the same building, they executed the warrant there instead and took the suspect into custody. The court held that police did not have to obtain a new arrest warrant when they learned of his address change. It held that the discrepancy in addresses was immaterial to the existence of probable cause to arrest the suspect because a valid arrest warrant need only to identify the person sought.

## EXECUTION OF SEARCH WARRANTS

Once the authorities have obtained a search warrant, they must adhere to certain guidelines in executing it. As previously mentioned, rules and the issue of staleness limit when a search warrant can be executed. In addition, procedural rules specify that a warrant shall be executed in the daytime unless there is some justification to execute it at some other time. "The warrant shall be served in the daytime, unless the issuing authority, by appropriate provision in the warrant and for reasonable cause shown, authorizes its execution at times other than daytime" (Federal Rules of Criminal Procedure 41(c)(1)).

There have been a number of cases dealing with the issue of whether the police are required to knock before "forcibly" entering. In Wilson v. Arkansas (1995), a unanimous Court held that no-knock entry should be evaluated according to the reasonableness clause of the Fourth Amendment. The Court indicated that officer peril or destruction of the evidence might provide the necessary justification to constitute reasonableness and thus justifies a no-knock entry. However, in Richards v. Wisconsin (1997), the Court refused to create a per se exception to the knock requirement for drug searches. Police need to have reasonable suspicion that knocking and announcing would be dangerous, futile, or result in the destruction of the evidence. The fact that property was damaged during the entry did not increase the justification for dispensing with a knock (United States v. Ramirez, 1998).

Another warrant-related issue has to do with whether the police can detain an occupant while executing a search warrant. In Michigan v. Summers (1981), the Court held that a search warrant for a house carries with it the authority to detain its occupants until the search is completed. Detention does not include searching because the Court in Ybarra v. Illinois (1979) refused to allow officers armed with a warrant to search a bar to frisk the patrons of that bar without some sort of additional justification.

In Illinois v. McArthur (2001), the police were at a home to assist the defendant's wife while she removed her belongings. On exiting, she informed the police that her husband had marijuana under the couch. When the husband refused to consent to a search, one officer left to obtain a search warrant and the other officer remained with the husband, restricting his access to the home. He was allowed to go into the house only if accompanied by the officer. A search warrant was obtained two hours later. The issue in this case was the restriction imposed on the husband. The Court held that the restriction was reasonable because it was limited to two hours, and only restricted his access to the home, no search occurred until the warrant was obtained, and the police had good reason to believe that he would destroy the marijuana if he were not restrained.

## EXECUTION OF ARREST WARRANTS

In Maryland v. Buie (1990), police officers armed with an arrest warrant were allowed to do a protective sweep of the home. They could search the immediate vicinity of the arrest from which an attack could be launched. If there is reasonable suspicion to believe that there are accomplices in the home, the protective inspection can also be extended to other places within the home. In limiting this protective sweep, the Court said:

We should emphasize that such a protective sweep, aimed at protecting the arresting officers, if justified by the circumstances, is nevertheless not a full search of the premises, but may extend only to a cursory inspection of those spaces where a person may be found. The sweep lasts no longer than is necessary to dispel the reasonable suspicion of danger and in any event no longer than it takes to complete the arrest and depart the premises.

Tennessee v. Garner (1985) dealt with the issue of whether it was appropriate to use deadly force to effectuate a felony arrest. The Court turned to the reasonableness clause of the Fourth Amendment, balancing the type of force with the societal need for it. The majority concluded that, notwithstanding probable cause, it was unreasonable to use deadly force simply to apprehend a fleeing felon from the scene of a nighttime burglary. The majority felt that deadly force was only appropriate when there was an immediate threat to the officer or others. Not surprisingly, given the subjective nature of the balancing approach, the dissent felt that it was reasonable to allow the use of deadly force as a last resort to apprehend a fleeing suspect.

In Wilson v. Layne (1999), the Court held that officers exceeded the scope of a lawfully issued arrest warrant by allowing representatives of the media to accompany them as they executed the warrant. The Court expressed the importance of the sanctity of the home and given that principle, it indicated that the scope of the warrant should be carefully limited to its justification. There was no justification for media representation in this case. The Court indicated that it might be appropriate to have a third party who aided in the execution of the warrant as opposed to individuals who were not related to the objectives of the warrant.

There is one final point about the execution of a warrant with regard to the particularity requirement. As previously indicated, this requirement limits the scope of an authorized search. If, however, the police, acting within the scope of the warrant (it does not matter if it is a search or arrest warrant) see an item that they know is contraband or related to a crime, the police are permitted to seize this item. This is known as a plain view seizure. Thus, officers executing a warrant for a stolen 19-inch television monitor could not seize drugs found in a desk drawer because it would clearly exceed the scope of the search to look in a desk drawer for a large television set. In order for there to be a plain view seizure, the officer must be acting within the scope of the authorized search, and it must be immediately apparent to the officer that the item is contraband or related to a crime. This principle will be more fully discussed in the section on analyzing warrant exceptions.

## ENDNOTES

1. United States v. Litteral, 910 F.2d 547 (9th Cir. 1990); People v. White, 117 Ill.2d 194 (1987); United States v. Reese, 83 F.3d 212 (8th Cir. 1996).
2. United States v. Ranvitz, 770 F.2d 1458 (9th Cir. 1985).

# Analysis—Warrant Exceptions

## INTRODUCTION

The Court in recent history has expressed a preference for a warrant in its decisions. Despite this expressed preference, the Court, by its deeds, has expanded on the opportunities for warrantless police activity. Exceptions to this preference must be justified and the scope of the warrantless searches should be limited to their justification. Historically, exceptions to requiring a search warrant were based on practicality concerns, primarily the concern that a warrant could not be secured in time to accomplish the objective of the search. Recent years have seen the basis for exceptions move from practicality concerns to such factors as a reduced expectation of privacy, as is the case with the automobile exception.

In analyzing various exceptions to the warrant requirement, we are reminded of the relationship between the two clauses of the Fourth Amendment discussed in the history section. United States v. Rabinowitz (1950) presents an excellent example of a debate between Justice Minton and Justice Frankfurter, which highlights the differing approaches to the Fourth Amendment. Minton, for the majority, maintained that the reasonable clause should be read separately and distinctly from the warrant clause so that the existence of a warrant was only one possible factor relevant to the reasonableness of a search. This interpretation viewed the existence of a warrant as important in determining reasonableness, but not as an absolute requirement. Frankfurter, in dissent, argued that the two clauses should be read together so that warrantless searches are per se unreasonable. Frankfurter's preference for a warrant stated that "searches conducted outside the judicial process, without prior approval by judge or magistrate, are per se unreasonable under the Fourth Amendment—subject only to a few specifically established and well-delineated exceptions" (This language was picked up in later cases, including Katz v. United States, 1967.)

In applying the Frankfurter analysis, exceptions to warrants were limited to the practicality concerns that required the warrant exception in the first place.

However, although the Court has continued at times to articulate a preference for the warrant requirement, its rulings have in fact expanded the opportunities for conducting warrantless searches. Justice Stevens, dissenting in California v. Acevedo (1991), characterized the majority as paying only "lip service" to the warrant requirement. Although the Court has not greatly expanded on the number of warrant exceptions, it has been more willing to find those exceptions and has greatly extended their scope. Thus, the Court has found a way to limit the thrust of the exclusionary rule by increasing the opportunities for warrantless searches.

The Court's unpredictability in this area was described by Justice Scalia, who pointed out in *Acevedo*, that the Court has "lurched back and forth between imposing a categorical warrant requirement and looking to reasonableness alone." He further maintained that "the 'warrant' requirement [has] become so riddled with exceptions that it [is] basically unrecognizable."

In other sections of this treatise, allowance for warrantless activity is discussed. This includes both the administrative and consent sections. In this section, however, we will discuss exceptions to the warrant requirement and their scope, mostly in the context of criminal activity, although there is some discussion of warrantless activity in an administrative context that has not previously been addressed.

All the exceptions to a warrant were originally based on practicality concerns, the need for a police officer to act quickly, thus obviating the need for a search warrant. We will see this practicality concern when we look at the automobile exception, which was originally based on the mobility of a vehicle, and the search incident to arrest exception, which was based on the need to prevent destruction of evidence and to protect police officers. Since arrests and automobile searches occur frequently, the Court has created separate categories for these exceptions.

The first category we will examine, the emergency search exception, encompasses a myriad of situations that do not fit comfortably in either the search incident to arrest or automobile exception categories. In fact, the emergency exception to the warrant requirement provides the best examples of the practicality concerns underlying the Court's provision for warrantless searches.

## EMERGENCY

Here, we will consider two types of emergency situations, warrantless searches of homes and bodily fluids. The Court has balanced its desire to maintain and protect the sanctity of the home with the recognition that certain circumstances require a warrantless intrusion. The Court has found the following circumstances particularly compelling: hot pursuit, destruction of evidence, and the necessity to prevent an escape or danger to others. In Warden v. Hayden (1967), a hot pursuit case, an armed robbery occurred at a taxi office. Two cab drivers in the vicinity followed the suspect to a particular address and so informed the dispatcher who, in turn, informed the police. Within minutes the police arrived at the home, knocked, and explained their presence. The occupant allowed them to search for the robber without objection. They searched throughout the house and ultimately found the suspect feigning sleep in an upstairs bedroom. In addition to finding the suspect, the police discovered various evidentiary items related to the robbery throughout the house, including clothing that was used in the robbery and found in the washing machine. In upholding the search for the suspect, the Court said, "The Fourth Amendment does not require police officers to delay in the course of an investigation if to do so would gravely endanger their lives or the lives of others. Speed here was essential." In this case, there was probable cause that a particular armed robbery suspect had entered a particular house within five minutes of the police arrival. Thus there was hot pursuit of a fleeing felon. With regard to the evidence found throughout the house, the Court justified the scope of the search as a weapons search that was necessary to protect the officer who was searching for an armed robber.

The term *hot pursuit* first appears in Johnson v. United States (1948), in which narcotics agents who recognized the smell of burning opium in a hotel hallway knocked on the defendant's door and requested access to her room. The agents did not have a warrant. The defendant allowed the officers inside, and once the police ascertained the defendant was the only person in the room, they arrested her and conducted a search incident to arrest, uncovering opium and smoking apparatus. In a footnote, the Court rejected the government's argument that the arrest was made in "hot pursuit" because the defendant was not in flight, made no attempt to escape, and was completely surrounded by agents.

In United States v. Santana (1976), officers had information that Santana was in possession of money used to buy heroin. The officers went to Santana's house where they found her standing in the doorway holding a paper bag. When the officers identified themselves as police, Santana attempted to retreat into the house, but the officers caught her in the vestibule. As she attempted to pull away, packets of heroin fell out of the paper bag, and a request that she empty her pockets revealed some of the marked money from the heroin buy. The Court held that, as in *Warden*, this was a case of hot pursuit sufficient to justify a warrantless entry. The police realistically expected that once Santana had seen them, any delay would result in the destruction of evidence. The fact that the pursuit here ended almost as soon as it started and did not go through the public streets did not sway the Court.

In Minnesota v. Olson (1990), the Court further elaborated on the factors that could be used to determine the emergencies that would justify a warrantless search of a home. In this case, officers who suspected Olson of being the getaway driver in a robbery-murder surrounded the house where they believed Olson was hiding and telephoned the women who owned the house, telling them that Olson should come out. When the officers heard a male voice say, "Tell them I left," they entered the home without permission and found Olson hiding in a closet. The Court, in upholding the Minnesota Supreme Court decision finding no emergency exception, characterized that decision as "essentially the correct standard." "The [Minnesota] court observed that 'warrantless intrusion may be justified by hot pursuit of a fleeing felon, or imminent destruction of evidence, or the need to prevent a suspect's escape, or the risk of danger to the police or to other persons inside or outside the dwelling.'" The Court further observed that without hot pursuit, there must be probable cause to believe that the other factors existed. In assessing those factors, the seriousness of the crime and the possibility of the suspect being armed should also be considered.

The seriousness of the crime was an important consideration in an earlier decision involving hot pursuit or possibly imminent destruction of evidence. In Welsh v. Wisconsin (1984), a witness saw an erratically driven car swerve off the road and the driver walk away. He telephoned the police, indicating that the driver was either inebriated or very sick. After checking the car's registration, officers went to the defendant's house without a warrant. The defendant's stepdaughter admitted them and they found the petitioner asleep in bed and arrested him. In a decision by Justice Brennan, the author of the *Warden* decision, the Court, moved by the sanctity of the home for Fourth Amendment purposes, seemed to limit the emergency exception to only serious offenses: "Before agents of the government may invade the sanctity of the home, the burden is on the government to demonstrate exigent circumstances that overcome the presumption of unreasonableness that attached to warrantless home entries. When the government's interest is only to arrest for a minor offense that presumption of unreasonableness is difficult to rebut . . . ."

Concern for the sanctity of a home also played a role in Mincey v. Arizona (1978), in which homicide detectives conducted a four-day long warrantless search of defendant's apartment. During a narcotics raid on the petitioner's apartment, the petitioner and two other persons in the apartment were wounded and an undercover officer was shot and killed. The state attempted to justify the search by arguing for a "murder scene warrant exception," but the Court soundly rejected this argument. The Court upheld the search to the extent that it was necessary to resolve the emergency situation but indicated that the warrantless search must be "strictly circumscribed by the exigencies which justify its initiation." It therefore refused to accept any portion of the search that went beyond this justification.

A unanimous Court recently rejected another attempt by a state to reinstitute a murder scene exception. In Flippo v. West Virginia (1999), the Court pointed out that the state's argument squarely conflicts with *Mincey*:

[w]e rejected the contention that there is a "murder scene exception" to the Warrant Clause of the Fourth Amendment. We noted that police may make warrantless entries onto premises if they reasonably believe a person is in need of immediate aid and may make prompt

warrantless searches of a homicide scene for possible other victims or a killer on the premises, but we rejected any general "murder scene exception" as "inconsistent with the Fourth and Fourteenth Amendments . . . *Mincey* controls here.

In the administrative search category, a fire presents an emergency situation. In Michigan v. Tyler (1978), the Court recognized the legitimacy of a warrantless entry to immediately investigate the fire's source in order to prevent its reoccurrence. However, the scope of this search was limited to its justification. "Fire officials are charged not only with extinguishing fires, but with finding their causes. Prompt determination of the fire's origin may be necessary to prevent its recurrence . . . Immediate investigation may also be necessary to preserve evidence from intentional or accidental destruction . . . For these reasons, officials need no warrant to remain in a building for a reasonable time. . ."

In Michigan v. Clifford (1984), investigators did not search the house until several hours after the fire had been extinguished. The Court recognized that when investigators search a house to determine the cause of a fire, "the scope of the search may be no broader than reasonably necessary." After finding evidence of arson in the basement, they proceeded to search the upstairs of the house for more evidence, all without a warrant. The Court found that the basement search required an administrative warrant because the search was not the continuation of an earlier search and because the defendants maintained a significant privacy interest in their residence. The Court went on to say that the search of the upstairs rooms was clearly conducted to gather further evidence of arson and thus, absent exigent circumstances, required a criminal warrant. "The scope of such a search is limited to that reasonably necessary to determine the cause and origin of a fire and to ensure against rekindling. As soon as investigators determined that the fire had originated in basement . . . the scope of their search was limited to the basement area."

What should police do when faced with a situation in which there is a possibility that evidence will be removed or destroyed, yet they are not sure they have the justification to do a warrantless search? In Segura v. United States (1984), an Assistant United States attorney authorized agents to arrest the defendant, whom officers had reason to believe possessed cocaine, but were informed that they could not obtain a search warrant for the defendant's apartment until the following day. Agents went to the petitioner's apartment, arrested him in the lobby, and took him to his apartment where they entered without asking for or receiving permission. Agents performed a limited security check of the apartment and then took all the occupants of the apartment to DEA headquarters. Two agents remained in the apartment until a search warrant was obtained 19 hours later due to an administrative delay. The Court held that, regardless of the legality of the initial entry into the apartment, the search was ultimately conducted according to a valid search warrant, and thus it was not necessary to exclude the evidence obtained during the search. This case suggests that the police can secure the premises, preventing persons from entering while an officer seeks a warrant. Similarly, in Illinois v. McArthur (2001), the police secured the premises while an officer sought a warrant, though the occupant was allowed limited access during this time. In this case, two officers stood outside while McArthur's wife removed her clothing from their trailer. While exiting, she told the police that McArthur had hidden drugs in the trailer. When McArthur refused permission to search, one officer remained on the porch with him while the other obtained a warrant. He could reenter only if accompanied by an officer. The Court allowed for this restriction by balancing the needs of law enforcement with the privacy concerns of the individual. The Court concluded that the intrusion on McArthur was reasonable.

Thus far we have been discussing warrantless searches of a home. A second type of search that may fall into the emergency search category is a search for bodily fluids. Schmerber v. California (1966) dealt with the issue of extracting blood to establish a blood alcohol level. There was a need for quick extraction so as to get the blood alcohol level before the alcohol dissipated into the individual's system and thus the need for warrantless activity. The Court allowed for this search, provided that the blood was extracted in a reasonable manner. It should be pointed out that when dealing with major bodily intrusions that endanger life or health, the government is often required to show not only probable cause that evidence will be found from the intrusion but also that the method of extraction will be reasonable. Given the significant scope of this type of intrusion, it is highly unlikely that it could occur without a warrant.

In Cupp v. Murphy (1973), the respondent objected to officers taking samples from his fingernails when he came to the station house voluntarily and without being arrested. Officers did, however, have probable cause to believe the respondent had committed a murder. The Court allowed for the scraping, which was a very limited intrusion, because of the possibility that the suspect would destroy the evidence. Since the suspect was not under arrest at the time, the search was not justified as a search incident to arrest.

## SEARCH INCIDENT EXCEPTION

The oldest exception to the warrant requirement is the search incident to arrest exception, "[A]lways recognized under English and American law, to search the person of the accused when legally arrested to discover and seize the fruits or evidence of crime" (Weeks v. United States, 1914). The original justification for this search is two-fold. First and foremost is the need to protect the police officer from any weapons that the arrestee might use to resist arrest. Second is the need to prevent the destruction of evidence within the arrestee's control. Given this accepted justification, the Court in Chimel v California (1969) held that the scope of the search would be that area within the arrestee's control, "construing that phrase to mean the area from within which he might gain possession of a weapon or destructible evidence." Here, the Court took an approach that is consistent with a warrant preference, that is, limiting the scope of the warrantless search to the justification that necessitated the exception in the first place. However, in subsequent years the Court expanded the scope of this exception.

In United States v. Robinson (1973), the defendant was arrested for operating a motor vehicle after revocation of his license. Police conducted a warrantless search incident to this arrest. The search included a crumpled cigarette package found in the defendant's coat pocket. There were capsules containing heroin in the cigarette package. Even though the cigarette package was unlikely to hold either evidence of the crime of driving after license revocation or a weapon, the Court found the search to be justified as one incident to arrest. The seizure and opening of the cigarette package were clearly beyond the then-existing justification for, and scope of, a warrantless search incident to arrest. However, in a decision by Justice Rehnquist, the Court opted for a standardized approach to the search incident exception:

A police officer's determination as to how and where to search the person of a suspect whom he has arrested is necessarily a quick *ad hoc* judgment which the Fourth Amendment does not require to be broken down in each instance into an analysis of each step in the search. The authority to search the person incident to a lawful custodial arrest, while based upon the need to discern and to discover evidence, does not depend on what a court may later decide was the probability in a particular arrest situation that weapons or evidence would in fact be found upon the person of the suspect.

Justice Thurgood Marshall, dissenting, observed that this standardized approach was inconsistent with limiting the scope of warrantless searches to their justification:

In determining whether the seizure and search were unreasonable [the Court's] inquiry is a dual one—whether the officer's action was justified at its inception and whether it was reasonably related in scope to the circumstances which justified the interference in the first place.

Following the standardized rationale of *Robinson*, the Court in New York v. Belton (1981), designed a bright line rule to be applied to automobile searches incident to a custodial arrest. In *Belton*, a car was stopped for speeding. The officer smelled marijuana. He directed the four occupants out of the car and placed them under arrest. He then proceeded to search the interior of the car, including the defendant's jacket, which was located in the backseat. The officer found cocaine in the jacket. The Court held that the police, as incident to a lawful arrest of an individual who immediately preceding the arrest had been in a vehicle, may search the interior (passenger compartment) of the vehicle, including containers (jacket) found therein. This decision did not recognize the limitations of an area, as was the case in *Chimel*, where the arrestee could not have reached the jacket in the backseat. The *Belton* Court, following *Robinson*, opted for a standardized approach that police could easily apply. The Court refused to limit the scope of the warrantless search based on the particular facts of *Belton*. Not only was the jacket beyond the reach of the arrestee, the police also had control of the jacket, similar to the control of a cigarette package in *Robinson*. Thus, the justification for a warrantless search incident to an arrest had evaporated.

As mentioned in the section analyzing warrants, the scope of a search incident to an arrest was further expanded to allow police to do a protective sweep when the arrest occurs in a home (Maryland v. Buie, 1990). Officers are allowed to search areas in the immediate vicinity of the arrest so as to protect themselves from an attack. When the police have reasonable suspicion that there are accomplices in the house, they may conduct a housewide search that is limited to the search for accomplices. This so-called protective sweep is not a full search of the house but a cursory inspection of places where accomplices may be found. It should last no longer than is necessary to address the danger.

The timing of a search incident to arrest must be contemporaneous with the arrest. As the Court said in Preston v. United States (1964), "Justification (for a search incident) rule [is] absent where a search is remote in time or place from the arrest." In addition, in order for the search incident exception to be applied, there must be an actual arrest. In Knowles v. Iowa (1998), a unanimous Court held that an officer who issues a traffic citation, even though he has the option pursuant to a state statute to arrest, may not conduct a search incident to arrest. The Court reasoned that the issuance of a citation did not implicate the dual rationale of *Chimel*, protecting the officer and preventing the destruction of evidence. The Court refused to extend the bright line approach of United States v. Robinson (1973) to a nonarrest situation because the concern for the officer's safety was not present to the same extent as an arrest and the concern for destruction of evidence was not present.

In sum, if there is a lawful arrest, the police may automatically conduct a thorough search of the arrestee including containers (e.g., cigarette packages) on his person. If the arrestee was in the car immediately before his arrest, the police may automatically search the interior of the car, including containers (pocket of a jacket) found therein. However, this exception applies only when there is an arrest, as opposed to the option to arrest.

There is one final point that makes this warrantless search doctrine such an important law enforcement tool. As indicated in the section on probable cause, the Court in Whren v. United States (1996) said that it will not inquire as to the motivation of individual police officers as long as there is probable cause. Thus, a police officer who desires to search an individual's purse or wallet can do so as long as the officer has probable cause to arrest. Further, the Court in Atwater v. City of Lago Vista (2001) allowed for the arrest pursuant to a state statute of an individual driving without a seatbelt. The Court, in a 5-4 decision by Justice Souter, held that the Fourth Amendment did not limit the power of arrest to crimes involving breach of the peace. "If an officer has probable cause to believe that an individual has committed even a very minor criminal offense in his presence, he may, without violating the Fourth Amendment, arrest the offender." Justice O'Connor, for the dissent, was worried about the amount of discretion this would give to the police:

Indeed, as the recent debate over racial profiling demonstrates all too clearly, a relatively minor traffic infraction may often serve as an excuse for stopping and harassing an individual. After today, the arsenal available to any officer extends to a full arrest and the searches permissible concomitant to that arrest.

## AUTOMOBILE EXCEPTION

There are many opportunities for warrantless searches of automobiles. These include inventory searches, which we will discuss in the analysis on administrative searches, search incident to arrest, which we will discuss in the next section, and stop and frisk searches, which we discussed in the chapter on the *Terry* standard. In this section, we will focus on the automobile exception when there is probable cause to search an automobile. Originally, the automobile exception to the warrant requirement was based on practicality concerns. It was simply impractical to obtain a search warrant for an automobile on the open road because of the mobility of the vehicle. This was clearly the concern of Carroll v. United States (1925), the decision that established the automobile exception:

[T]he guaranty of freedom from unreasonable searches and seizures by the Fourth Amendment has been construed, practically since the beginning of Government, as recognizing a necessary difference between a search of a store, dwelling house or other structure in respect of which a proper official warrant readily may be obtained, and a search of a ship, motor boat, wagon or automobile, for contraband goods, where it is not practicable to secure a warrant because the vehicle can be *quickly moved* out of the locality or jurisdiction in which the warrant must be sought.

In Chambers v. Maroney (1970), the Court moved away from practicality concerns by allowing for the search of an automobile that was no longer on the road but was instead secure in a police station. As long as probable cause to search the automobile existed, mobility was not important. In Maryland v. Dyson (1999), the Court *per curiam* explicitly abandoned all reliance on exigency in justifying automobile searches. The Court justified this expansion by characterizing cars as having a diminished expectation of privacy because of the pervasive regulations governing their use:

Automobiles, unlike homes, are subjected to pervasive and continuing governmental regulation and controls, including periodic inspection and licensing requirements. (California v. Carney, 1985)

Thus the exception to the warrant requirement will be activated as long as there is probable cause to search the car.

The automobile exception was extended to include mobile homes. In California v. Carney (1985), the Court found a motor home that was indeed readily mobile to be an automobile for purposes of the automobile exception. The vehicle was licensed to "operate on public streets" and was situated in such a way that "an objective observer would conclude that it was being used not as a residence, but as a vehicle."

The issue that has garnered much of the Court's attention has to do with the permissible scope of an automobile search once an officer has probable cause. In particular, the Court has focused on the relationship between automobiles and the containers and personal effects carried within. In United States v. Chadwick (1977), federal agents had probable cause to search a footlocker, which had been removed from a train and placed into the trunk of a car. At this point the agents seized the locker and brought it to a federal building where they opened it. The government argued that the luggage should be regarded as movable and thus analogous to an automobile. The Court rejected this approach and required a warrant. The *Chadwick* case was extended in Arkansas v. Sanders (1979), in which police had probable cause to search luggage that was in the trunk of a taxi. The police stopped the taxi and immediately opened the luggage. The *Sanders* Court held that a warrant is necessary when there is probable cause to search a container and the container is secured. The rationale for distinguishing containers from automobiles is related to the fact that containers are not inherently mobile once they are secured and there is no diminished expectation of privacy associated with them.

In United States v. Ross (1982), the container in question was a brown paper bag. The Court indicated that it drew no distinction between footlockers or paper bags, as both were repositories for personal items. In seeking to distinguish *Chadwick* and *Sanders*, the *Ross* Court held that the police could search a container without a warrant if they had probable cause to search an entire vehicle. In allowing a search of a container if there is probable cause to search the car, the *Ross* Court said, "If probable cause justifies the search of a lawfully stopped vehicle, it justifies the search of every part of the vehicle and its contents that may conceal the object of the search." However, a warrant was still required if their probable cause was limited to a particular container.

In California v. Acevedo (1991), the Court noted the confusion associated with this probable cause dichotomy. "Until today, this Court has drawn a curious line between the search of an automobile that coincidentally turns up a container and the search of a container that coincidentally turns up in an automobile." In *Acevedo*, the police had probable cause to believe that a brown paper package contained marijuana. They observed the package being picked up and brought to an apartment. About two hours later, they observed Acevedo leaving the apartment with the bag. He placed it in his trunk and drove off. The police stopped him, opened the trunk and bag, and found marijuana. Thus the Court had to decide whether to follow *Ross* or the *Chadwick/Sanders* line of cases.

The Court opted for providing "clear and unequivocal guidelines to the law enforcement profession." The Court held that police may search an automobile and a container within the automobile whenever they have probable cause to search either the car or the container. By their ruling, they explicitly overruled *Sanders*. The Court went on to point out that the scope of this search would be limited to the justification, probable cause. Citing *Ross*, the Court stated:

The scope of the warrantless search of an automobile . . . is not defined by the nature of the container in which the contraband is secreted. Rather, it is defined by the object of the search and the places in which there is probable cause to believe that it may be found.

Thus if there is probable cause to search for a large television, the scope of that search would be limited to areas within the car in which a large television could be found. The glove compartment would obviously be off limits.

The Court once again addressed the scope of an automobile search when the police have probable cause in Wyoming v. Houghton (1999). The issue here was whether the police could search a passenger's personal belongings, a purse in this case. The Court held that "a police officer with probable cause to search a car may inspect passenger's belongings found in the car that are capable of concealing the object of the search."

In sum, when there is probable cause to search an automobile, the police can search without a warrant at any location, whether on the street or in the secure setting of a police station. Actual mobility is no longer important. The scope of the search, that may extend to any container, including a passenger's purse, is limited only to the extent of probable cause.

## PLAIN VIEW EXCEPTION

This doctrine permits an officer, engaged in a lawful arrest or search, to seize an item that comes into view. This doctrine does not permit an extension of Fourth Amendment activity but only a seizure of something discovered pursuant to a lawful intrusion. The lawful intrusion could be based either on warrant or warrantless police activity. However, the police may not search in an area not covered by a warrant or an exception to a warrant.

The requirements of plain view were elaborated in Coolidge v. New Hampshire (1971). First and most importantly, the initial intrusion must be lawful. The second requirement is that the discovery of the evidence must be inadvertent. This requirement sought to prevent the police from using the initial valid search as a pretext to find other items. Horton v. California (1990) eliminated the inadvertent requirement because the Court, similar to the previously mentioned *Whren* decision, did not want to evaluate the subjective motivation of individual officers. *Horton*, in describing the seized object, said that it must be immediately apparent to the officer that it is incriminating. That means the police must have probable cause to believe that the thing they have encountered is either contraband (unlawful property such as drugs) or connected to criminal activity.

In Arizona v. Hicks (1987), the Court addressed both the immediately apparent requirement and the scope of a plain view seizure. In *Hicks*, the police, while lawfully searching an apartment for weapons and a victim of a recent shooting, noticed stereo equipment that they suspected was stolen. They lifted the stereo equipment to read the serial numbers and called them into headquarters. On being notified that the equipment was stolen, they seized it. The Court, in a 6-3 decision by Justice Scalia, held that moving the equipment constituted an expansion of the search. In order to seize or move the item, there must be probable cause that the item is related to criminal activity. The Court, citing *Coolidge*, stated that "the plain view doctrine may not be used to extend a general exploratory search from one object to another until something incriminating at last emerges."

The plain view term would indicate that it was limited to that which was seen. However, in Minnesota v. Dickerson (1993), the Court indicated a willingness to expand the doctrine to other senses such as feel and touch. In *Dickerson*, the police officer conducting a *Terry* weapons search (pat down search) felt a small lump in the front pocket of the suspect. Further feeling with his fingers led the officer to conclude that it was a lump of crack cocaine in cellophane. The Court refused to allow the seizure of the cocaine because the police officer overstepped the limitation of a pat down weapon search by "squeezing, sliding and otherwise manipulating the contents of the defendant's pocket." Nevertheless, in dicta, the Court indicated that the sense of touch during an otherwise lawful search was analogous to the plain view doctrine.

In sum, in order for a plain view seizure to be used, the original intrusion must be lawful, the item must be observed by the officer within the scope of the initial intrusion, and it must be immediately apparent (probable cause) that the item is related to criminal activity (contraband or evidence of a crime).

# Analysis—Consent

## INTRODUCTION

Consent is a very important law enforcement tool for avoiding the requirements of the Fourth Amendment. By obtaining consent, the police may conduct a search without the requisite justification (probable cause) and without the necessity for a warrant. In consenting, an individual, or in some instances a third party for an individual, is waiving the protections afforded by the Fourth Amendment. Therefore, the terms *consent* and *waiver* are used interchangeably here.

The Court, in its desire to aid the needs of law enforcement, has liberally interpreted the consent doctrine and generally finds consent, thereby avoiding the requirements of the Fourth Amendment. This approach implies a relaxing of Fourth Amendment requirements by allowing the police to obtain evidence without complying with the Fourth Amendment.

Shortly after the Mapp v. Ohio (1961) decision, the Court indicated that it viewed the Fourth Amendment as a kind of second-class protection. An example of this can be found in Linkletter v. Walker (1965), in which the Court refused to apply the full retroactive effect to *Mapp* that it had applied to decisions involving coerced confessions and right to counsel. *Linkletter* limited the retroactive effect to only those convictions occurring after *Mapp*. Before *Linkletter*, the Court applied its decisions to all cases still pending even if the case was decided before the constitutional ruling. The justification given for treating Fourth Amendment protected rights differently than Sixth Amendment (e.g., right to counsel) and Fifth Amendment (e.g., coerced confessions) protected rights was that the Fourth Amendment had nothing to do with the integrity of the fact-finding process. In other words, evidence obtained as a result of a Fourth Amendment violation will be useful or truthful evidence, thus contributing to the fact-finding process. However, evidence obtained as a result of a coerced confession will often be unreliable and thus will not contribute to the fact-finding process.

The fact that the Court has been less stringent with regard to the waiver of Fourth Amendment rights than with the waiver of other constitutionally protected rights demonstrates this second-class status. In Johnson v. Zerbst (1938), a case involving the Sixth Amendment, the Court held that, in order to establish waiver of a constitutional right, the state must demonstrate "an intentional relinquishment or abandonment of a known right or privilege." In Schneckloth v. Bustamonte (1973), the Court eliminated the knowledge portion for waiver of Fourth Amendment rights and observed that "The protections of the Fourth Amendment are of a wholly different order, and have nothing whatever to do with promoting the fair ascertainment of truth at a criminal trial." In addition, it is possible for waiver to be made by a third party, though this is not the case for other constitutional provisions.

## STANDARD

Schneckloth v. Bustamonte (1973) established the current standard for determining the validity of a waiver of Fourth Amendment protections. In this case, a police officer who stopped a car after observing that one headlight and a license plate light were burned out, asked Alcala, a passenger in the car who claimed that the car belonged to his brother, if he could search the car. Alcala agreed and actually helped in the search by opening the trunk and glove compartment. The officer discovered three stolen checks wadded up under the rear seat and these were later used as evidence against the defendant, another passenger in the car. The Court was faced with the question of whether knowledge of the right to refuse consent to a search was a requirement for a valid waiver. The Court held that, while knowledge of the right to refuse consent is one factor to be taken into account, it is not required to establish an effective consent. This ruling demonstrates that the Court recognizes the importance of consent as a law enforcement tool and treats Fourth Amendment protections differently from protections provided by other amendments. Instead, the standard to establish a valid waiver of Fourth Amendment protections was whether the waiver was voluntary rather than "the product of duress or coercion." This would be determined by a "totality of all the circumstances." There is no set formula to determine voluntariness under the totality of the circumstances test. Instead, the Court balances the needs of law enforcement against the right of an individual not to be coerced. Among the factors to be considered are the presence of subtly coercive police questions and various possible subjective characteristics of the person such as mental competence and age (Schneckloth v. Bustamonte, 1973).

A review of other cases provides a better understanding of the voluntary standard. In Bumper v. North Carolina (1968), the Court focused on what was meant by coercion. One of four police officers who arrived at the home of the defendant's grandmother, a 66-year-old widow living at the end of an isolated, rural dirt road, told her that they had a warrant to search her house. After she told them to 'Go ahead' and opened the door, police seized the rifle that was later used as evidence against the defendant at trial. The Court held that the officers showed authority to search by announcing that they had a search warrant and therefore, the consent obtained could not be considered voluntary.

A more recent case highlighting coercion is found in a per curium decision of Kaupp v. Texas (2003). In this case, a 17 year old boy was awakened in his bedroom at 3:00 AM by three police officers, one of whom stated, "we need to go and talk." The response of "okay" was not regarded as consent as the adolescent had no option given the circumstance. His "okay" response was a "mere submission to a claim of lawful authority."

In a case involving the Fifth Amendment, Colorado v. Connelly (1986), the Court elaborated on the *Schneckloth* standard. In this case, Connelly approached an officer and stated that he had murdered someone and wanted to talk about it. Despite the officer's immediate *Miranda* warnings, Connelly insisted he wanted to confess and was taken to the station where he detailed the murder to police and later pointed out the exact location of the murder. Subsequent interviews with a psychiatrist revealed that Connelly was suffering from chronic schizophrenia and believed that the voice of God had commanded him to confess to murder. Although the Colorado Supreme Court reasoned that this confession was not truly voluntary because of this perceived compulsion, the Court disagreed. According to the Court, a mental health issue is not in itself enough to establish a lack of voluntariness. The defense must show that the police actually used or exploited that condition. "[A]s interrogators have turned to more subtle forms of psychological persuasion, courts have found the mental condition of the defendant a more significant factor in the voluntariness calculus. But this fact does not justify a conclusion that a defendant's mental condition, by itself and apart from its relation to official coercion, should ever dispose of the inquiry into constitutional "voluntariness.""

In Florida v. Bostick (1991), the Court indicated the importance of informing an individual of his right to refuse consent. Although notifying an individual in this way is not a requirement for a valid consensual search, it certainly receives considerable weight by the Court in determining whether a search is actually consensual. In *Bostick*, officers boarded a bus as a routine part of a drug interdiction effort, questioned Bostick, and requested to search his luggage for drugs. The officers advised him of his right to refuse consent. Bostick, however, gave permission for the search and police found cocaine in his luggage. The Court, in a somewhat confusing analysis in which they dealt with the issue of what constitutes a seizure and the consent issue, indicated that the cramped confines of a bus were a relevant factor in determining voluntariness, but not the only factor. The Court went on to define seizure in a way that suggests a similar standard as that used in determining the validity of consent. This is further discussed in the section analyzing reasonable suspicion and stops. "We adhere to the rule that, in order to determine whether a particular encounter constitutes a seizure, a court must consider all the circumstances surrounding the encounter to determine whether the police conduct would have communicated to a reasonable person that the person was not free to decline the officers' request or otherwise terminate the encounter" (Florida v. Bostick, 1991). Had the Court found a seizure, the consent would have been invalid as it was a result of the seizure.

In United States v. Drayton (2002), a case that also involved a bus search, the Court seems to have relaxed the considerable weight it gave to notifying the individual of his right to refuse consent. Both Bostick and Drayton seem to intermesh the analysis for consent and seizure, applying the same standard to each. In *Drayton*, three plainclothes police officers boarded a bus. With one officer at the back of the bus and the other at the front, a third officer moved through the bus indicating that they were conducting a "drug and weapons interdiction." He asked each passenger if he could search their bags. He further indicated that all the passengers consented to this request. Kennedy, for 6-3 majority, in holding that there was no seizure in this situation even though there was no indication from the officer that passengers were not required to consent, noted that there were no threats, intimidation, show of force, or blocked exits. He equated the confrontation with an officer approaching someone on the street. Souter in dissent (joined by Stevens and Ginsburg) reasoned that given the officer's position and the confined quarters of a bus, it was hard to imagine that the defendants felt free to decline the officer's request. This could be an indication of the Court's concern for public transportation in light of the events of September 11, 2001, and its resulting desire to free the hands of law enforcement.

The Court also considered the issue of seizure in Schneckloth v. Bustamonte (1973), which involved a noncustodial situation. In that case, consent was obtained before the actual arrest. The Court, in its holding, specifically mentioned "when the subject of a search is not in custody." The lack of custody therefore seems important. On the other hand, in United States v. Watson (1976), the defendant consented to an automobile search while in custody. The majority did not find this factor significant especially since the arrest took place in a public street. The dissent in *Watson* found the lack of custody to be very important in *Schneckloth*, as the *Schneckloth* Court repeatedly distinguished the case before it from one involving a suspect in custody.

Consent is a particularly important law enforcement tool in carrying out automobile searches. Consent can be used to do an extensive search of a car including the trunk. In Ohio v. Robinette (1996), an officer stopped a car for speeding, issued the driver an oral warning, and then asked if the driver had any illegal contraband, weapons, or drugs in his car. The driver answered that he did not and consented to the search of his car, during which the officer uncovered a small amount of marijuana and a pill. The Ohio Court ruled that in order to establish a consensual search, officers should have to meet a bright-line prerequisite by actually telling a driver that he is free to go after the traffic offense stop. The Supreme Court disagreed. Although recognizing the value of such information to the driver, the Court held that it was "unrealistic to require police officers always to inform detainees that they are free to go before a consent to search may be deemed voluntary." The Court pointed out that knowledge was a factor to consider in determining the voluntariness of consent under the totality of the circumstances test. It was not a *sine qua non* of an effective consent.

## SCOPE OF CONSENT

Even when a valid consent for a search is obtained, we need to consider the scope of the search. In Florida v. Jimeno (1991), the Court developed a standard by which to measure the scope of the search to which the individual had consented. In *Jimeno,* an officer overheard Jimeno arranging what appeared to be a drug transaction over a public telephone, followed Jimeno's car, and pulled him over for making a right turn at a red light without stopping. The officer told Jimeno that he had been stopped for a traffic infraction but then explained that he had reason to believe there were narcotics in the car and asked for permission to search. The officer advised Jimeno that he did not have to consent to the search, but Jimeno agreed, and the officer found cocaine inside a brown paper bag on the passenger side floorboard. In answering the question of whether permission to search the car included permission to open the paper bag, the Court developed an "objectively reasonable standard": "What would the typical reasonable person have understood the exchange between the officer and the subject to mean?" Since the officer indicated he was looking for narcotics, it was reasonable in this case to look in containers that might hold drugs. The opinion stated that "[t]he scope of a search is generally defined by its expressed objective." In discussing the relevance of the type of container, the Court went on to say that "it is very likely unreasonable to think that a suspect, by consenting to the search of his trunk, has agreed to the breaking open of a locked briefcase within the trunk, but it is otherwise with respect to a closed paper bag."

## THIRD-PARTY CONSENT

An individual with an expectation of privacy over the property or a third party who has some authority over the areas searched may waive Fourth Amendment protections. In the usual scenario, consent by a third party is used as a justification to introduce evidence against someone other than the third party. In Illinois v. Rodriguez (1990), the Court moved from the requirement that a third party needed to have actual authority over the premises to a requirement of only apparent authority. In this case, the police relied on the representation of a third party that she had common authority over the apartment when she unlocked the apartment and gave police permission to enter. It turned out that her representations were false and she did not have actual authority to enter the apartment. The Court nevertheless held that the warrantless entry was valid because the police reasonably believed the third party's representation. In deciding that apparent authority on the part of the third party is sufficient, the Court said the following: "As with other factual determinations bearing upon search and seizure determination of consent to enter must be judged against an objective standard: would the facts available to the officer at the moment . . . warrant a man of reasonable caution in the belief that the consenting party had authority over the premises?" Thus, as with the determination of voluntariness, the Court's decision that third-party–apparent authority is sufficient for valid consent marks a shift to a more expansive definition of consent.

# PART II

# Bibliographic Essay

## ANALYSIS—HISTORY

In his early work, *The History and Development of the Fourth Amendment to the United States Constitution* (1937), Nelson B. Lasson argues that the Framers used the reasonableness clause to give the Fourth Amendment greater scope for the prohibition of warrants. Professor Telford Taylor, in *Two Studies in Constitutional Interpretation* (1969), argues that, since the Framers' prime purpose was to prohibit the use of warrants, the reasonableness clause should be read separately and independently from the warrant clause. This position can also be found in the work of Akhil Amar. Amar argues that the Fourth Amendment, at the time of its adoption, did not require warrants, probable cause, or exclusion but did require reasonableness. Therefore reasonableness should be the standard for evaluating Fourth Amendment violations.

Professor Anthony Amsterdam, in *Prospectives of the Fourth Amendment* (58 Minn. L. Rev. 349, 1974), argues that the reasonableness clause demonstrates that the Framers intended to deal with evils beyond general warrants. He characterizes those evils as indiscriminate searches by police officials. He further argues that warrants and probable cause help to address these evils. Therefore, he argues that the reasonableness clause should be read with the warrant clause. Tracy Macklin agrees with this approach. Macklin sees the Fourth Amendment as a way to deal with an oppressive central government. He would argue that warrants are a way to address this oppression as it interposes a neutral judge between the police and the individual.

In the last decade, two significant works on the history of the Fourth Amendment were published. *The Fourth Amendment: Origins and Original Meaning* is an unpublished doctoral dissertation by William John Cuddihy from the Claremont Graduate School. Interestingly, Leonard Levy was Cuddihy's thesis advisor. Thomas Davies' *Recovery of the Original Fourth Amendment* (98 Mich. L.

Rev. 547, 1999), also represents a significant contribution to Fourth Amendment scholarship.

In her dissent in *Vernonia*, Justice O'Connor characterized Cuddihy's dissertation as "the most exhaustive analysis of the original meaning of the Fourth Amendment ever undertaken" (Vernonia School District 47J v. Acton, 1995). Cuddihy's analysis is much more broad ranging than previous scholarship. For example, he traces the concept of unreasonable searches and seizures from the seventh century, before the existence of the Magna Carta. Cuddihy recognizes that the Framers' prohibition against general warrants was part of a larger desire to prevent categorically general searches that were characterized by a lack of both justification and limitations on the scope of the searches. The requirement for probable cause was an indication that individualized suspicion was required to make a search reasonable and was also a rejection of general warrants. In addition, specific warrants used during that time were seen as the preferred method of conducting searches. By 1787, specific warrants had become the common device for searches in a number of states. This bit of history provides support for the warrant preference approach. Cuddihy suggests that "privacy was the bedrock concern of the amendment not general warrants." Thus the concerns of the Framers were much broader than just concerns over general warrants, the primary evil of the time.

Davies largely agrees with much of Cuddihy's work, especially with regard to the importance of specific warrants. He points out that the Fourth Amendment not only condemned the use of general warrants, it also represented a preventative strategy by prohibiting warrants that did not meet the probable cause and specificity requirements found in the Fourth Amendment. The main point of disagreement concerns the meaning of the reasonableness clause of the Fourth Amendment. Davies contends that Cuddihy's historical accounts are similar to Lasson. Davies instead argues that the term *unreasonable,* which at the time was used as a synonym for illegal, refers directly to general warrants and was not intended to give broader meaning to the Fourth Amendment.

Leonard W. Levy, in *Origins of Bill of Rights* (Yale University Press, 1999), does a superb job of tracing the history of the Fourth Amendment up until its adoption. He points out the importance of the concept of dwelling in the Fourth Amendment, including the origins of its importance and the concern for government intrusion. Although many have thought that "a man's house is his castle" came from the Magna Carta, Levy points out that it actually came from later embellishments of the Magna Carta. These same embellishments made the Magna Carta, "a talismanic symbol of freedom."

He also traces the influence of colonial and English history on the Framers. In examining English history, he discusses the Wilkes cases and their effect on the colonies. His examination of colonial history points out how John Adams was influenced by the Otis argument in the Paxton case. In addition, he carefully analyzes English and colonial legislation as well as the declarations of rights in the individual colonies. Finally, he considers the actual adoption of the Fourth Amendment, including the debate between the Federalists and Anti-Federalists as to the necessity for a bill of rights. It is a very thorough and fact-laden presentation.

For a cross-section of the debate over the Framers' intent when drafting the Fourth Amendment, see Akhil Reed Amar, *Fourth Amendment First Principles* (107 Harv. L. Rev. 757, 1994).

Amar contends that most of the Supreme Court jurisprudence with regard to the Fourth Amendment is historically flawed. He takes issue with the way the Court has created and handled the preference for a warrant. He also disagrees with the utilization of the probable cause standard and with the exclusionary rule remedy. He goes further than most historians in pointing out that the Framers were opposed not just to general warrants but to any type of warrant because they indemnified officials from lawsuits (trespass actions at common law), the only way to correct abuses by officials. He further argues that probable cause was the standard only for warrants and should thus be limited to searches that involve warrants. He would read the two clauses of the Fourth Amendment separately, and he argues that since the Fourth Amendment does not require warrants, probable cause, or exclusion but does require reasonableness, reasonableness should be the standard for evaluating Fourth Amendment violations.

Tracy Macklin's *Central Meaning of the Fourth Amendment* (35 Wm. & Mary L. Rev. 197, 1993) takes issue with the Court's adoption of the reasonableness approach to the Fourth Amendment. He points out that it is not a good idea to focus on the literal wording of the Fourth Amendment because the separate reasonableness clause was largely a mistake. He argues that reasonableness does not capture the intent of the Framers. He argues for a broader approach, which was concern for the oppressive central government. Warrants are one way to address this oppression because they place a neutral judge or magistrate in between the police power of the government and the individual. This addresses the concern of the Framers about the dangers of discretionary police activity.

In *When the Cure for the Fourth Amendment Is Worse than the Disease* (68 USC 1, 1994), Macklin criticizes Amar's approach to Fourth Amendment history. He relies considerably on the Cuddihy dissertation. He agrees that the Framers never had a warrant preference view. Nevertheless, he argues that they were concerned with abusive searches by the executive. He argues that the vague text of the Fourth Amendment allows for liberal construction and the opportunity to look to broad motivational principles. Opposition to writs of assistance indicates one of these principles, a concern to limit arbitrary power. Thus the Fourth Amendment was adopted to deter police officers from exercising unrestrained power.

Tracy Macklin, in *Let Sleeping Dogs Lie: Why the Supreme Court Should Leave Fourth Amendment History Unabridged*, 82 BU Law Rev. 895 (2002), argues that there is no consensus in the Supreme Court on the use of historical analysis in modern Fourth Amendment jurisprudence. He points out that the Justices utilized history when it suits their goals. Thus no principled basis for historical analysis has emerged and the "use of history in Fourth Amendment cases has been unpredictable and inconsistent."

## ANALYSIS—EXCLUSIONARY RULE

Of all the elements of the Fourth Amendment that have generated academic attention, none has been the subject of as intense or varied a debate as the exclusionary rule. It should be pointed out that although some of the articles deal directly with the exclusionary rule, articles involving substantive Fourth Amendment issues will often examine the importance of the exclusionary rule in the Court's approach to the Fourth Amendment. Many authors argue about the necessity of the rule and how to revise it. There is also much debate over the source of the rule. The following articles provide a glimpse into some of the areas of debate that have garnered significant attention.

For articles discussing the theoretical basis of the exclusionary rule and how this basis affects its application see Lawrence Crocker, *Can the Exclusionary Rule Be Saved?* (84 Journal of Criminal Law and Criminology 310, 1993).

Crocker focuses the majority of his article on how the development of, and the present lack of, a constitutional authorization for the exclusionary rule largely explains the confusion and contention surrounding the rule. Essentially, Crocker expands on a theory created by John Kaplan in his article, *The Limits of the Exclusionary Rule* (26 Stan. L. Rev. 1027, 1974), filling in the gaps in Kaplan's theory that have drawn criticism, specifically focusing on the absence of constitutional authorization. Crocker argues that in order to save the exclusionary rule the Court must point to an enforcement clause, sensitive to contingencies, which is implicit within the Fourth Amendment. It is interesting to note that Crocker admits he is "less than enthusiastic" about the solution he presents, implying that it may not be worthwhile to save the exclusionary rule. He argues, however, that saving the exclusionary rule may not be a worthwhile endeavor at all, but argues it is the best of the solutions the court is likely to consider.

Crocker argues that from the alternatives expressed in Mapp v. Ohio, the Court has ended up relying on essential deterrent sanction. The first two alternatives, the "implied privilege" and "extended violation" theories were completely undermined by the Court's later cases that relied entirely on an altered form of the third foundation, the "essential deterrent sanction." An important problem with this reliance, however, is that in United States v. Calandra, the Court characterized the rule as "judicially created," thus casting doubt as to whether it was essential. What then is the authority for the existence of the exclusionary rule? Crocker theorizes that the exclusionary rule should be seen as a contingent consequence or an implicit result of the Fourth Amendment. It is legitimate because we have no other more effective deterrent measures that are practical. If such alternative were found, the exclusionary rule would lose its constitutional authorization and could be replaced.

Presenting another view are Arnold H. Lowey, *Police-Obtained Evidence and the Constitution: Distinguishing Unconstitutionally Obtained Evidence from Unconstitutionally Used Evidence* (87 Mich. L. Rev. 907, 1989), and Yale Kamisar, *Does (Did) (Should) the Exclusionary Rule Rest on a "Principled Basis" Rather than an "Empirical Position"?* (16 Creighton L. Rev. 565, 1983). According to Lowey, there are two theories under which police-obtained evidence can be excluded from a criminal trial. First, police have unconstitutionally obtained the evidence, and exclusion should be used to deter such police behavior in the future. Second, evidence is excluded because the Constitution guarantees the defendant the procedural right to exclude the evidence. Lowey feels that the Court's failure to recognize this important difference between unconstitutionally obtained evidence (not necessarily forbidden by the Constitution) and evidence whose use is forbidden by the Constitution is one source of the continued confusion surrounding the Fourth Amendment. Lowey argues that the Court's present approach to the Fourth Amendment, to date, is fundamentally unsound because Fourth Amendment rights are substantive as opposed to procedural because the Fourth Amendment is concerned with obtaining not using the evidence. The exclusionary rule is a remedial device to make the substantive right a reality—that is to say that the right to be free of unreasonable searches and seizures applies to all people and not only to those individuals charged with a crime. Lowey argues that the exclusionary rule is inadequate because it cannot compensate for the substantive rights violated by an unreasonable search and seizure.

Kamisar seeks to reinstitute the judicial integrity argument mentioned in *Mapp*. He essentially argues that participants in the ongoing debate over the effectiveness of the exclusionary rule have lost sight of the real principled basis and purpose of the rule. Because Kamisar believes the Framers intended the Fourth Amendment to prevent the government from profiting from its own lawlessness and thus to minimize the chance that the people would lose their trust in government, he argues that any possible deterrence of police violations was originally really only a hoped-for effect of the exclusionary rule and not the reason for or basis of its existence. Kamisar goes on to discuss in depth the development of and problems with the deterrence rationale—that is, the view that the exclusionary rule's existence is based on its supposed deterrent effect on police officials. Kamisar argues that the Court has an important responsibility to preserve the judicial process from contamination and thus should not sanction unconstitutional activity by the executive. In this way, the exclusionary rule is simply another version of judicial review as established in Marbury v. Madison. Therefore, the exclusionary rule is based on principle and not on how substantially the exclusion of evidence might affect officers. The debate over its empirical value is unfortunate because it distracts attention from the true purpose and basis of the rule. In addition, the rule's value cannot hope to stand up under the present cost benefit analysis. The costs of the exclusionary rule are immediately apparent, whereas the intended benefits, maintaining individual privacy and security, are only conjectural. Kamisar thus argues that the Court must view the exclusionary rule as a command of the Constitution if it is to have any power and not be swallowed up by the growing list of exceptions. Furthermore Kamisar suggests that the very purpose of the Bill of Rights is to place certain subjects beyond the reach of cost-benefit analysis in order to protect certain rights from the value judgments of certain eras and certain judges.

Christopher Slobogin, in *Why Liberals Should Chuck the Exclusionary Rule* (U. Ill. L. Rev. 363, 1999), argues that the exclusionary rule should be severely limited and replaced by an administrative damages regime. He argues that evidence should still be excluded when an officer has flagrantly violated an individual's Fourth Amendment rights, but that monetary penalties should be the primary recourse in all other situations. According to Slobogin, no one will conclusively win the empirical debate over whether the exclusionary rule actually deters police from conducting illegal searches and seizures. He therefore premises his argument on behavioral and motivational theory, attempting to show that the exclusionary rule will continually fail to deter individual police officers. Slobogin argues that an administrative damages regime, under which actions would be brought directly against individual officers and departments, would more effectively deter Fourth Amendment violations. He furthers asserts that this regime would encourage the use of warrants, revitalize judicial review, diminish racism on the beat, curb perjury, improve hiring and training practices, and promote respect for the system.

Craig M. Bradley, in *Two Models of the Fourth Amendment* (83 Mich. L. Rev. 1468, 1985), enthusiastically advocates the complete abandonment of current Fourth Amendment law that, due to "constant tinkering" by the Court, has become a completely unsalvageable mass of contradictions and misconceived exceptions. Bradley argues that the source of the present confusion is the Court's attempt to reconcile two competing desires: the wish to have clear rules for police to follow and the desire to respond flexibly or reasonably to each case. Therefore, Bradley argues, the Court must adopt and adhere to one of the only two viable ways of looking at the Fourth Amendment, either the "no lines" approach or the "bright line" approach.

Under the "no lines" approach, the Court would simply consider whether a search or seizure is reasonable on a case-by-case basis. This approach would allow both police and the reviewing court to consider all relevant factors including whether there is probable cause or a warrant, the nature of the property being seized, or the nature of the entry. Under the "bright line" approach, the Court would actually enforce the warrant requirement that it has only paid lip service to in recent years. This could be achieved by making magistrates available 24 hours a day and allowing officers to radio in for warrants. Although Bradley realizes that police officers would initially feel unduly constrained by this procedure, he argues that they would adjust as they have to reading *Miranda* rights before questioning suspects. These two models would prevent the Court from encountering the clear rule versus flexibility dilemma in which it now finds itself entangled. Bradley concluded by recognizing that either model is likely to appear undesirable to people with certain views but insists that a strong solution has become necessary and either approach will have some benefits for law enforcement, defendants, and the public perception of the exclusionary process.

Robert M. Bloom, in *The Supreme Court and Its Purported Preference for Search Warrants* (50 Tenn. L. Rev. 231, 1983), suggests that because of the Court's disenchantment with the exclusionary rule, it has distorted other Fourth Amendment doctrine. He specifically points out that, despite the Court's articulated preference for search warrants, it has in fact increased the opportunities for warrantless searches. The Court had done this by ignoring the practicality rationale for warrantless searches. Warrantless activity was initially limited to the practicality justification. The Court has greatly expanded on warrantless activity by ignoring the practicality justification. He further points out that "these basic doctrines are not being disrupted on their merits, but rather because they stand in the way of the Court's determination to limit the exclusionary rule."

Much of the debate over the efficacy of the exclusionary rule has revolved around its effectiveness as a deterrent to police misconduct. Several authors have conducted empirical studies in an effort to fully determine the effectiveness of, and pitfalls of, the exclusionary rule. For an extremely comprehensive but not unbiased review of these studies, see Timothy L. Perrin, Mitchell H. Caldwell, Carol A. Chase, and Ronald W. Fagan, *If It's Broken, Fix It: Moving Beyond the Exclusionary Rule* (83 Iowa L. Rev. 669, 1998).

In addition to describing previous studies done on the impact of the exclusionary rule, the authors discuss their own extensive study designed to advance an understanding of the rule's deterrent effect. The study involved a questionnaire administered to six law enforcement agencies in Ventura County, California. Although the authors candidly admit that their study does not provide final or comprehensive answers to many of the questions that surround the exclusionary rule, their results do confirm the results of other studies that indicate that the rule does not effectively deter police misconduct. The study showed that officers who had previously had evidence excluded did not understand the exclusionary rule any better than other officers did and that the rule may actually foster misconduct in the form of officer deception. The authors go on to propose a modification for "fixing" the exclusionary rule by supplementing it with a new civil administrative remedy for those wronged by police misconduct. They present a detailed explanation for how such a remedy would work, detailing everything from the standard of proof to the statute of limitations. The authors conclude that empirical studies will not be able to definitively resolve the debate over the effectiveness of the exclusionary rule as a deterrent, but insist that further studies are still important to provide better understanding and perspective. Ultimately they insist that the exclusionary rule can no longer function as the sole remedy for constitutional violations and argue that the proposed administrative remedy will successfully achieve deterrence.

A number of authors, including William Heffernan, Myron Orfield, and William Stuntz, have expressed concerns over the exclusionary rule's effects on the integrity of law enforcement practices and courtroom proceedings. For more information, see William C. Heffernan and Richard W. Lovely, *Evaluating the Fourth Amendment Exclusionary Rule: The Problem of Police Compliance with the Law* (24 U. Mich. L. Rev. 311, 1991).

In an attempt to evaluate the present and potential effectiveness of the exclusionary rule, Heffernan and Lovely conducted a study examining both police officers' knowledge of the rules of search and seizure and the extent to which officers actually engaged in the behavior they believed was prohibited. The study therefore presented officers with the actual situations addressed in several different cases in the Court, and asked them to evaluate the legality of a search and then to state their willingness to intrude. A second part of the questionnaire contained multiple choice questions about search and seizure law that dealt only with knowledge of the law. The authors also gave the questionnaire to groups of laypersons and lawyers in order to create comparison points for the officers' responses.

Not too surprisingly, the study revealed that even the most knowledgeable officers and lawyers made substantial mistakes in dealing with the rules of search and seizure. The authors clearly point out that deterrence can only be effective if the subjects understand what is expected of them. The complexity of the rules of search and seizure significantly narrow the possibility of deterring police illegality. The authors are quick to recognize, however, that simplifying the rules of search and seizure would not be an easy task. They do point out that training does improve officers' knowledge of the law. The authors do also point out that exclusion reminds officers of the importance of acting constitutionally and provides incentive for officers to learn the constitutional limitations that should govern their actions. Most interesting, however, is the portion of the study in which a substantial minority of the responses indicated a deliberate disregard for the law. The authors go on to discuss the impact and effectiveness of exclusion and to evaluate the idea of a general good faith exception in light of the study's findings. Ultimately, the article concludes that exclusionary rule actually is "the least undesirable" remedy for violation of the Fourth Amendment and that it would be a mistake for the Court to adopt a general good faith exception.

Myron W. Orfield, in *Deterrence, Perjury, and the Heater Factor: An Exclusionary Rule in the Chicago Criminal Courts* (63 U. Colo. L. Rev. 75, 1992), details the results of a two-part study he conducted. The first study included 26 officers of the Narcotics Section of the Organized Crime Division of the Chicago Police Department, and the second study included judges, prosecutors, and public defenders in the Chicago court system. Orfield's article is interesting both for its description of the factors affecting the actual application of the exclusionary rule in court and for the anecdotes and quotes provided by the participants in the study. By conducting interviews with each subject Orfield is able to present a uniquely personal view of the exclusionary rule, although the limited number of subjects in his study means his empirical findings can be given little weight. Interestingly, and contrary to several other studies discussed, Orfield points out that respondents felt that police officers actually have a good understanding of Fourth Amendment rules and that the present doctrine is not too complicated for officers to understand. Orfield instead focuses largely on the issue of perjury by police. He notes that while the police officers interviewed felt perjury is a minor problem, the subjects in the court portion of the study revealed that they see police perjury as a common occurrence. Orfield discusses in depth the points in the procedural process at which police officers may choose to lie and what participants perceive as a systemic toleration and even encouragement of perjury. Orfield argues that the results suggest that perjury has become such an ingrained and accepted part of the process that some participants in the criminal justice system do not even recognize police perjury as violating the law. Orfield goes on to discuss the so-called "heater" cases, big cases that would arouse public ire if the defendant were allowed to walk for a technical or procedural reason. Judges were less likely to suppress evidence in heater cases, and Orfield presents several arguments as to why this might be the case. At the close of his article Orfield stresses that the participants in his study overwhelmingly favor retention of the exclusionary rule because they believe it has dramatically improved police behavior and no more effective alternative presently exists. Participants specifically judged that a tort remedy would not be as effective and could even be disastrous. Though Orfield recognizes the imperfections of the exclusionary rule, he concludes the article by calling it a "substantial success." This view of how we should perceive the exclusionary rule and judge its effectiveness differs substantially from other views such as the one presented in the Kamisar article. This difference reflects the continuing debate over whether and how the empirical question of the exclusionary rule as a police deterrent can be answered.

While the debate continues over whether and how the empirical question of the exclusionary rule's effectiveness as a police deterrent can be answered, the previously mentioned Kamisar article presents a vastly different view of how we should perceive the exclusionary rule and judge its effectiveness.

William J. Stuntz, *The Virtues and Vices of the Exclusionary Rule* (20 Harvard Journal of Law and Public Policy 443, 1997), provides a brief, yet informative, view of some of the issues surrounding the exclusionary rule. Most notable in this article is the author's focus on how the exclusionary rule affects other aspects of the criminal justice system. Stuntz focuses on how criminal defense lawyers choose which claims or arguments to raise on behalf of their clients. Specifically, he focuses on the time and financial constraints faced by public defenders and argues that the exclusionary rule, while valuable for its efficiency, can negatively impact defendants whose cases would be better tried on the merits. Stuntz argues that this tradeoff does more than allow the Fourth Amendment to occasionally release a guilty defendant. The reallocation of resources likely contributes to the jailing of innocent defendants where the trial on the merits gets less attention. Thus Stuntz concludes that because regulatory law must displace something else in our selective system of limited resources, we may be sacrificing resources that could be spent on determining whether a defendant actually committed a crime.

## INDIRECT CUTBACKS—STANDING

Like the exclusionary rule, the Court's interpretation of the Fourth Amendment's standing requirement has generated a substantial amount of criticism and debate. As many of these articles will point out, the Court's attitude to the exclusionary rule generates much of the standing jurisprudence. The four articles discussed next present a sample of the variety of ways in which authors have approached what they see as the problems inherent in the Court's approach to the standing requirement and the variety of potential solutions different authors have developed.

In Melvin Gutterman's *Fourth Amendment Privacy and Standing: Wherever the Twain Shall Meet* (1 N. Carolina L. Rev. 1, 1981), Professor Gutterman argues that the Court has, mainly through the *Rakas* opinion, merged the substantive Fourth Amendment determination with the concept of standing to produce a confusing and inappropriate analysis which fails to provide any meaningful guidance to lower courts. To arrive at this conclusion Gutterman analyzes Fourth Amendment privacy issues in four areas: privacy rights in papers, misplaced confidences, required confidences, and privacy expectations in cars and other containers. Gutterman explains that the standing concept has been used by the Court in an attempt to mitigate some of the costs of the exclusionary rule. Gutterman presents an informative historical overview of the development of the standing doctrine, highlighting the importance of cases like Jones v. United States (1960), Katz. v. United States (1967), and Rakas v. Illinois (1978). Specifically, Gutterman argues that the Court has consistently failed to attribute appropriate weight to the reasonable privacy expectations of the people as a whole. For example, he explains that the Court's decision in *Rakas*, that passengers in a car have no privacy expectations because they do not control the vehicle, is completely contrary to the view he feels the public would express, that a passenger in a car with the owner's consent expects privacy in the vehicle. Gutterman also stresses the idea that the Court has, most noticeably in *Payner*, given insufficient weight to the important Fourth Amendment concern of preserving judicial integrity. In situations in which the government has deliberately violated an individual's Fourth Amendment rights in order to secure evidence against a third party, Gutterman feels that the Court must broaden the standing doctrine to include the "targeted" individual. Unfortunately, the Court's desire to limit the exclusionary rule wherever possible has caused it to resist enlarging the group of people who may invoke the exclusionary rule. He concludes by stating "that the protections afforded by the Fourth Amendment begin to approach the evaporation point."

Richard B. Kuhns, *The Concept of Personal Aggrievement in Fourth Amendment Standing Cases* (65 Iowa L. Rev. 493, 1980), begins his article by stating that his objective is to provide a "comprehensive basis for evaluating the standing requirement," a basis that he believes the Court has failed to provide thus far. Kuhns goes on to explain two perspectives on the Fourth Amendment first characterized by Professor Anthony Amsterdam as the "atomistic perspective" and the "regulatory perspective." Under the atomistic perspective, the Fourth Amendment is viewed as a protection of certain individual rights. Under the regulatory perspective, the Fourth Amendment is viewed as "a regulatory canon requiring government to order it[s] law enforcement procedures in a fashion that keeps us collectively secure ... against unreasonable searches and seizures." Although Kuhns argues that these two perspectives are not logically inconsistent, the Court's failure to deal with how the relationship between the two has created problems and confusion, particularly with regard to the standing doctrine. Kuhns argues that the Court's focus on deterrence and judicial integrity in its discussion of the exclusionary rule clearly demonstrates a regulatory perspective. On the other hand, the concept of personal aggrievement, which is the core of the standing doctrine, is essentially atomistic. Kuhns suggests that the Court's reliance on the "legitimate expectation of privacy test" in Rakas v. Illinois (1978) is undesirable because it fails to provide a bright line test. He is justifiably worried that it will gives judges who already dislike applying the exclusionary rule a great deal of flexibility. Kuhns also examines the potential impact of the Court's apparent abandonment of standing as a separate issue in *Rakas*. He seems frustrated by the Court's failure to characterize standing in a more atomistic fashion that reflects personal aggrievement. He argues that until the "Court either abolishes the exclusionary rule" or somehow clarifies the relationship between the regulatory and atomistic perspectives of the Fourth Amendment, standing will be a mess.

In an effort to expand on the standing requirement, Mary I. Coombs, in *Shared Privacy and the Fourth Amendment, or The Rights of Relationships* (75 Calif. L. Rev. 1593, 1987), discusses the Court's doctrine relating to derivative standing and third-party consent cases through the lens of feminist jurisprudence and its emphasis on interconnectedness. She argues that the Court's focus on the privacy rights of individuals and neglect of the ways in which privacy embodies chosen sharing have resulted in a distortion of the focus and use of the Fourth Amendment. She proposes that if Fourth Amendment jurisprudence explicitly considered shared privacy in determining when a search has occurred and who can challenge it, the Court's decisions would more accurately reflect how people behave and should be allowed to behave. Coombs provides a brief yet informative discussion of the evolution of the expectation of privacy standard and argues that, although the indeterminacy of the Court's standard is likely unavoidable, it must still make an effort to create standards that adequately reflect the lives of the people who are involved in Fourth Amendment cases. To meet this challenge, Coombs first looks at the Court's decisions relating to shared privacy issues and then examines these issues in a more general sense. She proposes that a derivative claimant who has no possessory or property interest of his own should still be allowed to challenge a search when he can reasonably assume that the person with possessory or property interest would seek to exclude the public from the thing searched and that this person would take the derivative claimant's interest into consideration in the exclusion. Essentially, Coombs suggests that there should be a rebuttable presumption of shared privacy for some relationships which confer standing absent the government's ability to show that shared privacy did not exist. For other relationships, the Court would consider specific concrete facts the defendant produced to show a shared expectation of privacy. Coombs points out that the Court would also have to determine whether the defendant's claim could be extended to the particular areas searched. To answer this question, she proposes that reasonable expectations of privacy are directly proportional to the intimacy and extensiveness of each relationship. Finally, Coombs argues that because third-party consent and derivative standing both depend on the nature of the relationship, the same test should govern each doctrine.

Eulis Simien, Jr., in *The Interrelationship of the Scope of the Fourth Amendment and Standing to Object to Unreasonable Searches* (41 Ark. L. Rev. 747, 1988), presents a critique of the Court's interpretation of the standing requirement and suggests a more effective alternative approach. In his critique of the standing requirement since *Rakas*, Simien constructs an insightful description of how the Court's decisions have led to the virtual elimination of the standing requirement, and why this change has severely limited the protections of the Fourth Amendment as a whole. In particular it is worth examining his comparison of the Court's present doctrine with their decisions in Jones v. United States and Katz v. United States, cases that represent the height of Fourth Amendment standing expansion. Essentially Simien argues that the Court's present analysis incorrectly allows the question of the government's reasonableness to become part of the standing inquiry. The Court's reasoning thus unfortunately becomes "the claimant would lose on the merits, therefore no standing." Interestingly, Simien points out that the Court's present analysis also seems to assume that the Court may distinguish between the protection of different property interests based on whether such interests are legitimate (i.e., property interest in cocaine is illegitimate). Yet the historical basis of the Fourth Amendment was to prevent searches and seizures of effects that England had refused to recognize as legitimate, smuggled goods, particularly molasses. Like many other critics of the Court's standing doctrine, Simien argues that the Court's dislike of the exclusionary rule has tainted their standing analysis by encouraging them to limit the number of people who will be able to invoke the rule. Also like other authors, Simien argues that the Court's emphasis on the deterrence rationale as the basis for the exclusionary rule is flawed and misplaced.

In constructing his alternative approach Simien demonstrates the importance of property interest in his standing analysis and discusses what he sees as the proper role and scope of privacy interests. By requiring that original concepts in the Fourth Amendment have a binding effect, while simultaneously allowing for changes in the way these concepts are advanced, the Court would allow for the effective operation of the Fourth Amendment in a constantly changing and progressing society. Most notable in this portion of the discussion is the author's emphasis on the collective "right of the people" aspect of the Fourth Amendment. Under this theory a defendant who failed to meet the burden of showing his individual Fourth Amendment rights were violated could still be entitled to standing for his collective rights.

## INDIRECT CUTBACKS—DERIVATIVE EVIDENCE

As discussed, the Court has created a number of exceptions to the fruit doctrine. For the viewpoint that these exceptions have undermined the warrant requirement, see Craig M. Bradley, *Murray v. United States: The Bell Tolls for the Search Warrant* (64 Indiana Law Journal 907, 1989) and Robert M. Bloom, *Inevitable Discovery: An Exception Beyond the Fruits* (20 American Journal of Criminal Law 79, 1992).

In his article, Bradley addresses what he terms "the hypocrisy of claiming that there is a warrant requirement and then not enforcing it." Bradley argues that the Court misses a crucial point by applying the independent source exception to situations where a warrant is based on information "wholly unconnected" to a previous search, but ignoring the fact that the parties conducting the subsequent search also conducted the illegal search. Thus the seizure cannot be considered "wholly unconnected" in the same way as it would be in a traditional independent source case. Bradley stresses that there is no deterrence for future violations after *Murray*. He goes on to suggest that by basically allowing initial warrantless searches, the *Murray* decision is incompatible with the warrant requirement of the

Fourth Amendment. Interestingly, Bradley does not necessarily disagree with the Court's result in *Murray*, but only insists that "instead of claiming that there is a warrant requirement and then, as illustrated by *Murray*, repeatedly finding ways to ignore it," the Court should either dispense with the warrant requirement altogether or actually enforce the warrant doctrine. What is important, Bradley explains, is not which of these options the Court chooses but simply that they chose one and no longer leave police and courts guessing as to whether a warrant is required in any given situation.

Bloom raises a similar point about the warrant requirement in his article. In talking about the inevitable discovery exception, he suggests that it will result in a diminution of an already diluted warrant requirement. He further suggests that the rationale for expanding the exceptions to the fruit doctrine is directly related to the Court's attitude toward the exclusionary rule.

## ANALYSIS—GOVERNMENT ACTION

John M. Burkoff, in *Not So Private Searches and the Constitution* (66 Cornell L. Rev. 627, 1980), would like to see a more expansive approach to private searches so as to bring them under the authority of the Fourth Amendment. This article argues that the exclusionary rule should apply to more private searches than is currently the case. Burkoff discusses the origins of the government action doctrine and the early use of the *silver platter doctrine*, which allowed for the use of evidence that private individuals turned over to the government on a silver platter. The silver platter doctrine also refers to the turning over of illegally obtained evidence for state prosecutions before the exclusionary rule applied to the states. Although the silver platter doctrine has largely been disregarded (at least with regard to states), the government continues to allow the admission of evidence collected through private searches. Burkoff argues that these private searches should be considered unconstitutional because the admission of the fruits of these private searches implicates the same liberty concerns as is the case when states actors carry out a search: "Victims of unlawful private conduct care little whether they have fallen prey to illegal law enforcement conduct or nominally private searches." This article argues that applying the exclusionary rule to private searches will have a deterrent effect on private searches. He argues that this effect will come from eliminating the advantage that private actors gain (punishing criminals) from their unlawful conduct. He is especially troubled by the actions of security officers or private law enforcement officials because these actors seem to have the authority of the state, yet they are not bound by Constitution. Ultimately, this article argues that by allowing the evidence into trials, the judiciary compromises itself by playing an accomplice after the fact. This judicial integrity argument is discussed in the chapter on the exclusionary rule.

Michael Wukmer, in *The Fourth Amendment Following Private Searches: Is There a Privacy Interest to Protect?* (52 U. Cincinnati L. Rev. 172, 1983), provides a nice overview of many of the major cases with regard to government action in Fourth Amendment litigation. It has a good, detailed discussion about many of the particular details that differentiate the cases in this area. Wukmer discusses these issues in the context of a diminished expectation of privacy when shipping through common carriers such as FedEx and others.

Emily M. Stout, in *Bounty Hunters as Evidence Gatherers: Should They Be Considered State Actors Under the Fourth Amendment When Working with the Police?* (65 U. Cincinnati L. Rev. 665, 1997), again examines the gray area of when private action becomes government action. It focuses on the special case of bounty hunters, who in searching for fugitives often incidentally discover evidence as part of their hunt. However, federal courts have agreed that bounty hunters are private actors. This author argues that bounty hunters should be considered agents of the government.

Anthony G. Scheer, in *A Search by Any Other Name: Fourth Amendment Implications of a Private Citizen's Actions in State v. Sanders* (69 N. Carolina L. Rev. 1449, 1991), discusses how State v. Sanders (327 N.C. 319, 1990) deals with an informant who entered a defendant's home to elicit evidence necessary for the police to obtain a search warrant. In this case, the North Carolina Supreme Court declined to apply the exclusionary rule to the evidence obtained, holding that the informant acted as a private citizen, not an agent of the government. This article looks at the Court's reasoning and analysis in determining whether an agency relationship exists.

## ANALYSIS—APPLICABILITY OF THE FOURTH AMENDMENT— EXPECTATION OF PRIVACY

Chris Slobogin and Joseph Schumacher examined expectation of privacy in *Reasonable Expectations of Privacy and Autonomy in Fourth Amendment Cases: An Empirical Look at "Understandings Recognized and Permitted by Society"* (42 Duke Law Journal 727, 1993). Although the Court often says that community values about intrusiveness and expectations of privacy dictate the Court's decisions with regard to the scope of the Fourth Amendment, Slobogin and Schumacher argue that, in fact, the Court's conclusions about the scope of the Fourth Amendment are often not in tune with commonly held attitudes about police investigative techniques. To demonstrate this point, Slobogin and Schumacher tested four hypotheses: (1) that the Court's conclusions about expectation of privacy do not correlate with citizens' actual understanding of privacy; (2) that people view searches of their own property as more intrusive than searches of others' property; (3) that a search with a specific objective (e.g., a frisk for drugs) was seen as less intrusive than a vague investigation; and (4) that crime control attitudes were inversely related to intrusiveness rankings. Slobogin and Schumacher urge judges to use their findings as a reminder that they may underestimate the intrusiveness of searching techniques and to reevaluate their analytical model for determining the reasonable expectation of privacy.

Robert Power, in *Technology and the Fourth Amendment: A Proposed Formulation for Visual Searches* (80 Journal of Criminal Law and Criminology 1, 1989), considers the impact of developing technology on Fourth Amendment jurisprudence. Although this article is from 1989, it offers some insight into issues that the courts should consider as they determine what technological intrusions into privacy will be allowed. Power presents four norms as a framework for an intrusion paradigm that he argues will limit the adverse effects of technology use in surveillance and serve as guideposts for the preservation of privacy as technology evolves. Power stresses that a clear and principled paradigm is critical because "technological change is constant . . . the principle that is valid for today's technology may be a laughable anachronism tomorrow." Currently, no bright line tests exist, and as police begin to use enhancing devices, people begin to fear totalitarian/Orwellian consequences. Power's four norms for developing a principle are (1) that the observation have a legitimate purpose (reasonable cause); (2) that the observations be reasonably implemented (reasonable law enforcement conduct); (3) that some objects be specifically protected from all observation (e.g., homes, public restrooms); and (4) that each enhancement device be considered in context over time.

For commentary on how the *Bond, Katz,* and *Kyllo* decisions have contributed to or detracted from the definition of a reasonable expectation of privacy, see Stacy E. Roberts, *Bond And Beyond: A Shift in the Understanding of What Constitutes a Fourth Amendment Search* (22 U. Toledo L. Rev. 457, 2002).

For insight into how the *Bond* decision has affected the Court's definition of what constitutes a reasonable expectation of privacy, Roberts' article approves the *Bond* Court's decision to expand individual Fourth Amendment rights by defining physical manipulation of luggage as a search. She contends that the Court has taken a step in the right direction by "expanding the scope of an individual's reasonable expectation of privacy." The author believes that the Court reasoned correctly in its conclusion that a bus passenger who places a bag in an overhead storage area does not reasonably expect that other bus passengers or law enforcement, for that matter, will examine the bag with their hands. Roberts implies that the Court can better protect Fourth Amendment rights when it has a better grasp on a reasonable person's expectation of privacy.

Roberts contends that before *Bond,* in cases like *Greenwood, Ciraolo*, and *Dow Chemical*, the Court had not defined privacy expectations as they would be defined by an average, reasonable person. She argues that the *Bond* Court did look to "prevailing societal norms" to decide what is a reasonable expectation of privacy. In its ruling, the Court manifested an understanding of privacy expectations "more attuned to what society actually regards as private." Looking ahead to the ramifications of this "laudable shift," Roberts predicts that the Court will be more likely to call something "private" if it could not be uncovered accidentally. She sees this broadened scope of privacy expectations as a positive shift in Fourth Amendment jurisprudence.

Richard H. Seamon, in *Kyllo v. United States and the Partial Ascendance of Justice Scalia's Fourth Amendment* (79 Washington University Law Quarterly 1013, 2001), examines the recent *Kyllo* decision and the effects that it has on how the Court has defined expectations of privacy.

Seamon contends that while *Kyllo*, on the surface, "does not break much new ground" in Fourth Amendment jurisprudence, he sees the decision as a reflection of the views of Justice Scalia, the author of the majority opinion. He argues that the decision is a subtle departure from *Katz's* proposition that all warrantless searches are presumptively unreasonable. Justice Scalia has argued in past decisions that *Katz's* reasonable expectation of privacy doctrine has developed as a way of avoiding the creation of more exceptions to the warrant requirement. If activity is not governed by the Fourth Amendment, it is not subject to the warrant requirement. Thus, the application of *Katz* in a perverse way preserves the warrant requirement.

Seamon points out that Scalia, based on his historical analysis, disagrees with *Katz's* presumption favoring warrants. In fact, the Court has demonstrated a tendency to narrow the warrant presumption, and to allow a wider range of warrantless searches without a presumption of unconstitutionality. *Kyllo*, because it involves the home to which the warrant requirement historically has applied, allows Scalia to comfortably apply *Katz* without buying into the warrant presumption.

In *Leading Cases* (115 Harvard Law Review 346, 2001), the author concedes that the Court's decision in *Kyllo* is a victory for privacy rights, especially with regard to the sanctity of the home. Nevertheless, the Court's focus on technology is at odds with the concept of protection of the home. In cases regarding intrusive technology, the location is supplanted by the reasonableness of a person's expectations, which is related to the general availability of the relevant technology. The *Kyllo* decision is grounded in the Court's reliance on privacy as a concept of expectation. Consequently, the reasonable expectation prong the Court applied to *Kyllo* to accommodate developments in technology is flawed because the evolutional perpetuity of technological advances will lead to a continuous diluting of Fourth Amendment protections over time. However, the Court clearly intended to protect the homeowner from compromised privacy interests in the face of technological advancement. Therefore, as a remedy, the author urges the Court to exercise its reliance on place, in this case the home, as a trigger for invoking the newly formed technology-focused rule to determine whether an expectation of privacy is reasonable and thus "restoring the Fourth Amendment protections of the home to the heightened status that the Founders envisioned."

With regard to the impact of *Kyllo*, we find differing opinions.

David Sklansky, in *Symposium: Back to the Future; Kyllo, Katz and Common Law*, 72 MISS L.J. 143 (2002), says that *Kyllo* is a touchstone for striking the difficult balance between an individual's privacy intent and societal need for security. He claims that *Kyllo* takes "long view" so as to provide guidance for future technology cases touching the Fourth Amendment. He argues that *Kyllo* focuses on the past in a more flexible manner. It focuses more on traditional or the core components of privacy, which the Framers had in mind.

Tracy Macklin, in *Katz, Kyllo, and Technology: Virtual Fourth Amendment Protection in the Twenty-first Century,* 72 MISS L.J. 51 (2002), disagrees with Sklansky as to the impact of *Kyllo* for the future. He would compare it with the impact of the *Katz* decision, which he describes as "slight." He predicts that *Kyllo* like *Katz* will be interpreted narrowly and not prevent law enforcement from using sophisticated technological devices.

## ANALYSIS—ARREST AND CRIMINAL SEARCHES— JUSTIFICATION—PROBABLE CAUSE

The definition and application of the probable cause concept have consistently occupied both the Court and legal scholars. Two articles dealing with the *Whren* decision discuss the importance of considering an officer's subjective and objective motives when determining if probable cause existed for a search are:

David A. Harris, in *"Driving While Black" and All Other Traffic Offenses: The Supreme Court and Pretextual Traffic Stops* (87 Journal of Criminal Law and Criminology 544, 1997), specifically considers the impact of the Court's decision in Whren v. United States that because officers have probable cause to pull drivers over for committing traffic infractions, it makes no difference that the officer's "real purpose" in the stop is to investigate a hunch that the occupants of the car were involved in a crime. Harris argues forcefully that the Court's decision is a step in the wrong direction, allowing pretextual invasions of citizens' Fourth Amendment rights and legitimizing racist policing. Harris devotes the majority of his article to examining the disparate impact that the police discretion allowed by *Whren* will have on African-American and Hispanic drivers. He presents several specific examples, arguing that police already target African-Americans and Hispanics in pretextual traffic stops and will only increase this practice after *Whren*. Harris then suggests that we should address the Court's mistake by encouraging police departments to create administrative regulations to control racially biased traffic enforcement tactics and to collect data on all traffic stops so that a more rigorous analysis can be conducted in the future.

Craig M. Glantz, in *Could This Be the End of Fourth Amendment Protection for Motorists?* (87 Criminal Law and Criminology 864, 1997), expresses concern that the current Court's bright line rule with respect to traffic stops enunciated in *Whren*—that they pass Fourth Amendment scrutiny so long as they are objectively based on probable cause—allows police officers to use traffic violations as pretexts for searches really based on impermissible motives such as race.

There are two competing standards of review for traffic stops, according to Glantz. The objective standard, adopted by the current Court will find an investigative stop of a motor vehicle constitutional "if the officer *could* have stopped the vehicle for a traffic infraction." Under this standard, worries Glantz, subjective motivations of officers, including race, are not important to the analysis.

Glantz argues that Fourth Amendment jurisprudence has developed a number of safeguards against arbitrary search and seizures. He contends that the *Whren* Court, because it was willing to defer to police judgment and allow stops based on minor traffic violations, has undermined these safeguards by leaving the door wide open for officers to use minor traffic offenses to legitimize otherwise impermissible searches and seizures.

The standard that Glantz argues should be adopted instead is a more subjective one that asks whether "under the same circumstances a reasonable officer *would* have made the stop in the absence of invalid purpose." According to Glantz, this more subjective standard allows "advantageous judicial review of discretionary police conduct," while at the same time still providing for an "objective inquiry into Fourth Amendment action."

Glantz argues that this "would" standard would allow the Court to examine traffic stops based on the "totality of the circumstances" standard found in Terry v. Ohio (1968). He contends that this extension of the *Terry* reasonableness standard into the area of probable cause–based traffic stops is necessary in order to ensure that police officers are not using minor traffic violations as pretexts for otherwise impermissible searches. He argues that the *Terry* standard has been shown to be versatile enough to be applied to a wide range of encounters and that it would be "no more arduous" to apply the subjective standard to traffic stops than it is to on-the-street stop and frisk encounters.

Another case that has generated significant interest within the legal community for its reformulation of the probable cause standard is Illinois v. Gates. For commentary on how the case has affected the Court's interpretation of the standard, see Charles E. Moylan Jr., *Illinois v. Gates: What It Did and What It Did Not Do* (20 Criminal Law Bulletin 93, 1984); Yale Kamisar, *Gates, Probable Cause, Good Faith, and Beyond* (69 Iowa L. Rev. 551, 1984); and Joseph D. Grano, *Probable Cause and Common Sense: A Reply to the Critics of Illinois v. Gates* (17 Journal of Law Reform 465, 1984).

In his discussion, Judge Moylan presents a clear and practical assessment of the impact of Illinois v. Gates on the warrant-issuing function and warrant-reviewing function in Maryland. Judge Moylan argues that despite the "sweeping rhetoric" of the majority in the *Gates* opinion, the basic two-pronged test of *Aguilar* remains intact. Moylan argues that the majority's only real contention is with *Spinelli* and only with the *Spinelli's* "very particularized implication . . . that overkill on one prong will not compensate for a deficit in the other." Though the Court found that the basis of knowledge prong could not be satisfied by the informant's letter in *Gates*, the Court was determined that the search would be found reasonable and thus had to modify the *Spinelli*-derived idea that the two prongs were completely independent. Essentially Judge Moylan argues that judges now should continue to apply the *Aguilar-Spinelli* analysis and only resort to *Gates'* "totality of the circumstances" test when "the Spinelli supplementation of Aguilar appears to come tantalizingly close but might technically fail under the traditional analysis."

Kamisar examines what he sees as *Gates'* abandonment of the two-pronged test and looks at the scope and implications of the newly adopted practical and flexible "totality of the circumstances" test. In arguing that the Court's reasons for abandoning the two-pronged test are unsound and that problems with the two-prong test could be easily remedied, Kamisar presents an interesting look at the debate over whether police corroboration could overcome deficiencies in either or both prongs of the two-pronged test. He suggests that the two pronged test is indeed working and agrees with Justice White's concurrence in *Gates*. He also points out that the Court has always adhered to the need for flexibility in assessing probable cause. He further argues that, in reading the entire opinion, there is still a need to substantially follow the so-called two-pronged test. Finally, he discusses how the totality of the circumstances test coupled with the good faith exception to the exclusionary rule would act as a double dilution of the probable cause standard.

Grano presents a vastly different view of the Court's "totality of the circumstances" test. Grano also examines the impact of *Gates,* focusing on the case as a reflection of competing conceptions of probable cause and concluding that the majority has moved probable cause review in the direction that common sense dictates. He argues that *Gates* raises a question as to what standard should be used to determine probable cause. The majority appears to advocate a substantial possibility standard or perhaps even a reasonable suspicion standard, whereas Justice Stevens' dissent advocates a more-probable-than-not standard. Grano goes on to argue that common sense and the history of probable cause indicate that probable cause should continue to be a flexible concept that can be adjusted to the circumstances. The "more probable than not" standard is unreasonable, he explains, because it places too much emphasis on the individual and does not adequately balance individual interests against important societal interests. On a separate note, it is also worth examining Grano's article for his interesting and detailed historical perceptive of probable cause in both England and America.

Ronald J. Bacigal, in *Dodging a Bullet, but Opening Old Wounds in Fourth Amendment Jurisprudence*, 16 Seton Hall L. Rev. 597, 1986), Bacigal explores the history behind what he views as the likely repercussions of the Court's decision in Winston v. Lee (1985), a case in which the Court refused to allow the government to "seize" a bullet lodged in the shoulder of an armed robbery suspect. Ultimately, Bacigal argues that although *Winston* may be seen as a victory for the substantive right to privacy in the short run, the Court's return to a focus on the substantive content of the reasonableness clause will damage the clarity needed for successful application of the warrant clause.

To reach this conclusion, Bacigal begins by presenting an in-depth analysis to answer the question: "Is the reasonableness clause a 'blank check' that the Court may fill in with whatever substantive values it considers appropriate, or is constitutional reasonableness defined by the "bright line" procedural requirements of the warrant clause?" To answer this question, Bacigal takes us back to the history chapter when we discussed the relationship between the two clauses of the Fourth Amendment. Bacigal focuses on what he sees as the Court's move toward a sliding scale of probable cause, and the way this approach has blurred the line between the reasonableness clause and the warrant clause. Bacigal argues that the decisions are merely ad hoc determinations of reasonableness based on the totality of the circumstances. To be effective, Bacigal insists that the balancing process must somehow define the government interests and assign actual value to them. The Court's Fourth Amendment decisions appear unprincipled in large part because of this lack of set values.

Patrick S. Yatchak, in *Breaching the Peace: The Trivialization of the Fourth Amendment Reasonableness Standard in the Wake of Atwater v. City of Lago Vista* (25 Hamline L. Rev. 329, 2001), argues forcefully that the *Atwater* decision—creating a per se rule allowing custodial arrest when probable cause exists that even a minor traffic violation has occurred—"trivialized" the Fourth Amendment's requirement of reasonableness.

Yatchak points out that a central feature of the Fourth Amendment's safeguards against unreasonable search and seizures is the requirement that an intrusion be justified by a legitimate government interest. He argues that in *Atwater*, the intrusion on Atwater's personal liberty far outweighed the state's interest in placing her under custodial arrest. The government may have a strong interest in conducting arrests in situations involving probable cause for violent crimes, but he argues that it has nowhere near the same interest in arresting for minor traffic stops. Yatchak contends that a fine for a seat belt violation would have served the government interest.

He expresses concern that the *Atwater* per se rule will invite abuse in the form of pretextual traffic stops and racial profilings by police officers. Yatchak worries that so long as police officers can justify a custodial arrest with probable cause of a violation of any type of crime, they will have the ability to use that justification as a cover for ulterior motives.

As a solution, he proposes a "reasonable articulable suspicion" standard for custodial arrests incident to traffic stops. Under this rule, an officer could only issue a statutorily required citation for minor traffic violations, unless he could point to reasonable, articulable grounds for doing more. This standard, he argues, would take into consideration the proper balancing of interests required by Fourth Amendment jurisprudence.

## ANALYSIS—STOPS—JUSTIFICATION—REASONABLE SUSPICION

Although *Terry* and the cases that have developed the *Terry* doctrine have shown the "reasonable suspicion" standard to be a flexible, widely applicable one, legal scholars have argued both for its modification and its expansion to other areas of Fourth Amendment jurisprudence.

Anthony C. Thompson, in *Stopping the Usual Suspects: Race and the Fourth Amendment* (74 N.Y.U. L. Rev. 956, 1999), argues that the *Terry* reasonable suspicion framework is deficient to the extent that it does not factor in the effects of racial motivation. According to Thompson, the fact that the Court does not look into an officer's consideration of race when evaluating a *Terry* stop represents a fundamental flaw in its "reasonable suspicion" Fourth Amendment analysis. Current Court jurisprudence looks to the Fourteenth Amendment, not the Fourth, as the safeguard against racially motivated searches and seizures. Thompson argues that this choice by the Court was a "wrong turn," and that the Fourth Amendment should instead be "squarely at the heart" of constitutional analysis of the issue.

Examining the facts behind the landmark *Terry* case, Thompson points out that the two men deemed to have been engaging in suspicious behavior by Officer McFadden—John Terry and Richard Chilton—were African-American, yet the Court ignored this fact as a possible source of McFadden's motivation for approaching them. Because the Court constructed the now-famous "reasonable suspicion" stop and frisk *Terry* standard on race-neutral considerations, argues Thompson, it left the door open for racially motivated searches and seizures justified by pretext. By factoring race out of its analysis in *Terry* and its progeny, Thompson argues that the Court has been operating in an unrealistic "constructed reality" in which officers do not act based on considerations of race. Thompson contends that the logical conclusion of what *Terry's* race-neutral analysis started was reached in *Whren*, where the Court "overtly" removed race considerations from Fourth Amendment analysis. Further, he argues that in *Whren* (discussed in the probable cause chapter) the Court declared that racial motivations are irrelevant to search and seizure considerations if a stop is premised on probable cause.

Thompson argues that this "raceless" approach to Fourth Amendment jurisprudence is misguided for two reasons. First, he provides social science data to show that race considerations are very much at the heart of police officers' motivations when making *Terry* stops. Second, he argues that historically, the Fourth Amendment was intended by the Framers to prevent against the targeting of minority members of "disfavored groups" in society and that it should therefore do so today.

As a solution, Thompson argues that courts should engage the issue of race in Fourth Amendment analyses head-on. He calls for the Court to provide a set of guidelines regarding the types of situations in which race could be a factor in determining reasonable suspicion and then to take an active role in scrutinizing those motivations in the same way it does other factors in a *Terry* stop analysis. This way, a *Terry* analysis would truly reflect a consideration of the "totality of the circumstances" surrounding a particularized incident of search and seizure.

Craig M. Glantz, in *Could This Be the End of Fourth Amendment Protection for Motorists?* (87 Journal of Law and Criminology 864, 1997) (discussed more fully in the probable cause chapter) argues that the *Terry*-style "totality of circumstances" standard should be used by the Court to examine probable cause traffic stops. He proposes that the Court do this by inquiring whether "under the same circumstances a reasonable officer *would* have made the stop in the absence of the invalid purpose." According to Glantz, this more subjective standard allows "advantageous judicial review of discretionary police conduct" while at the same time still providing for an "objective inquiry into Fourth Amendment action." He contends that this extension of the *Terry* reasonableness standard into the area of probable cause-based traffic stops is necessary in order to ensure that police officers are not using minor traffic violations as pretexts for otherwise impermissible searches. He argues that the *Terry* standard has been shown to be versatile enough to be applied to a wide range of encounters and that it would be "no more arduous" to apply the subjective standard to traffic stops than it is to on-the-street stop and frisk encounters.

Margaret Raymond, in *Down on the Street: Considering the Character of the Neighborhood in Evaluating Reasonable Suspicion* (60 Ohio State Law Journal 99, 1999), expresses concern that "character of the neighborhood" considerations have grown from being one of many factors in a reasonableness analysis of a *Terry* stop into, in some cases, *the* determinative factor. She argues that this is a departure from the heart of what a *Terry* stop analysis is supposed to focus on— the specific behavior of a suspect at a given time. While conceding that the character of a neighborhood can play an important role in an officer's justification for a stop, Raymond worries that some suspects are being stopped merely for being found in a certain area, rather than as a result of particularized observations of their behavior.

Raymond argues that the Court has somewhat forgotten this important requirement of a legitimate *Terry* stop, that it be based on particularized, individualized suspicion, rooted in specific, articulable facts. When a court finds a *Terry* stop to be legitimate based primarily on character-of-neighborhood considerations, Ray-

mond believes that this represents a departure from this "particularized" requirement, and instead allows more generalized, probabilistic justifications for stops.

As a solution, Raymond argues that character-of-neighborhood considerations
should be allowed as a basis for reasonable suspicion only when the behavior of
the suspect is "not common among persons engaged in law-abiding activity at the
time and place observed." By adding this requirement, Raymond believes that
*Terry's* requirement of a consideration of the "totality of the circumstances" surrounding a stop will be better satisfied. Raymond argues that requiring more
focus on the individual suspect in this way will "enhance the accuracy and logical
consistency of the reasonable suspicion standard.

Steven A. Saltzburg, in *Terry v. Ohio: A Practically Perfect Doctrine* (72 St.
John's L. Rev. 911, 1998), discusses how in April 1998, St. John's University
School of Law hosted a conference to mark the thirtieth anniversary of the *Terry*
case. The articles from the conference were published in Volume 72, a symposium issue of *St. John's Law Review*. Topics range from praise for the *Terry* standard's flexibility to criticisms of its vagueness. Looking at *Terry* and its
"reasonable suspicion" framework 30 years after its creation, scholars commented on how it has developed in light of issues ranging from race to drug
enforcement to community policing.

As the title suggests, Saltzburg argues that the *Terry* standard has proven to be
versatile, well reasoned, and applicable to a wide range of police-suspect encounters. He contends that the "reasonable suspicion" doctrine has developed in logical, practical ways as it has been stretched to apply to more and more types of
situations. Saltzburg points out that the *Terry* standard of "reasonable suspicion"
has largely remained uniform. He comments that a side benefit of the struggle to
clarify the *Terry* standard has resulted in a clearer explanation of the probable
cause standard.

Saltzburg's major concern with *Terry*, however, is what he sees as a lack of
attention by subsequent courts to the *Terry* frisk standard. Saltzburg notes that a
narrow reading of *Terry* would allow a frisk only when an officer felt endangered.
He argues that the right to frisk under the *Terry* reasonable suspicion standard
should be viewed more leniently as a self-protective measure for the police.

Christopher Slobogin, in *Let's Not Bury Terry: A Call for Rejuvenation of the
Proportionality Principle* (72 St. John's L. Rev. 1053, 1998), points out that *Terry*
puts forth a framework in which a search or seizure is reasonable when its level of
intrusion is "roughly proportionate" to the justification behind it. Slobogin contends that to the extent courts are inconsistent about the application of *Terry*, it is
due to a lack of consensus among courts on how to interpret this standard. The
murkiness of the *Terry* standard, however, does not mean that it is unworkable;
instead, a better proportionality framework is necessary.

Slobogin argues against those who support Justice William Douglas's *Terry*
dissent in saying that there should be no reasonable suspicion standard and that

all Fourth Amendment activity should be based only on probable cause. He argues that that would be an unworkable standard, one that would place courts under pressure to narrowly construe the Fourth Amendment applicability threshold so police could act without probable cause. He also contends that having a sole probable cause standard would only encourage states to pass numerous new traffic and loitering laws designed to give police the probable cause necessary to make arrests.

A better solution, contends Slobogin, is for the Court to refocus on the *Terry* standard's principle of proportionality. It is clear from *Terry*, he argues, that the level of intrusion created by a search or seizure must be proportional to the government interest served by the intrusion. Therefore, the more a person's autonomy, property rights, or privacy are infringed, the more justification the government must have. He proposes that a workable standard to measure Fourth Amendment activity on this "sliding scale" would be to look at how much explanation would be necessary to convince an innocent person of the reasonableness of a given intrusion.

In order to maintain the proportionality principle, Slobogin calls for a standard of judicial review analogous to the scrutiny currently given to Fourteenth Amendment activity, requiring that the government convincingly show its justification for a search or seizure. This, he argues, coupled with a better, more hierarchical definition of which activities are intrusive and to what degree would make the *Terry* standard better applicable to real life situations and therefore easier to apply.

For insight into the *Terry* standard and its relationship to the issue of race in law enforcement practices, see Tracy Macklin, *Terry v. Ohio's Fourth Amendment Legacy: Black Men and Police Discretion* (72 St. John's L. Rev. 1271, 1998); Honorable Jack B. Weinstein and Mae C. Quinn, *Terry, Race and Judicial Integrity: The Court and Suppression During the War on Drugs* (72 St. John's L. Rev. 1323, 1998); and Jonathan Bender, *Illinois v. Wardlow: The Supreme Court Dodges the Race Bullet in Fourth Amendment Terry Stops* (78 Denv. U. L. Rev. 125, 2000).

Macklin offers a critique of *Terry*, saying that it effectively placed a constitutional stamp of approval on racially discriminatory police activity. He argues that it is ironic that the Warren Court, renowned for its role in furthering civil rights and protecting minorities, reached a decision in *Terry* that eroded that protection. Macklin contends that *Terry's* creation of a reasonable suspicion standard created a "predictable result"—that is, greatly increased police power and greatly decreased individual liberties. He argues that this had a disproportionately negative effect on minority groups, in that the standard provided a "springboard" for police activities that target minorities such as blacks.

Examining the *Terry* opinion, Macklin argues that the issue of race was far too "subordinate" in the text. Given the era in which the opinion was written and the fact that the suspects were African-American, he contends that race should have played a much more prominent role in the decision and the standard that it created. He argues that if the Court is willing to consider issues such as police safety in the "totality of the circumstances" when assessing reasonableness, it should be willing to examine racial motivations as well. Macklin believes that the *Terry* holding was flawed because it "lost sight of the larger picture it confronted."

Macklin's contention that *Terry* was wrongly decided stems from three main concerns. First, he argues that the law was already settled on the level of evidence necessary for a warrantless search before *Terry*. Second, he says that the opinion ignored the reality of on-street police encounters, and should have taken a more realistic approach to the issue. Third, he argues that the Court should have taken it on itself to write a decision that more actively addressed the need of minority groups for Fourth Amendment protection.

Judge Jack Weinstein argues that it is not the *Terry* standard, but racially motivated abuses *of* the standard, that have led to the discriminatory results to which Macklin points. He and Quinn defend the *Terry* standard by arguing that it is a workable one, but one that has led to inequitable results when used by a racially divided society. The authors argue that proof of this lies in the fact that were the Court to change the *Terry* standard and adopt a rule that more closely controlled police activity, there would be no real change. They contend that experiences like the "War on Drugs" and the policing of minority neighborhoods have shown that racial discrimination occurs at an alarming rate regardless of the law enforcement methods that are used. According to the authors, it is a societal flaw, not a flaw inherent in the *Terry* standard, that has led to racially motivated abuses of the stop and frisk rule.

Bender criticizes the *Wardlow* Court's refusal to consider race in its decision regarding the impact of the Fourth Amendment on unprovoked flight situations. He argues that the Court erred in following what it had done in *Terry* and *Whren*, where it had also factored race out of its "reasonable suspicion" analysis.

Pointing to Justice John Paul Stevens' dissent in *Wardlow,* Bender contends that in poor, minority neighborhoods, unprovoked flight can be based simply on mistrust of the police. Therefore, he says, flight is not a surefire indicator that crime is afoot, and courts must look deeper into the *Terry*-required "totality of the circumstances" in Fourth Amendment inquiries.

Bender argues that if four of the justices in *Wardlow* were willing to look at subjective flight motivations (why an individual might have run) in this way, why shouldn't the Court be willing to look at law enforcement's subjective, race-based motivations for giving chase? He further points out that the Court has already indicated that "character of neighborhood" considerations can play a role in a Fourth Amendment inquiry and wonders why equally subjective racial considerations are therefore overlooked. Noting these apparent inconsistencies, Bender argues that race can and should be a factor used by the Court to assess the legitimacy of claims of reasonable suspicion.

Peter Erlinder, in *Florida v. J.L.—Withdrawing Permission to "Lie with Impunity": The Demise Of "Truly Anonymous" Informants and the Resurrection of the Aguilar/Spinelli Test for Probable Cause* (4 U. Pa. J. Const. L. 1, 2001), discusses the reasonable suspicion standard as it relates to searches based on anonymous tips. He examines the Court's decision in Florida v. J.L., where it found that an anonymous phone tip did not justify reasonable suspicion because it was not sufficiently identifiable to be accountable. Erlinder cites with approval the *J.L.* Court's reasoning that for an anonymous tip to justify reasonable suspicion as defined by *Terry,* it must make reliable assertions of illegal behavior. This is consistent with *Terry's* oft-cited requirement of specific, articulable facts. Further, Erlinder agrees with the concurrence in J.L. that allowing truly anonymous tipsters to justify reasonable suspicion is dangerous because there is no mechanism for judges to assess the credibility of completely anonymous informants.

For Erlinder, the *J.L.* decision reaffirms what he sees as the Fourth Amendment's vital separation of powers function. He argues that the principal purpose of the Fourth Amendment is that it creates a system in which a "neutral, detached magistrate" evaluates the validity of an officer's inferences. By requiring that anonymous tips require "standard indicia of reliability" beyond simply an accurate description of a suspect, Erlinder believes that the *J.L.* Court strengthened this separation of powers function.

## ANALYSIS—ADMINISTRATIVE SEARCHES—JUSTIFICATION— REASONABLE STANDARDS

The administrative search issue has been a part of the larger discussion concerning how to clarify and restructure the Fourth Amendment. For an especially comprehensive look at the changes that resulted from the Court's expansion of the Fourth Amendment to include administrative law, see Scott E. Sundby, *A Return to Fourth Amendment Basics: Undoing the Mischief of Camara and Terry* (72 Minn. L. Rev. 383, 1988).

In this article the author argues that the Fourth Amendment, as a result of the balancing approach used in the decisions in *Terry* and *Camara*, has become makeshift, lacking in continuity of design or purpose. Its effect has gone well beyond the stop and frisk and administrative situations. The author describes the Court's balancing test as "ill defined" and expresses concern with what he perceives as the resulting weakening of the probable cause requirement. He points out that reasonable suspicion, instead of probable cause, is now treated as the acceptable compromise between government interest and individual privacy interests. Although the Court has attempted to address these issues and preserve the traditional role of probable cause, the author argues that these attempts have proven unworkable and have only exacerbated the Court's piecemeal approach to Fourth Amendment analysis. Sundby concludes by presenting his proposed

"Composite Model" to reconcile the reasonableness and warrant requirements and to adequately define reasonableness.

Several other authors have also provided alternative models for what they perceive as important weaknesses in the Court's present methods of analysis. For an example, see Nadine Strossen, *The Fourth Amendment in the Balance: Accurately Setting the Scales Through the Least Intrusive Alternative Analysis* (63 N.Y.U. L. Rev. 1173, 1988).

In this article the author criticizes the use of the balancing test because of its inherent subjectivity, its tendency to deprive constitutional rights of the special protection they deserve, and the likelihood that the test will produce inconsistent results. Strossen explains that courts often inaccurately identify and compare competing interests. However, Strossen believes that the court is not likely to abandon the balancing test and so suggests that the problems should be addressed through the addition of a least intrusive alternative component. Under this alternative model, the court would evaluate alternative law enforcement strategies for advancing the goals of the challenged measure in order to compare the relative intrusiveness and effectiveness of alternative measures. The state would have to show that the challenged measure was the least intrusive that was reasonably available to substantially promote its goals. Strossen then details her proposed procedures and rules for implementing a least intrusive analysis in the Fourth Amendment balancing test and thus adjusting the scales on which the Court balances.

Other authors have chosen to address more specific questions raised by the Court's developing Fourth Amendment analysis and the elements of the balancing approach, for example, Wayne R. LaFave, *Controlling Discretion by Administrative Regulations: The Use, Misuse, and Nonuse of Police Rules and Policies in Fourth Amendment Adjudication* (89 Mich. L. Rev. 442, 1990). In this article, LaFave examines the role that police discretion and policy making presently play, and can play in the future, in Fourth Amendment decisions. LaFave expresses the view that while police discretion is inevitable, it must be controlled. The most effective means of controlling discretion is to require that the police themselves create standardized policies and criteria. LaFave presents several interesting arguments for how police rulemaking can benefit the police, courts, and general public. The creation of policies by police has the advantages of creating greater protection for Fourth Amendment rights while at the same time ensuring that higher-ups contribute to policy making and become more aware for several reasons: the judicial branch has not sufficiently encouraged the police rulemaking process; judges do not evaluate rules well, or even at all; and litigants have failed to focus on the rules or their rationale. The author then looks at several issues and prospective solutions, which must be tackled in addressing these problems. He urges that, although the police are entitled to some deference as qualified professionals, the courts have an obligation to review their procedures with sufficient scrutiny to ensure fairness and accountability in the rule-making process.

The "special needs" doctrine has played a major role in the development of the Court's approach to administrative searches. For a cross-section of the vast scholarly research that exists on the topic, see Gerald S. Reamy, *When "Special Needs" Meet Probable Cause: Denying the Devil the Benefit of Law* (19 Hastings Const. L. Q. 295, 1992).

In this article the author examines those cases in which the presence of "special needs" was used to justify searches without probable cause or warrants. Reamy argues this line of cases is flawed because they fail to adhere to prior case law and require the Court to interpret the Fourth Amendment in an unprincipled and ad hoc fashion. Probable cause, if not totally eliminated as a requirement, has been relegated to the position where exceptions to probable cause are now the rule. Specifically the author provides an interesting view of the development of the special needs doctrine and its eventual "trump" of the probable cause requirement. The author warns that the special needs doctrine appears virtually unlimited and then proposes judicial process and constitutional ethics as a method of constructional decision making he feels is more consistent with the realities of politics.

Jennifer E. Smiley, in *Rethinking the "Special Needs Doctrine": Suspicionless Drug Testing of High School Student and the Narrowing of Fourth Amendment Protections* (95 Nw. U. L. Rev. 811, 2001), focuses specifically on the effect of the special needs doctrine on school drug testing programs, advocates abandoning the special needs doctrine and returning to the requirement that government actors demonstrate individualized suspicion before they conduct invasive searches. The author expresses the view that the special needs doctrine has failed to develop into a coherent and workable body of Fourth Amendment law and that its continued application presents real dangers. The author concludes that if the Court were to return to a standard that demanded individualized suspicion in all but the least intrusive administrative searches, suspicionless drug tests of high school students would clearly violate the Fourth Amendment.

William J. Stuntz, in *Implicit Bargains, Government Power, and the Fourth Amendment* (44 Stan. L. Rev. 553, 1992), argues that most of the court's special need decisions have been correct and are justified when viewed under a contract model. Stuntz contends that the question is "Would those innocent parties who are subject to the search have bargained for the search if given the choice?" To answer this question in the affirmative, the author suggests that there must be a relationship between the relevant government agent and the target of the search that exists independent of the search, and the government must have options not controlled by Fourth Amendment law that it might well exercise if searching is forbidden. These options would make innocent search targets worse off than they would be with the searches. Thus both the government and search target would probably prefer that the protection of the Fourth Amendment be minimized when the government had the option to do something else, often worse than the search itself.

The author goes on to distinguish those cases involving police roadblocks and group drug testing as governed, not by a contracts model but by politics, because groups of drivers (unlike solitary citizens) can protect themselves from overzealous police tactics at the polls.

Robert D. Dodson, in *Ten Years of Randomized Jurisprudence: Amending the Special Needs Doctrine* (51 S.C. L. Rev. 258, 2000), and Mary Jacq Watson, in *Chandler v. Miller: The Civil Liberties Sky Is Not Falling* (19 Mississippi 421, 1999), both offer insight into special needs.

In his article, Dodson expresses the idea that, although the Court has addressed the special needs doctrine several times in the past few years, it has failed to adequately define a special need or special government interest. The Court has thus failed to provide a framework for lower courts to use in determining what searches and seizures fall within the special needs doctrine. Dodson looks particularly at where the special needs doctrine stands after Chandler v. Miller. Although the author agrees with the outcome of the case, he feels that the Court's reasoning is flawed. The definition assigned to "special need," that it ensures public safety, is confusing and inconsistent with prior case law. The balancing test still heavily favors the government, and has become little more than a "judicial stamp of approval" on randomized drug testing. Dodson explains that despite the problems with the special needs doctrine, the Court is unlikely to abandon it. However, he feels the Justices are showing more willingness to revisit the special needs doctrine and tighten the requirements necessary to dispense with probable cause and warrant requirements of the Fourth Amendment. The author suggests ways the Court could clarify and correct the problems with the doctrine. Ultimately the author suggests that, although the Court made progress toward defining special needs in *Chandler*, it did not go far enough.

The Watson article, on the other hand, presents a vastly different view of what the *Chandler* decision means to the special needs doctrine. Watson concludes that *Chandler* actually demonstrates the Court's ability to apply the special needs doctrine clearly and effectively, and provides the needed definition for special needs. The author concludes that the Supreme Court's analysis should serve as "an exceptionally clear roadmap" for lower courts, and thus there should be little doubt about what is and is not a special need.

A number of authors have examined the two most recent administrative search decisions, *Edmond* and *Ferguson*, and explored the Court's approach of scrutinizing the "primary purpose" behind these types of searches.

For an insight into how the Court's recent jurisprudence applies to traffic checkpoint stops, see Theresa A. O'Loughlin, *Guerillas in the Midst: The Dan-*

*gers of Unchecked Police Powers through the Use of Law Enforcement Check-points* (6 Suffolk J. Trial & App. Advoc. 59, 2001).

O'Loughlin's article expresses concern with the dangers that checkpoint stops could pose to individual Fourth Amendment rights. While lauding the Court's decision in *Edmond* to invalidate a narcotic checkpoint as violative of the Fourth Amendment, she contends that the door may still be open for police to act on ulterior motives. She argues that the Court may have left open the possibility to use checkpoints with a legitimate primary purpose but with a secondary purpose of intercepting narcotics.

O'Loughlin writes that although it is certainly tempting to use checkpoint stops as an effective tool to combat things like drugs, the costs that such measures exact on society in terms of individual rights is far too great. She argues that in modern society, people are spending more and more time in their cars and that they therefore need to feel that they are safe from unreasonable searches or seizures while in them.

O'Loughlin agrees with the result of *Edmond*—that narcotics checkpoints violate the Fourth Amendment—but she is critical of the path the Court used to reach it. She argues that by evaluating the legitimacy of a checkpoint based on a "primary purpose" analysis, the Court may be making it possible for police to engage in pretextual checkpoint stops. So long as a checkpoint has a constitutionally legitimate "primary" purpose, it seems, it could have a whole host of illegitimate "secondary" purposes piggybacked on it, such as narcotics searches.

Finally, O'Loughlin proposes alternative means such as community policing or increased police presence in high crime areas as techniques that could be used instead of checkpoints as effective measures to stop crime.

For an exploration of how the Court's definition of an administrative search relates to the "special needs" doctrine, see Barbara J. Prince, *Casenote: The Special Needs Exception to the Fourth Amendment and How it Applies to Government Drug Testing of Pregnant Women: The Supreme Court Clarifies Where the Lines Are Drawn in Ferguson v. City of Charleston* (35 Creighton L. Rev. 857, 2002).

Prince's note highlights the recent Court's unwillingness to characterize searches as administrative when crime control has been the primary motivation. It examines the Court's decision in *Ferguson* to invalidate warrantless, suspicionless drug testing because it did not fall within either the "special needs" requirement or the definition of an administrative search. Prince argues that the Court was correct to note that the primary purpose of the drug testing policy in that case was to use law enforcement means to curb drug abuse by expectant mothers. Because the police were closely involved in the administration of the program (patients found to have drugs in their urine were reported to police if they refused drug treatment), it too closely resembled a law enforcement activity to be exempted from the Fourth Amendment's warrant requirement.

Thus, argues Prince, the Court was correct to strike down the program based on the fact that its "ultimate goal" was to gather evidence for law enforcement. She points out that even if the Court *had* found that there was some "special need" outside of law enforcement goals that existed for the testing, it still would not have survived a balancing test of the government's interest versus individual privacy rights. Prince contends that the governmental interest in the drug testing in *Ferguson* was simply not of the magnitude to justify a search without a warrant or probable cause.

## ANALYSIS—WARRANTS

A number of authors have expressed concern over the Court's willingness to allow reasonableness-based exceptions to the warrant requirement. These scholars, including Wayne Holly and Robert Bloom, have called on the Court to reemphasize a "warrant-centered" approach to Fourth Amendment jurisprudence.

Wayne D. Holly, in *The Fourth Amendment Hangs In the Balance: Resurrecting the Warrant Requirement Through Strict Scrutiny* (13 New York Law School Journal of Human Rights 531, 1997), stresses the concept that the warrant requirement is indispensable to the protections that the Fourth Amendment provides. He argues that the Court's shift from a warrant-centered reading of the Amendment to a reasonableness-based balancing approach has resulted in "insufficient protection to the individual's interest in privacy and personal security." Holly criticizes what he sees as the Court's willingness to allow warrantless searches. He argues that the Court's exceptions to the warrant requirement are so numerous that they have rendered it "almost unrecognizable." A proper reading of the Fourth Amendment, according to his article, is one that strongly emphasizes its warrant requirement in order to protect individual liberties.

He contends that Fourth Amendment rights are "fundamental" in the sense that First Amendment rights are and that they should therefore be afforded an equal level of protection by the Court. Just as First Amendment rights have long enjoyed "heightened judicial attention," Holly argues that Fourth Amendment rights should have the same type of judicial scrutiny, including a requirement that the government show a "compelling interest" when infringing on those rights.

Holly proposes that warrantless searches be examined by the Court on a "strict scrutiny" basis. Under this standard of review, the government would be required to show that a warrantless search was necessary to the achievement of a compelling government interest and was the least intrusive alternative to a warrant reasonably available. This standard, he argues, will provide much-needed emphasis on the warrant-centered approach to the Fourth Amendment. In doing so, he contends that a proper balance can be struck between allowing police the ability to do their job, while protecting citizens from overzealous law enforcement at the same time.

Robert M. Bloom, in *Warrant Requirement—The Burger Court Approach* (53 U. Colo. L. Rev. 691, 1982), explores what he labels the "considerable confusion" that has resulted from the Court's inconsistent reading of the Fourth Amendment's warrant requirement. Surveying the shift in Fourth Amendment jurisprudence from the Warren Court to the Burger Court, Bloom expresses concern that the Burger Court has undermined the Warren Court's focus on the Fourth Amendment's warrant clause. Bloom contends that in doing this, the Burger Court showed much more concern with expanding law enforcement powers, and less concern with protecting individual privacy.

Bloom's article criticizes the Burger Court's "expectation of privacy"–centered approach to Fourth Amendment issues. He examines the Court's use of a "sliding scale" of various degrees of privacy expectations to determine the reasonableness of a search or seizure, whether warrantless or otherwise. He argues that these "incomprehensible categories" of privacy expectations have resulted in a high degree of confusion as to when exactly a warrant is required for a search or seizure.

As a solution, Bloom calls for a consistent application of the warrant-centered approach to search and seizure issues, coupled with an elimination of the "expectation of privacy" approach. This, he argues, would provide a more workable Fourth Amendment standard that would ensure the Fourth Amendment rights of the individual. It makes more sense, he argues, for the Court "to determine whether or not it was practical to secure a warrant" than it does to engage in the "abstract distinctions" of an expectation of privacy-based rationale.

For an exploration of the warrant requirement as it applies to anticipatory search warrants, see Robert A. Messina, *Anticipatory Search Warrants: Striking a Balance Between Privacy Rights and Police Action* (22 S. Ill. U. L. J. 391, 1998).

Messina's article points out that anticipatory search warrants are the "new frontier of search and seizure law" and therefore have yet to be as well-examined by courts as other types of warrants. Examining the case law, he finds two main requirements for an anticipatory warrant: evidence of an ultimate destination or sure course of delivery and execution of the warrant conditioned on the occurrence of specific events. The fulfillment of these requirements, he writes, are often based on information provided by law enforcement officials who also vouch for the reliability of the source from which the information was obtained.

In order for the anticipatory search warrant standard to become a reliable one, Messina argues that the "predetermined event" requirement needs to be better defined by the Court. This aspect of an anticipatory search warrant—that certain predetermined events must occur in order for a warrant to be executed—has yet to be circumscribed. He contends that in order to ensure that Fourth Amendment rights are fully protected, a "universal rule" for what types of events must be set forth in a warrant is necessary. Thus, Messina concludes that while anticipatory search warrants are an effective law enforcement tool, their Fourth Amendment costs may be "too high to bear" if the Court does not adequately define how and when they may be used.

## ANALYSIS—WARRANT EXCEPTIONS

Barbara C. Salken, in *Balancing Exigency and Privacy in Warrantless Searches to Prevent Destruction of Evidence: The Need for a Rule* (39 Hastings L. J. 283, 1988), begins her article by recognizing that, although the Court has concluded that the need to prevent the destruction of evidence is one type of exigent circumstance that may justify warrantless action, it has not defined the point at which the fear that evidence might be destroyed is sufficient to justify such warrantless action. The circuit courts have thus created their own approaches to this question, which Salken believes can be grouped into three distinct categories. These categories differ according to how the courts address two important issues. The first issue is whether the threat of destruction of evidence is genuine and imminent or merely speculative. The second issue is whether the threat was foreseeable or otherwise avoidable. So, for example, one court may require factual proof that a threat that evidence would be destroyed actually existed, whereas another may uncritically accept the government's contention that such a threat existed. She points out, however, that these different approaches lead to inconsistent results across circuits, and the lack of guidance by the Court has allowed certain circuits to interpret the circumstances that justify warrantless entry extremely broadly. Salken examines these lower court approaches very carefully, specifically pointing out and illustrating through examples the strengths and weaknesses of each approach, as well as analyzing the degree to which each approach is consistent with the limited Court precedent. She then constructs her own hypothetical to clearly illustrate the dramatically different results that may occur depending on the court addressing the case. Salken emphasizes that the need for uniformity is particularly strong because destruction of evidence may, like the automobile exception and search incident to arrest, soon become its own exception to the warrant requirement, independent of the exigent circumstances exception. She insists that Fourth Amendment values will be compromised by the creation of a separate exception, and the destruction of evidence exception should therefore remain limited to truly exigent circumstances. Salken thus concludes by presenting a four-part rule detailing the circumstances under which the police may make a warrantless entry into private premises. The rule is designed to encourage officers to use warrants but also allows them to make informed decisions before making warrantless entries.

## SEARCH INCIDENT EXCEPTION

A number of scholars have examined the issue of searches incident to arrest in light of the *Belton* decision and have raised questions about the effects of that decision's rule. David Rudstein analyzes the *Belton* decision and other ways the Court could have approached the issue. David Silk looks at the way the lower courts have interpreted *Belton*.

David S. Rudstein, in *The Search of an Automobile Incident to Arrest: An Analysis of New York v. Belton* (67 Marq. L. Rev. 205, 1984), argues that the Court went beyond the scope of the reasoning justifying a search incident to arrest and thereby unnecessarily reduced Fourth Amendment protection. Although Rudstein acknowledges that the validity of a search incident to arrest of the actual person is well established, he feels the Court has gone too far in extending the permissible scope of the search to the place where an arrest is made.

Rudstein questions the Court's decision to attempt to apply a bright line test to this area of search and seizure law when it allows determinations of so many other search and seizure issues to be made on a case-by-case basis. Instead of attempting to resolve confusion in lower courts by imposing this bright line, Rudstein argues that the Court could have resolved lower court contradiction by addressing a number of control issues, specifically whether "control" should be defined as at the time of an arrest, or at the time a search commences, and what factors should be used to determine "control." This portion of Rudstein's argument is particularly helpful in understanding why the Court felt prompted to apply a bright line standard and what alternative approach may have been available.

Rudstein also presents a very detailed and thorough analysis of the possible interpretations of the *Belton* decision. Rudstein examines several of the questions raised by Justice Brennan and analyzes his own question of whether the *Belton* rule would apply if the arrestee had recently been in an automobile but was not actually inside when the arrest took place. Rudstein urges the Court to reconsider its decision in *Belton*, abandon its attempt to apply a bright line test, and return to the test of *Chimel*. The fact and situation–sensitive approach will both provide adequate guidance to police and continue to protect the Fourth Amendment rights of motorists and their passengers.

David M. Silk, in *When Bright Lines Break Down: Limiting New York v. Belton* (136 U. Pa. L. Rev. 281, 1987), takes a retrospective look at the impact of the *Belton* rule, analyzing the ability of lower courts to apply the bright line approach set out in the Court's opinion. Although Silk finds courts have been able to apply the *Belton* rule when an occupant of a vehicle is arrested, they have been less successful in situations in which the person arrested has recently exited a vehicle. Notably, Silk finds that the courts have not been able to confine the rule to applications in the automobile context. This was precisely one of the concerns that Rudstein raised in his article three years earlier.

Silk delivers an especially interesting and comprehensive look at the criticism leveled at the *Belton* decision, both for its theoretical basis and practical application. Silk analyzes how the lower courts have had difficulty in applying the *Belton* doctrine, as much of the criticism predicted, because of the difficulty of limiting the decision to the context in which it was decided. Although Silk acknowledges that some courts have managed to apply the bright line rule successfully, eliminating the case-by-case analysis of automobile searches incident to arrest, the failure of other courts to reasonably limit the application of the rule has significantly damaged any possible usefulness of the rule. Silk argues that the most plausible solution to this problem of overstepping the scope of the rule is for the Court to expressly adopt a narrow interpretation of the *Belton* rule, limiting its application to arrests of occupants of automobiles.

For insight into searches incident to arrest as they relate to the warrant exception, see Robert M. Bloom, *The Supreme Court and Its Purported Preference for Search Warrants* (50 U. Tenn. L. Rev. 231, 1983).

In this article, the author argues that the Burger Court strayed from its "warrant preference" approach to Fourth Amendment searches to an approach where it was more and more willing to allow exceptions to the warrant requirement. Bloom expresses concern that this approach resulted in a situation where a warrant-preference truly exists only with respect to a person's home, office, and personal communications.

He argues that the Court took a wrong turn by departing from the requirement that the scope of a warrantless search be proportional to the reason for the exception in the first place. In doing so, he predicts that the "permissible scope of the exception will inevitably swallow up the warrant requirement itself." Bloom contends that the Court's justification for discarding a warrant-preference approach—that there was a need to create a standardized approach to examine police activity instead—was merely a "thin veil" hiding the Court's dislike for the exclusionary rule and the sometimes unpalatable results it creates. Examining the stances of the Court's individual justices, he reasons that the Court's unwillingness to engage in step-by-step analysis of police activity could be at least partially explained by this theory. Bloom argues that because application of the exclusionary rule can often mean that a guilty person goes free based on the misconduct of an officer, the Court has attempted to limit the exclusionary rule's application. He writes that it has gone too far in this effort, however, by distorting substantive Fourth Amendment doctrine such as the warrant preference approach.

Other authors such as Robert Rigg have examined how the search incident to arrest rule applies to minor traffic citations. Rigg's article is a precursor to the *Atwater* decision, which is discussed in greater detail in the probable cause chapter:

Robert R. Rigg, in *The Objective Mind and "Search Incident to Citation"* (8 B.U. Pub. Int. L. J. 281, 1999), published a year before the *Atwater* decision, points out that the purpose of the Fourth Amendment is to interpose an objective, detached magistrate between citizens and the police. Thus, the warrant requirement makes sure that the judicial process will "pass on the desires of the police" before they invade a citizen's privacy and engage in a search. He argues that the current exceptions to the warrant requirement, especially if extended to include searches incident to citations, are completely undermining this function. Rigg argues that the exceptions to the warrant requirements for searches are supposed to be "specifically established and well-delineated" in order to allow for warrantless searches incident to arrest and searches of automobiles. However, the Court's exceptions have almost swallowed the rule.

According to Rigg, if the justification for a warrantless search is based on its necessity—namely, the safety of the officer—then in a citation situation, there is no justification for such a search. Thus, he argues that equating a citation and an arrest, given Fourth Amendment principles, is illogical. Rigg writes that "a search incident to citation presents no urgency that cannot be justified by a Terry pat down or other exigencies previously developed by the Court." Further, Rigg contends that in modern times, with communication devices providing almost instantaneous contact between officers and judges, it is a relatively simple matter to obtain a warrant. Therefore, he argues, requiring them in more situations will not be a hindrance to police techniques. He concludes that unless "other facts present themselves" that necessitate a search, the Court should not allow officers to engage in one based solely on the issuance of a citation. To allow otherwise, he writes, will "eviscerate the protection envisioned by the Fourth Amendment."

## AUTOMOBILE EXCEPTION

A number of authors have expressed concern that the automobile exceptions to the warrant requirement have undermined Fourth Amendment Protections, including Lewis R. Katz, in *Criminal Law: United States v. Ross: Evolving Standards for Warrantless Searches* (74 J. Crim. L. & Criminology 172, 1983).

In this article, Katz provides a detailed description of the background, procedure, and reasoning of United States v. Ross, as well as a useful explanation of the Court's progression in reasoning concerning the automobile exception generally. Katz's descriptions, however, are influenced by his opinion that the Court is stripping the Fourth Amendment of its effectiveness by expanding warrantless automobile searches. Specifically, Katz sees the *Ross* decision as indicative of the Court's movement toward a new, virtually limitless "public place-probable cause exception" to the warrant requirement.

Katz finds the Court's extension of this general exception to closed containers found within the car even more disturbing. Katz argues that allowing an officer with probable cause to search a car to also, as a matter of course, search any containers within the car equates a warrantless search to a search conducted with a warrant. According to Katz, "[T]his approach will, in the long run, be more pervasively destructive of the warrant requirement than any strained necessity argument would have been."

Katz concludes his article by examining Justice Marshall's complaint in his *Ross* dissent that the majority "takes a first step toward an unprecedented 'probable cause' exception to the warrant requirement." Although Katz is quick to point out that the *Ross* decision does not make this result unavoidable, he explains that certain reasoning in the decision gives weight to Justice Marshall's concern. For example, Katz reasons that in future Fourth Amendment cases, the Court could be called on to explain why packages in automobiles should be treated differently than packages found in public places other than automobiles. The Court could choose to resolve any conflict by finding the foundation for a public place–probable cause exception in *Ross*. Although he stresses that the Court continues at least to talk about the use and value of the warrant requirement, Katz undoubtedly sees the *Ross* decision as the foundation on which an expansive and destructive public place exception could be erected.

David A. Harris, in *Car Wars: The Fourth Amendments Death on the Highway* (66 George Washington L. Rev. 556, 1998), presents an even bleaker picture than does Katz of the future value of the Fourth Amendment in the automobile context. Harris begins his note with the assertion that in cases involving cars, "The Fourth Amendment is all but dead." He does, however, see some hope for its resurrection through a more appropriate balancing of public safety and citizen autonomy. Harris argues that the Court has strayed too far toward the public safety side of the equation, and as a result, has lost sight of the importance of preventing innocent people from being stopped, questioned, searched, and essentially treated like criminals. Harris points out that this imbalance is especially troubling because the cost of allowing such treatment will fall disproportionately on African-Americans and people of color.

Harris provides an overview of *Whren* (discussed in the probable cause chapter), *Robinette,* and *Wilson* (discussed in the *Terry* chapter), the three most recent cases concerning the automobile exception at the time this article was written. Although these cases did not represent a huge change in the state of the law, Harris stresses that they do convey a significant amount of discretionary power to the police. One of the important costs associated with this power is the cost of searching and seizing innocent parties. Harris further points out that the police will not use this discretionary power to stop just anyone but that evidence indicates they will apply it disproportionately to African-Americans and Hispanics.

Harris argues that, although unbounded police discretion should prompt concern in any area, unbounded discretion combined with disproportionate application on the basis of race creates a situation that is totally intolerable and demands a new approach. Harris suggests changes in the law that could help to reign in the cost of this discretion. He would limit traffic stops to their purposes and never allow for a pretext search such as that in *Whren*. In addition, he would limit consent searches to instances when the officers tell those searched that they have the right to refuse and limit the scope of the search. Finally, he would limit canine sniffs and other sophisticated detection devices to situations when there is some justification to believe contraband is present. Although Harris acknowledges that these restrictions would create their own cost by preventing police from finding some of the drugs transported in vehicles that they would find without the restrictions, he stresses that this cost does not compare with the present cost to freedom born by a disproportionate number of innocent citizens based on the color of their skin.

James A. Adams, in *The Supreme Court's Improbable Justifications for Restriction of Citizen's Fourth Amendment Privacy Expectations in Automobiles* (47 Drake L. Rev. 833, 1999), like Harris, considers the impact of any curtailment of Fourth Amendment rights on the community as a whole rather than restricting his analysis solely to the interaction of police and criminals. Adams argues that the Fourth Amendment strikes a balance in favor of individual security and privacy and insists that the Court has not given the requisite weight to this value in their balancing test. Adams uses the examples of Court decisions on the automobile exception because he believes this area clearly illustrates the Court's abandonment of the traditional Fourth Amendment focus on privacy. Adams argues that we should be especially concerned with the Court's approach to the automobile exception because of the possible application of this approach to all modern technology.

Specifically, Adams discusses the relevance of the approach underlying the automobile exception to technology like satellite photos, forward-looking infrared radar, parabolic microphones, and computers. To support his position that the Court's reasoning could be extended to these areas and thus present a danger to a free society, Adams delivers a detailed analysis of the main theories for warrantless automobile searches, including the diminished expectation of privacy rationale.

This article is particularly interesting for its broad approach to the possible ramifications of the Court's automobile exception decisions. Adams stresses the idea that even seemingly small erosions in the protection afforded by the Fourth Amendment will add up over time and significantly alter the meaning and value of the Fourth Amendment as a whole.

For commentary on how the *Houghton* decision has expanded the scope of permissible warrantless automobile searches, see David E. Steinberg, *The Drive Toward Warrantless Auto Searches: Suggestions from a Back Seat Driver* (80 B.U. L. Rev. 545, 2000), and George M. Dery III, *Improbable Cause: The Court's Purposeful Evasion of a Traditional Fourth Amendment Protection in Wyoming v. Houghton* (50 Case W. Res. L. Rev. 547, 2000).

Steinberg's essay criticizes the Court's continued unwillingness to require warrants for automobile searches. He argues that the *Houghton* decision has increased the possibility of "dangerous and unnecessary intrusions" on motorists by police. Steinberg contends that because automobile-based encounters between citizens and police are so frequent, Fourth Amendment warrant protections are especially important in those situations. His essay expresses concern that instead, given the numerous warrant exceptions the Court has created in automobile situations, warrantless searches can almost always be justified. "Under a warrantless auto search regime[n]," Steinberg contends, "the incentive for police is to search first and develop some justification for the search later."

According to Steinberg, since the Court seems unwilling to adhere to a warrant requirement, the best path to take after a case like *Houghton* is to call for a stricter application of the Fourth Amendment's reasonableness requirement. Steinberg argues that balancing law enforcement interests against privacy rights in automobile stops, although not the best route, is a better solution than creating more and more exceptions to the warrant requirement. A stronger focus on the reasonableness of such searches, he contends, would enable the Fourth Amendment to retain a somewhat vital role in this "anything goes" area of searches and seizures.

Dery's article argues that *Houghton* wrongly removed the "core requirement," probable cause, from the automobile warrant exception. By allowing police to search passengers' belongings when probable cause exists to search a car, he contends that "all containers are vulnerable to government intrusion" simply by virtue of their location. He raises the point that the decision greatly expands law enforcement search powers but at a "terrible cost." By essentially "lumping individuals together" in allowing a passenger's purse to be searched based on the actions of the driver, Dery argues that the Court ignored the fact that the Fourth Amendment provides individualized, personal rights to each and every citizen.

Dery criticizes not only the *Houghton* ruling but also Justice Scalia's reasoning in reaching this outcome. Examining the case, he argues that it wrongfully analyzed the automobile exception "in a vacuum" and that it "is a study in selective citation" in the way that it disregarded the focus of prior case law on the requirement of probable cause. Dery sees the *Houghton* decision as improperly engaging in a "balancing" analysis that should be reserved only for those situations involving governmental special needs. Employing a balancing analysis was inappropriate, he argues, because it was being applied to a "traditional criminal investigation" that should focus more strictly on probable cause instead. Dery concludes that *Houghton* has resulted in a "careless containment of scope"—one that has severely eroded Fourth Amendment protections.

## PLAIN VIEW EXCEPTION

Denise Marie Cloutier, in *Arizona v. Hicks: The Failure to Recognize Limited Inspection as Reasonable on Fourth Amendment Jurisprudence* (24 Colum. J. L. & Soc. Probs. 351, 1991), explicitly calls for the Court to overrule Hicks v. Arizona, abandon its attempt to draw a bright line test for the plain view exception, and instead refocus their inquiry on the overall reasonableness of the search. According to Cloutier, the Court's attempt to draw a bright line by requiring that the incriminating nature of an object be immediately apparent and thus that an officer have probable cause before moving the object actually adds to the confusion surrounding the limits and application of the Fourth Amendment. Opinions of lower courts illustrate this confusion as judges struggle to admit evidence seized in apparent violation of *Hicks*. Cloutier provides several examples of how lower courts have contorted the *Hicks* opinion, including accepting the plain feel doctrine and determining that the object moved was somehow included in the vague terms of the warrant. Most importantly, Cloutier stresses that this confusion is likely to result in a dilution of the probable cause standard. The lower courts that do apply *Hicks* may allow for a more flexible definition of probable cause in order to find the evidence obtained admissible.

In addition to creating confusion in its application by the lower courts, Cloutier argues that *Hicks* is itself inconsistent with prior Court opinions. She points out that prior opinions have already accepted a lower standard of justification than probable cause for searches involving lesser intrusions. If a limited inspection of an object in plain view is a lesser intrusion, then the lesser justification of reasonable and articulable suspicion, as in a *Terry* stop, should apply. Acceptance of a lesser standard would be more consistent with the Court's prior reliance on a balancing approach in considering the degree of intrusiveness when determining the necessary level of justification.

Cloutier attributes the Court's failure to apply the balancing approach partly to its inconsistent approach to "searches" on one hand, and "seizures" on the other. In evaluating seizures, the Court focuses on the degree of police intrusion to determine the necessary level of justification, but in evaluating searches, the central focus is often not on the degree of intrusiveness but instead on the officer's safety. Thus in a *Terry* stop, the justification for the limited search is not really the lesser intrusion but rather the safety of the officer. Cloutier argues this distinction adds to the confusion in this area, and should be abandoned. Both searches and seizures should be evaluated according to the level of intrusiveness and resulting level of necessary justification. Cloutier concludes that public policy favoring crime control supports recognition of limited inspection that would enhance Fourth Amendment rights by eliminating judicial incentive to dilute the probable cause standard.

Anne Bowen Poulin, in *The Plain Feel Doctrine and the Evolution of the Fourth Amendment* (42 Vill. L. Rev. 741, 1997), uses her article to argue for limitations to the plain feel doctrine that the Court recognized in Minnesota v. Dickerson. Poulin makes a point of differentiating the legitimacy of Fourth Amendment rules in theory from Fourth Amendment rules in application. Although the doctrine of *Dickerson* represents "no remarkable" erosion of Fourth Amendment rights in theory, Poulin feels that the sloppy reasoning and overly deferential fact finding typical in its application pose a serious threat to Fourth Amendment rights.

In arguing for her interpretation of *Dickerson*, Poulin examines two rules that existed before *Dickerson*. First, the rule of the *Terry* stop allows officers to seize weapons and items resembling weapons. Second, the rule of a search incident to arrest allows officers to seize all items concealed on or near the arrestee. In light of the prior existence of these two doctrines, the plain feel doctrine need only apply to seizure of a nonweapon-like item, recognizable by feel, when there is no probable cause to arrest. Therefore, Poulin argues the plain feel doctrine should be evaluated as a search incident to arrest in which the pat down itself yields probable cause immediately when the officer recognizes the nonweapon contraband by feel. In this analysis, the actual seizure of the nonweapon doesn't occur until after probable cause is established by the pat down, and the seizure is thus simply one incident to arrest. Poulin argues that the Court's decision to instead associate plain feel with plain view has resulted in a contorted and confusing analysis. Most importantly, Poulin stresses that in a plain view situation the officer is already present and in a position to seize an item without further invasion. In contrast, in a plain feel situation, an officer is not in a position to seize without some degree of further intrusion, such as reaching into a pocket.

Poulin goes on to explain that, since it has been used as an important weapon in the war on drugs, the plain feel exception has had a notable impact on both law enforcement and the courts. Law enforcement officers can use the doctrine to exploit a chance to see what is hidden in a person's clothing or a container, and may probe more aggressively than they otherwise would. In addition, officers in court may exaggerate claims of tactile sensitivity and even commit perjury in order to avoid suppression of seized evidence. The courts, Poulin argues, have been too lax in applying the "immediately apparent" requirement the Court imposed in *Dickerson*. Poulin examines how to define the allowable scope of a search in different possible situations, including a stop and frisk, consent search, and authorized temporary or inadvertent contact with a container. Essentially, Poulin feels that Courts are too deferential to officers' claims that they instantly knew what the nonweapon contraband was without exceeding the scope of the allowable search. Courts should be skeptical of officers' testimony and constantly aware that tactile data is inherently uncertain. Poulin then concludes with a concise model for how courts should approach the question of whether the identity of an object was "immediately apparent." First, examine the object itself. Second, ask what the tactile information would convey to an impartial observer. Third, ensure that the officer did not exceed the scope of the justified initial touching.

## ANALYSIS—CONSENT

Peter Goldberger, in *Consent, Expectations of Privacy, and the Meaning of "Searches" in the Fourth Amendment* (75 J. Crim. L. & Criminology 319, 1984), Goldberger discusses the inadequacy of the definition of "search" developed by the Court in *Katz* and suggests that the lack of clarity in this definition provided no meaningful distinction between situations where no search has occurred and situations where consent to search has been given. As a result, the prosecution has been in a position to decide whether to argue the no search versus the consent issue. The prosecution, Goldberger suggests, often argues the no search issue because it is easier to demonstrate that no search has occurred on the basis of the assumption of risk than to demonstrate authoritative third-party consent. (However, it should be pointed out that this article was written prior to Illinois v. Rodriguez, which made it easier to show third-party consent.) Throughout the article, Goldberger presents comparisons of several cases in which, although factually almost identical, the Court focused on the issue of consent in one case and focused on whether a "search" had even occurred in the other case, often arriving at different conclusions as to whether Fourth Amendment protections had been violated.

Goldberger suggests that the Court's approach to consent is essentially satisfactory, but an alternative interest-based definition of "search" needs to be adopted in order to remedy this inconsistency. Goldberger's alternative focuses on the four types of protected interests he sees identified in the language of the Fourth Amendment. He excludes the subjective element of expectation of privacy and the idea of "assumption of risk" entirely from his search definition. Instead, Goldberger argues that these concepts can more effectively and clearly be accommodated in the determination of whether a search was voluntary and authoritatively consented to and therefore reasonable without a warrant or probable cause. Goldberger goes on to examine several issues surrounding third-party consent, including whether apparent authority should be sufficient for consent to search. Particularly interesting in this portion of the article is the author's discussion of joint access without sharing and his suggestion that in this type of relationship, neither party should have authority to consent until control becomes exclusive. This approach was not the one taken by the Court in *Rodriquez*.

For commentary on the issue of third-party consent, see Tammy Campbell, *Illinois v. Rodriguez: Should Apparent Authority Validate Third-Party Consent Searches?* (63 U. Colo. L. Rev. 481, 1992); Gary Wimbish, *The United States Supreme Court Adopts "Apparent Authority" Test to Validate Unauthorized Third Party Consent to Warrantless Search of Private Premises in Illinois* (20 Capital U. L. Rev. 301, 1991); and Franck C. Capozza, *Whither the Fourth Amendment: An Analysis of Illinois v. Rodriguez* (25 Ind. L. Rev. 515, 1991).

In this note, Campbell examines the Court's opinion in Illinois v. Rodriguez and argues that the Court's adoption of the reasonable belief standard seriously damages Fourth Amendment rights for individuals. Campbell highlights language and ideas in the *Rodriguez* opinion, as well as in other Court decisions that are not clearly explained and thus suggest logical questions and inconsistencies surrounding the "apparent authority" concept. Campbell provides a concise yet informative look at the development of the third-party consent doctrine, as well as the dissenting opinion in *Rodriguez*. Her conclusion is simple and direct. She asserts that consent does not render a search reasonable under the Fourth Amendment; it waives a Fourth Amendment right and places the search outside Fourth Amendment protections. Thus the Court's reliance on a reasonable belief rationale is inherently misplaced, and all the reasonableness in the world cannot compensate for the fact that without a diminished expectation of privacy on the part of the subject of the search, consent from a third party is meaningless.

Wimbish presents an interesting background for, and analysis of, the basis for the third-party consent exception. Wimbish's article is particularly interesting for his analysis of how the *Rodriguez* opinion represents a departure from the Court's prior decisions. Wimbish discusses the cases relied on by the majority in their analysis and points out why their claims of support in prior decisions are misplaced or based on flawed analysis of prior opinions. He then joins other authors on this topic in declaring both that *Rodriguez* continues the potentially disastrous erosion of Fourth Amendment rights and that it opens the door for potential police abuse. Notably, Wimbish discusses several cases unrelated to the consent doctrine in which the Court expressed doubt as to whether police officers can be objective in their pursuit of subjects. He then points out that the "apparent authority" doctrine relies primarily on the ability of the police to remain objective in determining whether a person appears to have authority. Rather than actually remaining objective in these cases, Wimbish believes that police will use this new method to avoid the warrant requirement with increasing frequency, and the erosion of Fourth Amendment rights will intensify.

Capozza recognizes that regardless of whether he agrees with the Court's decision in *Rodriguez*, it is unlikely that the "reasonable" standard adopted will change in the immediate future. For this reason, Capozza's ultimate goal in this article is to explain to defense attorneys how they can protect their clients from invasions of their Fourth Amendment rights. Capozza suggests that defense counsel turn to their state constitutions to find this protection, and in so doing he presents an analysis of the Court's discussion of its jurisdiction. In *Rodriguez*, Justice Scalia specifically sets forth the standard of Michigan v. Long in which the Court held that it will not review decisions based on adequate and independent state grounds. Although there is no guarantee that state constitutions will grant more protection than the federal constitution, they cannot grant less, and the state expansion of protection is at least one possibility for the defense attorney to explore.

# Table of Cases

# Index

## ABOUT THE AUTHOR

ROBERT M. BLOOM is Professor of Law at Boston College Law School. He is the author of *Ratting: The Use and Abuse of Informants in the American Justice System* (Praeger, 2002), *Criminal Procedure* (2nd edition, 1996), and *Constitutional Criminal Procedure* (1992).